Hidden Histories of Major Cities

Shah Rukh

Published by Shah Rukh, 2024.

While every precaution has been taken in the preparation of this book, the publisher assumes no responsibility for errors or omissions, or for damages resulting from the use of the information contained herein.

HIDDEN HISTORIES OF MAJOR CITIES

First edition. June 27, 2024.

Written by Shah Rukh.

Table of Contents

Prologue

In the bustling heart of every metropolis, amidst the glittering skyscrapers and the hum of modern life, lie the echoes of stories long past. These cities, celebrated for their grandeur, are more than just economic or cultural hubs; they are the keepers of secrets, bearers of legacies, and witnesses to the myriad tales that have shaped our world. Each city is a living, breathing entity, with layers of history buried beneath its streets, waiting to be unearthed.

This book, "Hidden Histories of Major Cities," is a journey across the globe, traversing continents and cultures to uncover the fascinating, often overlooked narratives that have been woven into the fabric of these urban landscapes. From the ancient ruins of Rome to the vibrant streets of Buenos Aires, each chapter delves into the unique stories that have molded these cities into the icons they are today.

Our exploration begins in Rome, the Eternal City, where whispers of emperors and gladiators still linger among the ruins of the Colosseum. Here, the shadows of a once-mighty empire stretch across the millennia, telling tales of grandeur and intrigue that have captivated imaginations for generations.

Traveling east, we arrive in Cairo, the cradle of civilization, where the pyramids stand as silent sentinels guarding the mysteries of the pharaohs. The sands of Egypt have seen the rise and fall of dynasties, each leaving behind monuments and myths that continue to astonish and inspire.

As we journey through the vibrant alleyways of Athens, the birthplace of democracy, we uncover the philosophical musings and political upheavals that have left an indelible mark on human thought and governance. The Parthenon, a beacon of ancient wisdom, stands testament to a legacy that continues to influence the modern world.

Each city we visit offers a portal to the past, a glimpse into the lives of those who walked its streets and shaped its destiny. In Jerusalem, the holy land, we find a confluence of faiths and cultures, a city that has seen centuries of conflict and reconciliation, where every stone is steeped in spiritual significance.

Our narrative winds through the alleys of Beijing, where the Forbidden City once concealed the intrigues of imperial China, and through the vibrant heart of Mexico City, where the echoes of Aztec warriors still resonate beneath the modern metropolis. Istanbul, the city straddling two continents, reveals a rich tapestry of cultures and empires that have left their mark on its shores.

In Paris, the City of Light, we uncover the revolutionary fervor that transformed a nation and inspired the world. From the artistic boulevards of Montmartre to the revolutionary fervor of the Bastille, every corner of Paris tells a story of passion, innovation, and upheaval.

Kyoto's serene temples and gardens offer a stark contrast, inviting us into a world of samurai and shoguns, where tradition and modernity coexist in a delicate balance. Meanwhile, in the vast expanses of Moscow, the shadows of the Tsars and the revolutionaries whisper tales of power, struggle, and resilience.

Delhi's Mughal marvels narrate a tale of conquest and culture, blending the grandeur of empires with the rich traditions of India. And as we explore the remnants of the Berlin Wall, we confront a powerful symbol of division and reunification, a testament to the resilience of the human spirit.

Throughout this book, we will wander through the streets of London, the heart of an empire; delve into the rhythms of Buenos Aires; uncover the colonial echoes of Lagos; and sail through the stories of Sydney's harbor. Each chapter offers a unique lens through which to view the complexities and wonders of our shared human history.

These cities, and many more, stand as silent witnesses to the triumphs and tragedies, the conquests and revolutions, that have shaped our world. They are the settings for countless tales of love, loss, and perseverance. Their histories, hidden in plain sight, offer a profound understanding of the forces that have shaped human civilization.

"Hidden Histories of Major Cities" invites you to embark on a voyage of discovery, to unearth the secrets that lie beneath the surface of these magnificent urban centers. As we peel back the layers of time, we reveal the intricate tapestry of stories that have crafted the world we know today. Through this journey, we hope to inspire a deeper appreciation for the rich heritage and enduring spirit of these cities, and to remind us that, beneath the modern facade, there lies a profound and compelling past, waiting to be explored.

Chapter 1: Rome: Echoes of the Eternal City

Rome, often referred to as the Eternal City, stands as one of the most historically rich cities in the world. Its history spans over two millennia, from its legendary founding by Romulus and Remus in 753 BC to its role as a vibrant modern capital. The echoes of Rome's past can be heard in every corner of the city, where ancient ruins, medieval churches, Renaissance palaces, and Baroque fountains coexist in a timeless tableau. The city's significance as the heart of the Roman Empire, a center of the Catholic Church, and a cradle of Western civilization is reflected in its architectural and cultural heritage.

The Roman Forum, located at the heart of ancient Rome, was the political, commercial, and religious center of the city. Walking through its ruins, one can almost hear the debates of senators, the proclamations of emperors, and the hustle and bustle of daily life. The Forum's temples, basilicas, and public spaces were the backdrop for key events in Roman history, such as the assassination of Julius Caesar and the speeches of Cicero. The Colosseum, Rome's iconic amphitheater, stands as a testament to the grandeur and brutality of the Roman Empire. Completed in AD 80, it hosted gladiatorial games, animal hunts, and mock naval battles, entertaining thousands of spectators with spectacles of violence and heroism.

Rome's architectural legacy continued into the medieval period, with the construction of numerous churches and basilicas that remain important pilgrimage sites. The Basilica of San Clemente, for example, offers a unique glimpse into Rome's layered history. Beneath its 12th-century church lies a 4th-century basilica, and beneath that, a 1st-century Roman house and Mithraic temple. This stratification of history is a common theme in Rome, where modern buildings often rest on ancient foundations. The Renaissance brought a cultural rebirth to Rome, as the city became a hub for artists, architects, and scholars. The Vatican, the seat of the Catholic Church, played a central role in this revival. St. Peter's Basilica, designed by Bramante, Michelangelo, and Bernini, stands as a masterpiece of Renaissance architecture. The Sistine Chapel, with Michelangelo's iconic ceiling frescoes, is a testament to the era's artistic achievements.

The Baroque period added another layer to Rome's architectural splendor. The cityscape was transformed by grandiose churches, elaborate fountains, and majestic piazzas. Bernini's work, in particular, left an indelible mark on Rome. His fountains, such as the Fontana dei Quattro Fiumi in Piazza Navona, are celebrated for their dynamic compositions and dramatic interplay of water and sculpture. The Trevi Fountain, another Baroque masterpiece, continues to draw millions of visitors who toss coins into its waters, hoping to return to Rome. The political history of Rome is equally compelling. After the fall of the Roman Empire, the city experienced centuries of turmoil and transformation. It was sacked by Visigoths, Vandals, and Ostrogoths, and later became the center of the Papal States. The unification of Italy in the 19th century saw Rome become the capital of a new nation, symbolizing the country's historical continuity and its aspirations for the future.

In the 20th century, Rome played a significant role in the rise of fascism and the subsequent establishment of the Italian Republic. The city witnessed the dramatic events of World War II, including the Nazi occupation and the Allied liberation. Today, Rome stands as a global city, blending its rich historical heritage with modernity. Its vibrant neighborhoods, such as Trastevere and Monti, offer a mix of old-world charm and contemporary culture. The city's cuisine, renowned for its simplicity and flavor, reflects its diverse history, with dishes like pasta alla carbonara and supplì showcasing the best of Roman culinary traditions.

Rome's museums and galleries house some of the world's greatest art collections. The Vatican Museums, with their vast array of treasures, including the Raphael Rooms and the Gallery of Maps, attract millions of visitors each year. The Capitoline Museums, located on the ancient Capitoline Hill, offer insights into Rome's classical past, while the Galleria Borghese boasts a stunning collection of Renaissance and Baroque art. The city's historical layers are not just confined to its buildings and monuments; they are also embedded in its streets and squares. The Via Appia Antica, one of the oldest and most important Roman roads, still bears the marks of ancient chariot wheels. The Pantheon, originally a temple dedicated to all the gods, remains remarkably well-preserved and continues to inspire awe with its massive dome and oculus.

Rome's religious significance is underscored by its many churches and basilicas, each with its own unique history and artistic treasures. The Basilica di Santa Maria Maggiore, with its stunning mosaics and relics, is a key site of Marian devotion. The Church of San Luigi dei Francesi houses Caravaggio's masterpieces, showcasing the dramatic chiaroscuro technique that revolutionized Baroque painting. In addition to its historical and cultural landmarks, Rome's natural beauty adds to its allure. The city's seven hills offer panoramic views, while the Tiber River weaves through its heart, providing a serene contrast to the urban landscape. The Villa Borghese gardens, with their lush greenery and elegant sculptures, offer a peaceful retreat from the bustling city.

Rome's enduring legacy is also reflected in its festivals and traditions. The city's calendar is filled with religious and cultural celebrations, from the solemn Holy Week processions to the exuberant Carnevale. These events provide a glimpse into Rome's vibrant community life and its ability to honor the past while embracing the present. The city's transport system, while modern and efficient, also provides a journey through history. The Rome Metro, with its archaeological finds during construction, offers commuters a unique connection to the city's ancient roots. The tram lines and buses navigate the narrow streets and broad avenues, bridging the gap between different eras.

Rome's educational institutions, including the University of Rome La Sapienza, one of the oldest universities in the world, continue to contribute to its intellectual and cultural vitality. The city's libraries and archives house invaluable manuscripts and documents, preserving the knowledge and wisdom of centuries. The Eternal City has inspired countless writers, poets, and filmmakers. From the verses of Ovid and Virgil to the novels of Alberto Moravia and the films of Federico Fellini, Rome's influence on literature and cinema is profound. Its streets and landmarks provide a backdrop for stories that explore the complexities of human experience and the passage of time.

The echoes of Rome's past are not just confined to its own borders; they resonate throughout the world. The city's contributions to law, engineering, and governance laid the foundations for Western civilization. The principles of Roman law continue to underpin legal systems globally, while the engineering marvels of Roman aqueducts and roads set standards for infrastructure development. In conclusion, Rome is a city where the past is ever-present, its echoes reverberating through its streets, buildings, and culture. The Eternal City remains a living testament to human achievement, resilience, and creativity. Its history, from the glory of the Roman Empire to the vibrancy of contemporary life, is a continuous narrative of innovation and tradition, making Rome a timeless and captivating destination for all who visit.

Chapter 2: Cairo: Secrets of the Pharaohs

Cairo, the sprawling capital of Egypt, is a city where ancient history and modern life coexist in a vibrant tapestry. Known as the City of a Thousand Minarets for its numerous mosques, Cairo's history stretches back thousands of years, with its origins deeply rooted in the age of the Pharaohs. The secrets of the Pharaohs are embedded in the very fabric of Cairo and its surrounding regions, offering a rich narrative of ancient civilization, architectural marvels, and cultural heritage that continues to captivate the world.

The Pyramids of Giza, just outside Cairo, are the most iconic symbols of ancient Egypt. These monumental structures were built during the Fourth Dynasty of the Old Kingdom, around 2580 – 2560 BC, serving as tombs for the Pharaohs Khufu, Khafre, and Menkaure. The Great Pyramid of Khufu, the largest of the three, was originally 146.6 meters tall and remained the tallest man-made structure in the world for over 3,800 years. The construction techniques used to build these pyramids remain a subject of fascination and debate among historians and archaeologists. The alignment of the pyramids with celestial bodies and their precise engineering reflects the advanced understanding of mathematics, astronomy, and architecture possessed by the ancient Egyptians.

The Sphinx, with its enigmatic smile and lion's body, guards the pyramids and has intrigued scholars and visitors alike for centuries. Carved from a single block of limestone, the Sphinx is believed to represent Pharaoh Khafre and serves as a testament to the grandeur of ancient Egyptian art and religious symbolism. Theories about its construction, purpose, and the weathering patterns on its body have spurred countless debates and investigations, adding to the mystique of the site.

The treasures of ancient Egypt are not confined to the Giza Plateau. Cairo's Egyptian Museum houses the world's most extensive collection of Pharaonic artifacts, including the treasures of Tutankhamun. Discovered in 1922 by British archaeologist Howard Carter, the tomb of Tutankhamun is one of the most significant archaeological finds of the 20th century. The young Pharaoh's burial chamber contained a wealth of artifacts, including his iconic golden death mask, chariots, thrones, and countless items intended to accompany him in the afterlife. These artifacts provide invaluable insights into the religious beliefs, artistic achievements, and daily life of ancient Egyptians.

The Step Pyramid of Djoser, located in Saqqara, is another remarkable monument from Egypt's Old Kingdom. Designed by the architect Imhotep, it is considered the earliest colossal stone building in Egypt and a precursor to the later pyramids at Giza. The Step Pyramid complex includes courtyards, temples, and ceremonial structures that offer a glimpse into the early development of pyramid construction and the centralization of religious and administrative functions in ancient Egypt.

Beyond its architectural wonders, the civilization of the Pharaohs left behind a rich legacy of hieroglyphic writing, art, and mythology. The Rosetta Stone, discovered in 1799 and now housed in the British Museum, was the key to deciphering ancient Egyptian hieroglyphs. The stone's inscriptions in Greek, Demotic, and hieroglyphic script enabled scholars like Jean-François Champollion to unlock the secrets of Egypt's written records, revealing detailed accounts of historical events, religious texts, and administrative documents.

Ancient Egyptian mythology and religious practices revolved around a pantheon of gods and goddesses, each associated with specific aspects of life and nature. Deities like Ra, the sun god; Osiris, the god of the afterlife; and Isis, the goddess of magic and motherhood, played central roles in the spiritual and cultural life of ancient Egyptians. The construction of temples, such as the Karnak and Luxor complexes in Upper Egypt, demonstrated the importance of religious worship and the Pharaohs' role as intermediaries between the gods and the people. These temples, with their massive columns, obelisks, and detailed reliefs, are masterpieces of ancient Egyptian architecture and artistry.

The Valley of the Kings, located on the west bank of the Nile near Luxor, served as the burial site for New Kingdom Pharaohs, including Tutankhamun, Seti I, and Ramses II. The tombs in the Valley of the Kings are renowned for their elaborate decorations, which depict scenes from the Book of the Dead and other religious texts intended to guide the deceased through the afterlife. The discovery and exploration of these tombs have provided a wealth of information about ancient Egyptian burial practices, beliefs about the afterlife, and the daily lives of the Pharaohs.

Cairo itself, though a bustling modern metropolis, is deeply influenced by its ancient heritage. The city's Islamic architecture, with its mosques, madrassas, and citadels, reflects a continuation of grand building traditions that began in the age of the Pharaohs. The Al-Azhar Mosque, founded in 970 AD, is one of the oldest universities in the world and remains a center of Islamic learning. The Cairo Citadel, built by Salah al-Din in the 12th century, offers panoramic views of the city and houses several important mosques and museums.

The Coptic Christian heritage of Cairo also connects to its ancient past. The Coptic Museum, located in Old Cairo, showcases a rich collection of artifacts, including textiles, manuscripts, and religious icons that highlight the continuity of Egyptian cultural traditions from Pharaonic to Christian times. The Hanging Church, one of the oldest Coptic churches in Cairo, is built above a Roman fortress gatehouse and features beautiful wooden screens and intricate artwork.

The Nile River, the lifeblood of ancient and modern Egypt, continues to play a central role in the daily life and economy of Cairo. The river's annual inundation was crucial for agriculture in ancient times, depositing fertile silt along its banks and ensuring bountiful harvests. Today, the Nile remains a vital source of water and a key transportation route, while the city's riverside promenades and floating restaurants offer a blend of traditional and contemporary experiences.

Cairo's vibrant bazaars and markets, such as Khan el-Khalili, echo the city's historical role as a hub of trade and commerce. The market's labyrinthine alleys are filled with shops selling spices, jewelry, textiles, and souvenirs, reflecting the diversity of Cairo's cultural influences and its position as a crossroads between Africa, the Middle East, and the Mediterranean.

Modern Cairo is a dynamic city that continues to grow and evolve, balancing its rich historical heritage with the demands of contemporary life. The city's skyline is dotted with high-rise buildings, luxury hotels, and modern infrastructure, yet the echoes of the Pharaohs are never far away. Archaeological discoveries continue to be made, offering new insights into Egypt's ancient past and attracting scholars and tourists from around the world.

The secrets of the Pharaohs, preserved in Cairo's monuments, artifacts, and cultural traditions, provide an enduring link to one of the world's oldest and most influential civilizations. The legacy of ancient Egypt, with its achievements in architecture, art, writing, and religion, remains a source of fascination and inspiration, ensuring that the stories of the Pharaohs will continue to be told and retold for generations to come.

Cairo's museums, including the upcoming Grand Egyptian Museum near the Giza Pyramids, are dedicated to preserving and showcasing the treasures of ancient Egypt. The Grand Egyptian Museum, set to be the largest archaeological museum in the world, will display thousands of artifacts, many of which have never been exhibited before. The museum aims to provide a comprehensive understanding of ancient Egyptian civilization, from its earliest periods to its interactions with other cultures and its lasting impact on the world.

In addition to its historical and cultural significance, Cairo is a city of contrasts and coexistence. The juxtaposition of ancient and modern, traditional and contemporary, creates a unique urban landscape where the past is constantly interwoven with the present. This dynamic interplay between history and modernity is evident in the daily life of Cairo's residents, who navigate the city's bustling streets, ancient sites, and modern amenities with a sense of continuity and adaptation.

Cairo's culinary scene is a testament to the city's rich cultural heritage. Traditional Egyptian dishes, such as koshari, ful medames, and molokhia, reflect the agricultural practices and dietary preferences that have evolved over millennia. The influence of various cultures and historical periods is also evident in Cairo's cuisine, with flavors and techniques borrowed from Mediterranean, Middle Eastern, and African traditions.

The city's artistic and literary scenes continue to thrive, drawing inspiration from Cairo's historical legacy and contemporary issues. Egyptian literature, cinema, and visual arts often explore themes related to identity, heritage, and social change, providing a platform for creative expression and critical reflection. Cairo's theaters, galleries, and cultural festivals contribute to the city's vibrant and dynamic cultural landscape.

Education and research are also central to Cairo's role as a custodian of ancient Egyptian heritage. Institutions such as the American University in Cairo, Cairo University, and various archaeological schools and research centers are at the forefront of studying and preserving Egypt's historical legacy. These institutions collaborate with international scholars and organizations to conduct excavations, conservation projects, and academic research that enhance our understanding of ancient Egyptian civilization.

The preservation of Cairo's historical sites and artifacts is an ongoing challenge that requires careful planning and international cooperation. Issues such as urban development, environmental factors, and tourism impact must be managed to ensure that the city's ancient treasures are protected for future generations. Conservation efforts, supported by both national and international organizations, play a crucial role in safeguarding Cairo's heritage and promoting sustainable tourism practices.

Cairo's significance as a global cultural and historical center is reinforced by its designation as a UNESCO World Heritage Site. The recognition of the city's outstanding universal value highlights the importance of its ancient monuments, historic neighborhoods, and cultural contributions. This designation also emphasizes the need for continued efforts to preserve and celebrate Cairo's unique heritage.

Chapter 3: Athens: Birthplace of Democracy

Athens, often hailed as the birthplace of democracy, stands as a testament to the enduring legacy of ancient Greece. This historic city, with its blend of classical ruins and vibrant modern life, offers a unique window into the development of democratic principles and practices that have influenced political systems worldwide. The story of Athens and its democratic evolution is a rich tapestry of social, political, and cultural achievements that continue to resonate through the ages.

The origins of Athenian democracy can be traced back to the late 6th century BC, during a period of social unrest and political upheaval. The city-state of Athens was initially governed by aristocrats who held power through hereditary privilege. This oligarchic system led to significant social inequalities and widespread dissatisfaction among the lower classes. The struggle for political reform culminated in the rise of influential leaders who sought to establish a more inclusive and participatory system of governance.

One of the earliest and most significant figures in this process was Solon, a statesman and poet who implemented crucial reforms around 594 BC. Solon's reforms aimed to address the economic disparities and social tensions that plagued Athens. He abolished debt slavery, where citizens were forced into servitude to pay off debts, and redistributed land to create a more equitable society. Solon also reorganized the political structure by establishing the Council of Four Hundred, which allowed broader participation in decision-making processes. These reforms laid the groundwork for the eventual development of a democratic system.

The true foundation of Athenian democracy, however, was established by Cleisthenes, who came to power in 508 BC. Often regarded as the "Father of Athenian Democracy," Cleisthenes introduced a series of radical reforms that transformed the political landscape of Athens. He reorganized the population into ten tribes based on geographic rather than familial affiliations, breaking the power of the traditional aristocratic clans. This reorganization fostered a sense of civic identity and unity among the diverse population of Athens. Cleisthenes also established the Council of Five Hundred, a representative body chosen by lot from each of the ten tribes. This council played a central role in the administration of the city-state, preparing legislation and overseeing various aspects of governance. The use of a lottery system to select council members ensured a more egalitarian and inclusive political process, reducing the influence of wealth and birthright.

The most distinctive feature of Athenian democracy was the Ecclesia, or Assembly, which was open to all male citizens over the age of 18. The Assembly met regularly on the Pnyx, a hill overlooking the Acropolis, and served as the primary decision-making body of Athens. Citizens could participate directly in the legislative process, debate policies, and vote on important issues such as war, peace, and public expenditures. This direct form of democracy empowered ordinary Athenians to play an active role in the governance of their city-state.

Pericles, a prominent statesman and general, further strengthened Athenian democracy during the 5th century BC. His leadership marked the height of Athenian political and cultural power, a period often referred to as the "Golden Age of Athens." Pericles expanded the participation of citizens in the democratic process by introducing pay for public officials, enabling poorer citizens to serve in government roles. He also championed the arts, philosophy, and architecture, fostering an environment of intellectual and cultural flourishing that left a lasting impact on Western civilization.

One of the most enduring contributions of Athenian democracy is the concept of legal equality and the rule of law. The Athenians developed a sophisticated legal system with laws that applied equally to all citizens. The principle of isonomia, or equality before the law, was a cornerstone of Athenian democracy. Citizens had the right to seek justice through the courts, and legal disputes were often resolved through jury trials. Juries were composed of large panels of citizens chosen by lot, ensuring a broad representation of the populace and minimizing the potential for corruption and bias.

Athenian democracy was not without its limitations and exclusions. Citizenship was restricted to adult males who had completed their military training, excluding women, slaves, and foreigners (metics) from political participation. Despite these limitations, the democratic system of Athens was revolutionary in its time, providing a model of citizen engagement and public accountability that influenced later democratic developments.

The philosophical and intellectual environment of Athens also played a crucial role in the development and critique of democratic principles. Thinkers such as Socrates, Plato, and Aristotle engaged in rigorous debates about the nature of justice, governance, and the role of the individual in society. Socrates, known for his method of dialectical questioning, challenged the assumptions and beliefs of his fellow citizens, encouraging critical thinking and self-examination. Plato, a student of Socrates, was more skeptical of democracy, arguing in his work "The Republic" that it could lead to mob rule and the rise of demagogues. Plato's critique highlighted the potential weaknesses of direct democracy and the need for a balanced and just political system. Aristotle, in his "Politics," offered a more nuanced view, recognizing the strengths of democracy while advocating for a mixed system that combined elements of democracy, oligarchy, and monarchy.

The cultural achievements of Athens during its democratic period were equally remarkable. The city became a center of artistic and intellectual activity, producing works of literature, drama, philosophy, and art that continue to inspire and influence. The construction of the Parthenon, a magnificent temple dedicated to the goddess Athena, symbolized the glory and civic pride of Athens. The theater of Dionysus hosted the plays of great dramatists like Aeschylus, Sophocles, and Euripides, whose works explored complex themes of human nature, morality, and the divine. These cultural contributions reflected the values and ideals of Athenian democracy, emphasizing the importance of civic participation, individual expression, and the pursuit of knowledge.

The Peloponnesian War, a protracted conflict between Athens and Sparta, marked a period of crisis and decline for Athenian democracy. The war strained the resources and resilience of Athens, leading to internal political strife and the eventual overthrow of the democratic system by the oligarchic regime known as the Thirty Tyrants in 404 BC. However, democracy was restored in 403 BC, demonstrating the resilience and enduring appeal of the democratic principles that had been established.

The legacy of Athenian democracy extends far beyond the borders of ancient Greece. The ideas and practices developed in Athens influenced the Roman Republic, the Enlightenment thinkers of the 18th century, and the framers of modern democratic constitutions. The principles of popular sovereignty, civic participation, and legal equality that emerged in Athens continue to underpin democratic systems around the world.

In modern Athens, the echoes of its democratic heritage are still present. The city is home to numerous archaeological sites, museums, and cultural institutions that preserve and celebrate its ancient past. The Acropolis Museum, the National Archaeological Museum, and the Ancient Agora are just a few of the places where visitors can explore the rich history and achievements of Athens. The city also serves as the capital of Greece, a democratic republic that upholds the values of political freedom and civic engagement that were first articulated in ancient Athens.

Athens' enduring legacy as the birthplace of democracy is a source of pride and inspiration for people around the world. The principles and practices developed by the Athenians continue to inform and shape contemporary political thought and institutions. The story of Athens and its democratic evolution is a testament to the power of collective action, the importance of civic responsibility, and the enduring quest for justice and equality.

As we reflect on the history of Athens, we are reminded of the profound impact that democratic ideals can have on shaping societies and fostering human flourishing. The achievements of ancient Athens, both in governance and culture, stand as a beacon of what is possible when citizens come together to build a just and inclusive society. The legacy of Athenian democracy serves as a guiding light, illuminating the path towards a future where the principles of equality, participation, and the rule of law are upheld and cherished by all.

Chapter 4: Jerusalem: Crossroads of Faith

Jerusalem, one of the oldest cities in the world, is a place of immense religious, historical, and cultural significance. Often referred to as the "Crossroads of Faith," Jerusalem is a sacred city to Judaism, Christianity, and Islam, making it a focal point of religious devotion and conflict for millennia. The city's history is a complex tapestry of conquests, cultural exchanges, and spiritual milestones, each layer adding depth to its significance in the hearts and minds of millions around the world.

For Jews, Jerusalem is the holiest city, the site of the ancient Temples and the eternal capital promised to them by God. The history of Jewish Jerusalem dates back to King David, who established the city as the capital of the United Kingdom of Israel around 1000 BCE. His son, King Solomon, built the First Temple on Mount Moriah, the site where Abraham was believed to have prepared to sacrifice his son Isaac. The Temple became the center of Jewish worship, housing the Ark of the Covenant. Jerusalem's significance grew with the construction of the Second Temple after the Babylonian Exile, which stood until its destruction by the Romans in 70 CE. The Western Wall, a remnant of the Second Temple, remains a place of pilgrimage and prayer for Jews worldwide.

Christianity reveres Jerusalem as the site of Jesus Christ's crucifixion, resurrection, and ascension. The city is central to the narrative of the New Testament, where many key events of Jesus' life and ministry occurred. The Church of the Holy Sepulchre, one of Christianity's holiest sites, is believed to encompass both Golgotha, where Jesus was crucified, and the tomb from which he rose. Christian pilgrims have journeyed to Jerusalem for centuries to walk the Via Dolorosa, the path that Jesus is said to have taken to his crucifixion, and to visit the numerous churches and monasteries that commemorate events from his life.

For Muslims, Jerusalem is the third holiest city after Mecca and Medina. The Al-Aqsa Mosque and the Dome of the Rock, both located on the Temple Mount, or Haram al-Sharif, are sites of profound religious importance. The Dome of the Rock, with its iconic golden dome, enshrines the rock from which Muslims believe the Prophet Muhammad ascended to heaven during the Night Journey. The Al-Aqsa Mosque, also on the Temple Mount, is a significant place of worship and the destination of Muhammad's night journey from Mecca. The importance of Jerusalem in Islam is rooted in both the Quran and the Hadith, with numerous references that underscore the city's sanctity.

The city's significance to these three major religions has made it a focal point of historical and modern conflicts. The Crusades, a series of religious wars in the medieval period, saw Christian armies from Europe attempt to reclaim Jerusalem from Muslim control. The city's control shifted numerous times, each change bringing about periods of relative peace and intense conflict. The modern history of Jerusalem is equally complex, particularly following the establishment of the State of Israel in 1948. The city's status remains one of the most contentious issues in the Israeli-Palestinian conflict, with both sides claiming Jerusalem as their capital.

Despite its turbulent history, Jerusalem is also a city of extraordinary cultural and religious coexistence. The Old City, a UNESCO World Heritage site, is divided into four quarters: Jewish, Christian, Muslim, and Armenian. Each quarter has its own unique character and significant religious sites. The Jewish Quarter is home to the Western Wall and numerous synagogues and yeshivas. The Christian Quarter hosts the Church of the Holy Sepulchre and the Via Dolorosa. The Muslim Quarter includes the Al-Aqsa Mosque and bustling markets. The Armenian Quarter, while smaller, holds significant religious and historical sites for the Armenian Christian community, including the Cathedral of St. James.

Jerusalem's cultural landscape is as diverse as its religious heritage. The city's museums, such as the Israel Museum, which houses the Dead Sea Scrolls, and the Yad Vashem Holocaust memorial, offer profound insights into Jewish history and heritage. The Tower of David Museum, located near the Jaffa Gate, provides a comprehensive overview of Jerusalem's long and storied past through archaeological artifacts and interactive exhibits. The city's vibrant arts scene, with galleries, theaters, and music venues, reflects the modern and diverse nature of its population.

The Hebrew University of Jerusalem, founded in 1925, is one of the leading academic institutions in the Middle East. It has been a center for research and learning, attracting scholars from around the world. The university's contributions to science, humanities, and social sciences underscore Jerusalem's role as a hub of intellectual and cultural activity.

Modern Jerusalem is a city that balances its ancient heritage with contemporary life. Its streets are a blend of the old and the new, where historic stone buildings stand alongside modern architecture. The city's diverse population includes Jews, Muslims, Christians, and people of many other faiths and backgrounds. This diversity is reflected in the city's cuisine, festivals, and daily interactions, making Jerusalem a microcosm of the world's rich cultural mosaic.

The city's festivals and religious celebrations are a testament to its spiritual vibrancy. Jewish festivals such as Passover, Rosh Hashanah, and Yom Kippur see thousands of worshippers gathering at the Western Wall and synagogues throughout the city. Christian celebrations, particularly Easter and Christmas, bring pilgrims to the Church of the Holy Sepulchre and other holy sites. Muslim festivals such as Ramadan and Eid al-Fitr are marked by prayers at the Al-Aqsa Mosque and communal gatherings.

Jerusalem's spiritual significance is further enhanced by the presence of numerous religious institutions, seminaries, and schools. These institutions continue the traditions of study, worship, and community service that have been part of the city's fabric for centuries. The interfaith dialogue and cooperation fostered by these institutions are vital for promoting understanding and peace in a city that is often a flashpoint for conflict.

The future of Jerusalem remains uncertain, with its status and governance continuing to be subjects of international debate and negotiation. The city's significance to so many people around the world ensures that it will remain at the heart of global religious and political discussions. Efforts to promote peace, understanding, and coexistence are essential for ensuring that Jerusalem can continue to be a place of pilgrimage, worship, and cultural exchange for future generations.

Chapter 5: Beijing: Tales from the Forbidden City

Beijing, the capital of China, is a city of immense historical and cultural significance. Among its many iconic landmarks, the Forbidden City stands out as a symbol of imperial grandeur and mystery. The Forbidden City, also known as the Imperial Palace, served as the home of Chinese emperors and their households for nearly 500 years, from the Ming dynasty to the end of the Qing dynasty. Its vast complex of palaces, halls, gardens, and courtyards is a testament to the architectural, artistic, and cultural achievements of imperial China. The tales from the Forbidden City are filled with intrigue, power struggles, and the daily life of those who lived within its walls.

The construction of the Forbidden City began in 1406, under the orders of the Yongle Emperor, the third emperor of the Ming dynasty. The project took 14 years to complete and involved hundreds of thousands of workers. The location of the Forbidden City was carefully chosen according to the principles of Feng Shui, ensuring harmony with the surrounding environment. The palace complex is situated at the heart of Beijing, aligned along a central north-south axis that extends throughout the city.

Covering an area of 180 acres, the Forbidden City is the largest ancient palatial structure in the world. It is enclosed by a massive wall 10 meters high and surrounded by a moat 52 meters wide. The layout of the Forbidden City follows a strict hierarchical order, reflecting the rigid social structure of imperial China. The complex is divided into two main sections: the Outer Court and the Inner Court. The Outer Court, located in the southern part of the Forbidden City, was used for ceremonial and administrative purposes. It contains the most important buildings, including the Hall of Supreme Harmony, the Hall of Central Harmony, and the Hall of Preserving Harmony. The Inner Court, located in the northern part of the Forbidden City, was the residential area of the emperor and his family. It includes the Palace of Heavenly Purity, the Hall of Union, and the Palace of Earthly Tranquility.

The architecture of the Forbidden City is a masterpiece of traditional Chinese design. The buildings are constructed using wood, with intricate roof structures, elaborate carvings, and vibrant colors. The roofs are covered with yellow glazed tiles, symbolizing the emperor's supreme authority. The use of red walls and columns throughout the complex signifies happiness and good fortune. The layout of the buildings and the arrangement of spaces are carefully designed to reflect the Confucian ideals of harmony, order, and respect for hierarchy.

One of the most famous tales from the Forbidden City is the story of the eunuchs who served the emperors. Eunuchs were castrated men who were employed in various roles within the palace, from personal attendants to high-ranking officials. The practice of using eunuchs dates back to ancient times, but it reached its peak during the Ming and Qing dynasties. Eunuchs held significant power and influence within the Forbidden City, often acting as intermediaries between the emperor and the outside world. Some eunuchs, such as the notorious Wei Zhongxian of the late Ming dynasty, accumulated vast wealth and wielded immense political power, while others served faithfully and loyally throughout their lives.

The lives of the concubines in the Forbidden City also provide a glimpse into the complex social dynamics within the palace. The emperor's harem consisted of numerous women, ranging from empresses and noble consorts to lesser concubines and maids. The selection and promotion of concubines were governed by strict protocols and ceremonies, reflecting the hierarchical nature of the court. While some concubines enjoyed the favor of the emperor and lived in luxury, others faced intense competition, jealousy, and intrigue. The story of Empress Dowager Cixi, who rose from the rank of a lowly concubine to become the de facto ruler of China in the late 19th century, is a dramatic example of the power struggles and political maneuvering within the Forbidden City.

The daily life of the emperor and his court was governed by a complex system of rituals and ceremonies. The emperor was considered the Son of Heaven, the supreme ruler who held the Mandate of Heaven to govern the world. His actions and decisions were believed to affect the harmony of the universe, and he was expected to perform numerous rituals to ensure the well-being of the state and the people. These rituals included offerings to ancestors, prayers for good harvests, and ceremonies marking important events such as the emperor's birthday or the winter solstice.

The Forbidden City was not only a political and ceremonial center but also a cultural hub. The palace was home to a vast collection of art, literature, and historical documents. The emperors themselves were often patrons of the arts and scholars. The Qianlong Emperor of the Qing dynasty, for example, was an avid collector and connoisseur of art. He commissioned numerous works of painting, calligraphy, and poetry, and his reign is considered a golden age of Chinese art and culture. The palace workshops produced exquisite objects, including lacquerware, porcelain, jade carvings, and textiles, many of which are now housed in museums around the world.

The fall of the Qing dynasty in 1912 marked the end of imperial rule in China and brought significant changes to the Forbidden City. The last emperor, Puyi, continued to live in the Inner Court for several years under a special arrangement with the new Republic of China. However, in 1924, he was expelled from the Forbidden City, and the palace complex was converted into a museum. The establishment of the Palace Museum marked the beginning of a new chapter in the history of the Forbidden City, as it became a symbol of China's cultural heritage and a major tourist attraction.

In recent decades, extensive efforts have been made to preserve and restore the Forbidden City. The Palace Museum has undertaken numerous restoration projects to repair and conserve the historic buildings and artifacts. These efforts have been supported by international collaborations and advanced conservation techniques, ensuring that the splendor of the Forbidden City can be appreciated by future generations.

Today, the Forbidden City stands as a testament to China's rich history and cultural achievements. It attracts millions of visitors each year, offering a glimpse into the opulent and complex world of the Chinese imperial court. The tales from the Forbidden City continue to captivate and inspire, reflecting the enduring legacy of one of the greatest architectural and cultural treasures in the world.

The Forbidden City has also been the subject of numerous books, films, and television series, further cementing its place in popular culture. These works often explore the intrigues, romances, and dramas that played out within the palace walls, bringing to life the stories of the emperors, empresses, concubines, and eunuchs who once inhabited this magnificent complex. Through these narratives, the Forbidden City remains a source of fascination and wonder, a symbol of the enduring power and mystery of China's imperial past.

Chapter 6: Mexico City: Aztec Foundations

Mexico City, the sprawling capital of Mexico, is a metropolis with a rich and layered history. Beneath its modern urban landscape lies the story of Tenochtitlán, the majestic city built by the Aztecs. The Aztec civilization, known for its complex social structure, impressive architecture, and advanced agricultural techniques, laid the foundations for what would become one of the most populous cities in the world. The tales of Mexico City's Aztec origins are intertwined with legends, conquests, and the remarkable achievements of a society that thrived in the heart of Mesoamerica.

The story of Tenochtitlán begins in the early 14th century when the Mexica people, a nomadic tribe from northern Mexico, arrived in the Valley of Mexico. According to Aztec legend, their god Huitzilopochtli instructed them to settle where they saw an eagle perched on a cactus, devouring a snake. This prophetic vision was realized on an island in the middle of Lake Texcoco, and there they founded Tenochtitlán in 1325. The site, seemingly inhospitable with its swampy terrain, would soon be transformed into a thriving and formidable city.

The Aztecs demonstrated remarkable engineering skills in the construction of Tenochtitlán. To create a stable foundation for their city, they built a series of causeways and canals that connected the island to the mainland, facilitating transportation and trade. These causeways were equipped with removable bridges, which could be retracted to defend the city from invaders. The city itself was laid out in a grid pattern, with wide avenues, marketplaces, temples, and residential areas. The heart of Tenochtitlán was the Templo Mayor, a massive pyramid dedicated to the gods Huitzilopochtli and Tlaloc. The Templo Mayor stood as a symbol of the Aztecs' religious devotion and political power, serving as the center for religious ceremonies, including human sacrifices which were believed to appease the gods and ensure the city's prosperity.

Agriculture was central to the Aztec economy and the sustenance of Tenochtitlán's population. The Aztecs developed an innovative farming technique known as chinampas, or "floating gardens." These were artificial islands created by piling mud and vegetation onto woven reed mats anchored to the lakebed. The chinampas provided fertile soil and a reliable water supply, allowing the Aztecs to grow crops such as maize, beans, squash, and tomatoes year-round. This agricultural abundance supported a population that, at its height, is estimated to have been between 200,000 and 300,000 people, making Tenochtitlán one of the largest cities in the world at the time.

The social and political structure of the Aztec Empire was highly organized and hierarchical. At the top of the hierarchy was the emperor, or Tlatoani, who was considered both a political and religious leader. The emperor was supported by a council of nobles, priests, and military leaders who helped govern the city and the expanding empire. Below the nobility were the commoners, who included farmers, artisans, merchants, and soldiers. Despite the rigid class structure, there was some social mobility, particularly through success in warfare or commerce. The Aztecs placed a strong emphasis on education, with separate schools for noble and commoner children. The calmecac, or school for the nobility, focused on subjects such as astronomy, theology, and leadership, while the telpochcalli, or school for commoners, emphasized practical skills, military training, and basic literacy.

Trade was another vital aspect of Aztec society, with Tenochtitlán serving as a major commercial hub. The city's markets, particularly the grand Tlatelolco market, attracted merchants from across Mesoamerica. Goods such as gold, silver, jade, textiles, cacao, and exotic feathers were traded, showcasing the wealth and diversity of the Aztec Empire. The use of cacao beans as currency facilitated trade, and the pochteca, or professional merchants, played a crucial role in the economy by traveling long distances to acquire luxury goods and establish trade networks.

Religion permeated every aspect of Aztec life, and the pantheon of gods and goddesses reflected the natural world and the human experience. Huitzilopochtli, the god of war and the sun, was the patron deity of Tenochtitlán, symbolizing the city's martial prowess and divine favor. Tlaloc, the rain god, and Quetzalcoatl, the feathered serpent god of wind and learning, were also prominent figures in Aztec mythology. Religious ceremonies, including elaborate rituals and festivals, were conducted to honor these deities and ensure the favor of the gods. The Aztecs believed that human sacrifice was essential to appease the gods and maintain the cosmic order. These sacrifices, often involving prisoners of war, were performed at the Templo Mayor and other temples, reinforcing the power of the priesthood and the ruling elite.

The arrival of the Spanish conquistadors in the early 16th century marked a dramatic turning point in the history of Tenochtitlán and the Aztec Empire. In 1519, Hernán Cortés and his expedition reached the Valley of Mexico and were awed by the grandeur of Tenochtitlán. Initially welcomed by the Aztec emperor Moctezuma II, the relationship between the Spanish and the Aztecs quickly deteriorated. Tensions escalated, leading to the capture and death of Moctezuma, and eventually to the brutal siege of Tenochtitlán in 1521. The city's advanced defenses and formidable warriors were no match for the Spanish, who, with the help of indigenous allies and superior weaponry, managed to conquer Tenochtitlán after a bloody and protracted battle. The fall of the city marked the end of the Aztec Empire and the beginning of Spanish colonial rule.

In the aftermath of the conquest, the Spanish systematically dismantled the structures of Tenochtitlán, building Mexico City atop its ruins. Many of the stones from Aztec temples and buildings were repurposed for the construction of colonial buildings, churches, and plazas. The layout of modern Mexico City retains the grid pattern of its Aztec predecessor, and the Zócalo, or main square, occupies the same space as the ceremonial center of Tenochtitlán. Despite the destruction, remnants of the Aztec city have survived, and archaeological discoveries continue to reveal the rich history beneath the modern streets. The Templo Mayor, partially excavated and preserved, stands as a testament to the grandeur and spiritual significance of Tenochtitlán. The adjacent museum houses a vast collection of artifacts, including sculptures, jewelry, and ceremonial objects, providing valuable insights into Aztec culture and daily life.

The legacy of the Aztecs is also evident in the cultural and artistic heritage of Mexico. Aztec symbols, motifs, and themes are prevalent in Mexican art, literature, and national identity. The eagle, cactus, and serpent emblem from the founding legend of Tenochtitlán are prominently featured on the Mexican flag, symbolizing the continuity of the nation's history and its deep-rooted connection to its indigenous past. Festivals and celebrations, such as Día de los Muertos (Day of the Dead), incorporate elements of Aztec beliefs and customs, reflecting the syncretism that characterizes Mexican culture.

Today, Mexico City is a vibrant and dynamic metropolis, blending ancient traditions with modern innovation. Its rich cultural scene, diverse population, and historical landmarks make it a major center of art, education, and tourism. The city's museums, such as the National Museum of Anthropology and the Frida Kahlo Museum, showcase Mexico's indigenous heritage and artistic achievements, attracting visitors from around the world. The bustling markets, lively neighborhoods, and iconic landmarks, such as the Palacio de

Bellas Artes and the Chapultepec Castle, offer a glimpse into the city's multifaceted identity.

The story of Mexico City and its Aztec foundations is a tale of resilience, transformation, and enduring legacy. From the legendary founding of Tenochtitlán to the vibrant urban landscape of modern Mexico City, the history of this remarkable place reflects the dynamic interplay of cultures, peoples, and epochs. The Aztec foundations of Mexico City continue to inspire and inform the present, offering a rich tapestry of history and culture that shapes the identity and spirit of the Mexican people.

Chapter 7: Istanbul: Gateway of Civilizations

Istanbul, straddling the continents of Europe and Asia, is a city that has been at the crossroads of civilizations for millennia. Known historically as Byzantium and later Constantinople, Istanbul's unique geographic position has made it a vital cultural, political, and economic hub throughout its long history. The city's strategic location on the Bosphorus Strait, linking the Black Sea to the Mediterranean, has ensured its role as a gateway between East and West, a melting pot of cultures, and a center of trade and commerce. The rich tapestry of Istanbul's history is woven from the threads of various empires and civilizations, each leaving an indelible mark on the city.

The origins of Istanbul date back to the 7th century BCE when Greek colonists from Megara established the city of Byzantium on the European side of the Bosphorus. The city thrived as a trading port due to its advantageous location, facilitating the exchange of goods between Europe and Asia. Byzantium's early history was marked by periods of independence and subjugation, as it fell under the influence of powerful neighbors, including the Persian Empire and later the Macedonian Empire under Alexander the Great.

Byzantium's significance grew exponentially when it was refounded as Constantinople by the Roman Emperor Constantine the Great in 330 CE. Recognizing the strategic and economic advantages of the site, Constantine declared Constantinople the new capital of the Roman Empire, a decision that would shape the future of the city and the empire. As the capital of the Byzantine Empire, Constantinople became a center of political power, culture, and religion. The city's defenses were bolstered by the construction of massive walls, most notably the Theodosian Walls, which provided formidable protection against invasions for centuries.

Constantinople's significance as a religious center was cemented with the construction of the Hagia Sophia, an architectural marvel that served as the cathedral of the Eastern Orthodox Church. Commissioned by Emperor Justinian I and completed in 537 CE, the Hagia Sophia's massive dome and intricate mosaics exemplified Byzantine architectural and artistic prowess. The cathedral remained the largest Christian church in the world for nearly a thousand years and became a symbol of Byzantine cultural and religious identity.

The Byzantine Empire, with Constantinople at its heart, was a beacon of learning and culture during the medieval period. The city was home to numerous scholars, artists, and theologians who contributed to the preservation and transmission of classical knowledge. The University of Constantinople, founded in the 5th century, became a renowned center of education, attracting students from across the empire and beyond. The city's libraries, filled with manuscripts and texts from antiquity, played a crucial role in preserving the intellectual heritage of Greece and Rome.

The strategic importance of Constantinople made it a coveted prize for invaders, leading to numerous sieges and assaults over the centuries. One of the most significant events in the city's history was the Fourth Crusade in 1204, when Crusader armies diverted from their original mission and sacked Constantinople. The city was plundered, and the Byzantine Empire was temporarily fragmented, leading to the establishment of the Latin Empire. The Byzantine emperors eventually recaptured Constantinople in 1261, but the empire never fully recovered from the devastation of the Fourth Crusade.

The final and most transformative conquest of Constantinople came in 1453, when the Ottoman Sultan Mehmed II, known as Mehmed the Conqueror, captured the city after a prolonged siege.

The fall of Constantinople marked the end of the Byzantine Empire and the beginning of a new era under Ottoman rule. Mehmed II immediately recognized the city's potential and declared it the capital of the Ottoman Empire, renaming it Istanbul. The Ottomans embarked on a series of ambitious building projects, transforming the city into a vibrant and cosmopolitan center of the Islamic world.

Under Ottoman rule, Istanbul flourished as a hub of trade, culture, and administration. The Ottomans preserved and enhanced the city's architectural heritage, converting the Hagia Sophia into a mosque and constructing new landmarks such as the Topkapi Palace, the Suleymaniye Mosque, and the Blue Mosque. The Topkapi Palace, the residence of the Ottoman sultans, became the administrative and ceremonial heart of the empire, reflecting the grandeur and sophistication of Ottoman court life.

Istanbul's population grew rapidly as people from various ethnic and religious backgrounds settled in the city, contributing to its cosmopolitan character. The Ottomans practiced a policy of relative religious tolerance, allowing Christians, Jews, and Muslims to coexist and maintain their own places of worship. This diversity fostered a rich cultural exchange and made Istanbul a melting pot of languages, traditions, and customs.

The city's position at the crossroads of trade routes ensured its economic prosperity. The Grand Bazaar, one of the largest and oldest covered markets in the world, became a bustling center of commerce where merchants traded goods from across Europe, Asia, and Africa. Istanbul's markets were filled with spices, textiles, ceramics, and precious metals, reflecting the city's role as a major trading hub.

The Ottoman period also saw significant advancements in the arts and sciences. Istanbul became a center of Islamic scholarship, with numerous madrasas (Islamic schools) and libraries. The city's artisans and craftsmen produced exquisite works of art, including calligraphy, ceramics, textiles, and metalwork, which were highly prized throughout the empire and beyond. The architectural style that emerged during this period, characterized by grand domes, intricate tile work, and elegant minarets, became synonymous with Ottoman aesthetics.

The 19th century brought challenges and transformations to Istanbul as the Ottoman Empire faced internal strife and external pressures. The city experienced a period of modernization and reform, known as the Tanzimat, which aimed to reorganize and modernize the empire's administration, legal system, and infrastructure. These reforms included the construction of new roads, bridges, and public buildings, as well as the introduction of Western-style education and legal codes.

The decline of the Ottoman Empire culminated in its dissolution after World War I, and Istanbul found itself at the center of the Turkish War of Independence. The establishment of the Republic of Turkey in 1923 marked a new chapter in the city's history. Although the capital was moved to Ankara, Istanbul remained Turkey's cultural and economic powerhouse. The city underwent significant modernization and urbanization, transforming into a vibrant and dynamic metropolis.

Today, Istanbul is a city of contrasts, where ancient history and modernity coexist. The city's skyline is a blend of historic minarets and domes, contemporary skyscrapers, and bustling neighborhoods. The Bosphorus Strait continues to be a vital artery, with ferries and ships navigating its waters, connecting the European and Asian sides of the city. The city's cultural heritage is preserved in its many museums, galleries, and historic sites, attracting millions of visitors each year.

Istanbul's rich culinary scene reflects its diverse heritage, with a fusion of flavors and dishes from the Middle East, the Mediterranean, and beyond. Traditional Turkish cuisine, with its emphasis on fresh ingredients, spices, and diverse cooking techniques, is complemented by a vibrant street food culture and a growing array of international restaurants.

The city's cultural life is equally vibrant, with numerous festivals, concerts, and exhibitions showcasing Istanbul's artistic and creative spirit. The Istanbul Biennial, one of the most prestigious contemporary art events in the world, attracts artists and art lovers from around the globe. The city's music scene is diverse, ranging from traditional Turkish music to classical, jazz, and contemporary genres.

Istanbul's universities and research institutions continue the city's long tradition of scholarship and learning. The city's educational institutions attract students from Turkey and abroad, contributing to its dynamic intellectual environment. Istanbul's role as a center of media and publishing further reinforces its cultural and intellectual significance.

In recent years, Istanbul has faced challenges related to rapid urbanization, environmental concerns, and political tensions. The city's growth has put pressure on its infrastructure and natural resources, prompting efforts to balance development with sustainability. Despite these challenges, Istanbul remains a resilient and thriving metropolis, a testament to its enduring legacy as a gateway of civilizations.

Chapter 8: Paris: The Revolution's Heartbeat

Paris, the capital of France, has long been regarded as the heartbeat of the French Revolution, a transformative period that reshaped the nation's political, social, and cultural landscape. The French Revolution, which began in 1789 and lasted until 1799, marked the end of the monarchy, the rise of republicanism, and the establishment of the French Republic. The city of Paris was at the center of these seismic changes, serving as the stage for many of the Revolution's most dramatic and significant events. Paris's streets, squares, and buildings witnessed the rise and fall of revolutionary fervor, the clash of ideologies, and the birth of modern political thought.

The origins of the French Revolution can be traced to a combination of social, economic, and political factors that converged in the late 18th century. The French society was deeply divided into three estates: the clergy, the nobility, and the common people, or Third Estate. The Third Estate, which comprised the vast majority of the population, was burdened with heavy taxes and had little political power. Economic hardship, food shortages, and widespread discontent with the monarchy and the ruling aristocracy created a fertile ground for revolutionary ideas. Enlightenment thinkers such as Voltaire, Rousseau, and Montesquieu had already begun to challenge the traditional social and political order, advocating for reason, equality, and individual rights.

The Revolution's heartbeat can be heard in the convocation of the Estates-General in May 1789, the first such meeting since 1614. This assembly, called by King Louis XVI to address the kingdom's financial crisis, brought together representatives from all three estates. The Third Estate, frustrated by the inequitable voting system that favored the privileged classes, declared itself the National Assembly, vowing to draft a new constitution. This bold move marked the beginning of the Revolution, as the National Assembly represented the will of the people and challenged the authority of the king.

One of the most iconic events of the Revolution took place on July 14, 1789, with the storming of the Bastille. The Bastille, a medieval fortress and prison in Paris, symbolized the tyranny of the monarchy. Its capture by an enraged crowd of Parisians seeking arms and gunpowder was both a literal and symbolic blow against the old regime. The fall of the Bastille became a rallying point for the revolutionaries and is still celebrated today as Bastille Day, a national holiday in France. The storming of the Bastille signified the power of the people and their determination to overthrow the oppressive structures of the past.

The Revolution continued to gain momentum with the Declaration of the Rights of Man and of the Citizen, adopted by the National Assembly in August 1789. This groundbreaking document, inspired by Enlightenment ideals, proclaimed the fundamental rights of individuals, including liberty, equality, and fraternity. It asserted that all men are born free and equal in rights and that sovereignty resides in the nation, not in a monarch. The Declaration laid the foundation for modern democratic principles and became a cornerstone of revolutionary ideology.

Paris played a central role in the early phase of the Revolution, with its streets and public spaces becoming arenas for political action and popular protest. The Women's March on Versailles in October 1789 was a pivotal moment when thousands of Parisian women, angered by food shortages and high bread prices, marched to the royal palace in Versailles. They demanded that the king address their grievances and return to Paris. The march resulted in the royal family being brought back to the capital, where they were effectively placed under house arrest in the Tuileries Palace. This event underscored the influence of ordinary Parisians in shaping the course of the Revolution.

The Revolution entered a more radical phase with the rise of the Jacobins, a political club that advocated for republicanism and greater social equality. The Jacobins, led by figures such as Maximilien Robespierre, Jean-Paul Marat, and Georges Danton, gained significant influence within the National Convention, the revolutionary assembly that replaced the National Assembly. The Jacobins pushed for the abolition of the monarchy, which was achieved with the execution of King Louis XVI in January 1793. The king's death marked the definitive end of the monarchy and the establishment of the First French Republic.

Paris became the epicenter of the Reign of Terror, a period of political purges and mass executions aimed at eliminating counter-revolutionary elements. The Revolutionary Tribunal, established in Paris, conducted trials of suspected enemies of the Revolution, leading to the execution of thousands, including prominent figures such as Marie Antoinette, the former queen. The guillotine, installed in the Place de la Révolution (now Place de la Concorde), became a grim symbol of the Revolution's radical phase. The Reign of Terror, while intended to protect the Revolution, also exposed the internal divisions and extremes of revolutionary zeal.

Amidst the political upheaval, Paris was also a site of significant social and cultural changes. The Revolution brought about the secularization of society, with the confiscation of church property and the establishment of state control over religious institutions. Revolutionary leaders sought to replace traditional religious practices with secular and republican rituals, such as the Cult of Reason and the Cult of the Supreme Being. These new forms of civic worship were intended to foster a sense of collective identity and devotion to revolutionary ideals.

The Revolution also had a profound impact on the arts and intellectual life in Paris. The Louvre, originally a royal palace, was transformed into a public museum, symbolizing the democratization of art and culture. Revolutionary leaders recognized the importance of education and established institutions such as the École Polytechnique and the Conservatoire de Paris to promote scientific and artistic advancement. The period saw a flourishing of revolutionary art and literature, with artists and writers creating works that celebrated the ideals of liberty, equality, and fraternity.

The Revolution's heartbeat continued to reverberate through Paris as the city witnessed the rise of Napoleon Bonaparte, who emerged as a dominant figure in the latter stages of the Revolution. In 1799, Napoleon staged a coup d'état, overthrowing the Directory, the ruling executive body, and establishing himself as First Consul. This marked the end of the revolutionary government and the beginning of the Napoleonic era. While Napoleon's rule brought stability and many reforms, it also marked a departure from the more radical and democratic aspirations of the Revolution.

In the decades following the Revolution, Paris remained a center of political and cultural innovation. The city's infrastructure was transformed under the direction of Baron Haussmann in the mid-19th century, with the creation of wide boulevards, parks, and public spaces that reflected the ideals of order and progress. The revolutionary spirit of Paris continued to inspire movements for social and political change, both in France and around the world.

The legacy of the French Revolution is deeply embedded in the fabric of Paris, visible in its monuments, museums, and public spaces. The Panthéon, originally built as a church, was repurposed during the Revolution to honor the great figures of French history, embodying the revolutionary principle of meritocracy. The Place de la Bastille, where the Bastille prison once stood, remains a symbol of the Revolution's fight against oppression. The Arc de Triomphe, commissioned by Napoleon to commemorate his victories, also stands as a testament to the revolutionary and Napoleonic eras.

Paris's role as the heartbeat of the Revolution is commemorated and celebrated in various ways. Bastille Day, celebrated on July 14th, is a national holiday that features military parades, fireworks, and public festivities, honoring the revolutionary heritage of France. The Musée Carnavalet, dedicated to the history of Paris, houses extensive collections related to the Revolution, offering visitors a deeper understanding of this transformative period.

In contemporary Paris, the spirit of the Revolution lives on in the city's vibrant political and cultural life. Paris remains a global center for intellectual debate, artistic expression, and social activism. The city's universities, theaters, and cultural institutions continue to foster a climate of innovation and creativity, reflecting the enduring influence of revolutionary ideals.

Chapter 9: Kyoto: Samurai and Sacred Shrines

Kyoto, Japan, a city renowned for its breathtaking beauty and cultural heritage, offers a fascinating glimpse into the world of samurai and sacred shrines. Once the imperial capital of Japan, Kyoto has retained much of its historical significance and traditional charm. The city is dotted with ancient temples, shrines, and castles that echo the grandeur of its past, particularly during the time of the samurai.

The samurai, the warrior class that dominated Japanese society for centuries, left an indelible mark on Kyoto. These noble warriors adhered to a strict code of conduct known as Bushido, which emphasized honor, discipline, and loyalty. The samurai were not only skilled in martial arts and combat but also deeply engaged in cultural pursuits such as tea ceremonies, calligraphy, and poetry. This blending of martial prowess and cultural refinement is evident in the architecture and layout of Kyoto, where fortresses and serene gardens coexist harmoniously.

One of the most iconic symbols of samurai heritage in Kyoto is Nijo Castle, a UNESCO World Heritage Site. Built in the early 17th century by Tokugawa Ieyasu, the founder of the Tokugawa Shogunate, Nijo Castle served as the Kyoto residence for the shoguns. The castle's Ninomaru Palace is particularly noteworthy, with its intricate woodwork, gold leaf decorations, and the famous "nightingale floors" that chirp when walked upon, designed to alert inhabitants to intruders. The expansive gardens surrounding the castle are a testament to the samurai's appreciation for nature and tranquility.

In addition to the samurai legacy, Kyoto is also a city of sacred shrines, each with its own unique history and spiritual significance.

The Fushimi Inari Taisha, one of the most famous Shinto shrines in Japan, is dedicated to Inari, the god of rice, prosperity, and foxes. This shrine is renowned for its thousands of vermilion torii gates, which create a mesmerizing pathway up the sacred Mount Inari. Pilgrims and visitors alike traverse this path, seeking blessings and enjoying the serene beauty of the surrounding forest.

Another significant shrine is the Kiyomizu-dera, a Buddhist temple that offers stunning views of Kyoto from its wooden terrace. Founded in the late 8th century, Kiyomizu-dera is dedicated to Kannon, the goddess of mercy. The temple's name, which means "Pure Water Temple," derives from the Otowa Waterfall that flows beneath it. Visitors can drink from the waterfall's three streams, which are believed to confer health, longevity, and success. The temple complex also includes various halls, pagodas, and statues that reflect the deep spirituality and artistic excellence of Kyoto's past.

The Heian Shrine, with its striking red buildings and expansive grounds, commemorates the city's history as the former imperial capital. Constructed in 1895 to celebrate Kyoto's 1100th anniversary, the shrine is dedicated to Emperor Kanmu and Emperor Komei. The Heian Shrine's torii gate is one of the largest in Japan, and its meticulously maintained gardens are a popular spot for festivals and cultural events, particularly the annual Jidai Matsuri, which features a grand parade of participants in historical costumes representing different periods of Kyoto's history.

Kyoto's religious heritage is not limited to Shinto and Buddhism; the city also has a rich tradition of Zen Buddhism. The Zen gardens, or karesansui, of Kyoto are masterpieces of minimalism and contemplation. Ryoan-ji, perhaps the most famous of these, features a rock garden with 15 stones placed in such a way that only 14 are visible from any vantage point. This design invites meditation and introspection, embodying the Zen principles of simplicity and mindfulness. Similarly, the Silver Pavilion, or Ginkaku-ji, although never covered in silver, is renowned for its exquisite garden that includes the Sea of Silver Sand and the Moon Viewing Platform, which reflect the aesthetics and philosophy of Zen.

The interplay between the samurai and sacred shrines in Kyoto is also evident in the city's festivals and traditions. The Aoi Matsuri, held annually in May, is one of Kyoto's oldest festivals, dating back to the 6th century. This festival features a procession of participants dressed in the Heian period attire, parading from the Imperial Palace to the Kamo Shrines. The Gion Matsuri, another major festival, takes place in July and is renowned for its grand floats and lively street festivities. Originally a purification ritual to appease the gods during an epidemic, Gion Matsuri has evolved into a celebration of Kyoto's cultural heritage, blending religious devotion with communal joy.

Furthermore, Kyoto's tea culture, deeply intertwined with the samurai tradition, reflects the city's historical and spiritual depth. The Way of Tea, or Chado, was perfected by Sen no Rikyu in the 16th century, and Kyoto remains a center for this refined art. Tea houses such as the historic Shosei-en Garden offer serene settings for tea ceremonies, where every gesture and element, from the utensils to the garden view, is imbued with meaning. The philosophical underpinnings of Chado, emphasizing harmony, respect, purity, and tranquility, mirror the values that guided the samurai and are evident in Kyoto's sacred spaces.

Kyoto's role as a center of craftsmanship and artistry further underscores its historical significance. The city has been home to many traditional crafts such as kimono weaving, pottery, and lacquerware. These crafts were often patronized by samurai and the imperial court, leading to the development of exquisite techniques and styles. The Nishijin Textile Center, for example, showcases the rich history of Kyoto's weaving industry, where intricate silk brocades were produced for the garments of samurai and nobility. The combination of artistic excellence and cultural heritage makes Kyoto a living museum, preserving the legacy of its illustrious past.

The philosophical and ethical teachings that were integral to samurai culture also find expression in Kyoto's educational institutions. The city is home to several prestigious universities and schools, including Kyoto University, one of Japan's leading research institutions. These centers of learning continue the tradition of intellectual and cultural development that has characterized Kyoto for centuries, fostering a spirit of inquiry and innovation while remaining deeply connected to the city's historical roots.

Chapter 10: Moscow: Shadows of the Tsars

Moscow, the capital of Russia, is a city steeped in history, where the shadows of the Tsars still linger. This city has witnessed the rise and fall of empires, the transformation of Russian society, and the centralization of political power. The legacy of the Tsars, who ruled Russia for centuries, is embedded in Moscow's architecture, culture, and historical consciousness.

The Kremlin, the heart of Moscow, is perhaps the most iconic symbol of tsarist power. This fortified complex, with its imposing walls and golden-domed cathedrals, has been the seat of Russian power since the late 15th century. Ivan III, known as Ivan the Great, was instrumental in consolidating the Russian state and making Moscow its capital. Under his reign, the Kremlin was transformed into a grand citadel. Italian architects were brought in to build its cathedrals, palaces, and towers, blending Russian and European architectural styles. The Assumption Cathedral, where Russian tsars were crowned, stands as a testament to this era, with its intricate frescoes and iconostasis reflecting the grandeur of the Russian Orthodox Church.

Ivan IV, known as Ivan the Terrible, further expanded the Kremlin and left a lasting impact on Moscow. His reign marked the beginning of the autocratic rule that would define the Russian monarchy. Ivan's Oprichnina, a state policy that involved mass repressions, executions, and the confiscation of land from the nobility, instilled a climate of fear and absolute power. St. Basil's Cathedral, commissioned by Ivan to commemorate his victory over the Kazan Khanate, is one of Moscow's most famous landmarks. Its colorful, onion-shaped domes and unique architectural style make it a symbol of Russia. Legend has it that Ivan blinded the cathedral's architect to prevent him from creating anything as beautiful again, a story that underscores the brutal nature of his rule.

The Romanov dynasty, which began with the election of Michael I in 1613, brought a period of stability and expansion to Russia. The Romanovs ruled for over 300 years, and their influence on Moscow is profound. Peter the Great, although he moved the capital to St. Petersburg, initiated significant reforms that modernized Russia and left a lasting impact on Moscow. His efforts to westernize Russian society included changes in dress, government, and military organization. These reforms were reflected in the architecture and urban planning of Moscow, as the city began to adopt European styles and practices.

Catherine the Great, another prominent Romanov ruler, continued the process of modernization and expansion. Under her reign, Moscow saw the construction of many neoclassical buildings, reflecting the Enlightenment ideals of the time. The Pashkov House, an exquisite example of neoclassical architecture, became a symbol of Moscow's intellectual and cultural life. Catherine's reign also marked the establishment of many cultural institutions, including universities, libraries, and theaters, which contributed to Moscow's development as a center of learning and the arts.

The 19th century was a period of great change and turmoil for Moscow. The Napoleonic invasion of 1812 brought devastation to the city, as much of Moscow was burned to the ground during the French occupation. However, the city's resilience was evident in its rapid reconstruction and recovery. The Cathedral of Christ the Savior, built to commemorate Russia's victory over Napoleon, became a symbol of national pride. This monumental structure, with its massive dome and lavish interiors, reflected the grandeur and ambition of the Russian Empire.

The latter part of the 19th century saw the rise of revolutionary sentiments, as discontent with the autocracy grew among various segments of society. Moscow became a hotbed of political activity, with numerous secret societies and revolutionary groups forming within the city. The assassination of Alexander II in 1881 by the People's Will, a revolutionary organization, marked a turning point in Russian history. This event led to increased repression and the tightening of autocratic rule under subsequent tsars, further fueling revolutionary fervor.

The early 20th century brought the final years of the Romanov dynasty and the tumultuous events that led to the Russian Revolution. Nicholas II, the last tsar, faced immense challenges, including political unrest, economic hardship, and the disastrous involvement in World War I. The 1905 Revolution, sparked by events such as Bloody Sunday, saw widespread strikes, protests, and uprisings in Moscow. Although this revolution was ultimately suppressed, it highlighted the deep-seated issues within Russian society and the growing demand for change.

The February Revolution of 1917, which led to the abdication of Nicholas II, marked the end of tsarist rule and the beginning of a new era for Moscow and Russia. The Bolsheviks, under the leadership of Vladimir Lenin, seized power in the October Revolution of 1917, and Moscow once again became the capital of Russia in 1918. The Kremlin, which had been the seat of the tsars, now became the center of Soviet power. The transition from tsarist autocracy to communist rule brought profound changes to Moscow, but the shadows of the tsars remained.

The Soviet era saw the transformation of Moscow into a symbol of socialist ideology and a showcase of Soviet achievements. Many of the city's tsarist-era buildings were repurposed or demolished to make way for new construction. The Red Square, adjacent to the Kremlin, became the focal point of Soviet power, with Lenin's Mausoleum and the grand parades that celebrated communist achievements. Despite these changes, the legacy of the tsars was not entirely erased. The Kremlin's cathedrals, with their rich history and religious significance, continued to stand as reminders of Moscow's imperial past.

After the fall of the Soviet Union in 1991, Moscow underwent yet another transformation. The city embraced capitalism and democracy, leading to a resurgence of interest in its historical and cultural heritage. Efforts to restore and preserve tsarist-era buildings and monuments gained momentum, reflecting a renewed appreciation for Moscow's imperial past. The Cathedral of Christ the Savior, which had been demolished during the Soviet era, was rebuilt in the 1990s as a symbol of Russia's spiritual and cultural revival.

Today, Moscow is a vibrant metropolis that seamlessly blends its historical legacy with modern development. The city's skyline is dotted with both contemporary skyscrapers and historical landmarks, creating a unique urban landscape. The Kremlin and Red Square, now UNESCO World Heritage Sites, attract millions of visitors each year, eager to explore the rich history of the Russian capital. Museums, galleries, and cultural institutions across the city offer insights into Moscow's past, including the era of the tsars.

The influence of the tsars on Moscow is also evident in the city's cultural and artistic life. The Bolshoi Theatre, one of the most prestigious ballet and opera houses in the world, has its roots in the imperial patronage of the arts. The Tretyakov Gallery, with its extensive collection of Russian art, includes many works from the tsarist era, reflecting the cultural flourishing that took place under their rule. The city's universities and academies continue to uphold the tradition of excellence in education and scholarship that was established during the Romanov period.

Moscow's role as the political center of Russia has also remained constant. The Kremlin, once the residence of the tsars, now houses the offices of the Russian president. The continuity of power in this historic complex underscores the enduring significance of Moscow as the heart of Russian governance. The city's political landscape, shaped by centuries of autocratic rule, revolutionary upheaval, and communist dictatorship, continues to evolve in the context of modern Russian politics.

The shadows of the tsars in Moscow are a testament to the city's rich and complex history. From the grand architecture of the Kremlin and the opulence of the cathedrals to the revolutionary fervor that swept through its streets, Moscow has been a witness to the rise and fall of empires. The legacy of the tsars, with their contributions to Russian culture, politics, and society, remains an integral part of Moscow's identity. As the city continues to grow and change, the echoes of its imperial past serve as a reminder of the enduring influence of the tsars on the history and soul of Moscow.

Chapter 11: Delhi: Mughal Marvels

Delhi, the capital of India, is a city that bears the magnificent legacy of the Mughal Empire, one of the most powerful and influential dynasties in Indian history. The Mughal marvels in Delhi are a testament to the grandeur, architectural genius, and cultural renaissance that characterized the Mughal era. Spanning over three centuries from the early 16th to the 19th century, the Mughal dynasty left an indelible mark on Delhi's landscape through its stunning monuments, gardens, and urban planning.

The arrival of the Mughals in India marked a new era of architectural brilliance. Babur, the founder of the Mughal dynasty, laid the foundation for Mughal architecture, but it was under his successors that Delhi saw the rise of some of its most iconic structures. Humayun's Tomb, built in the mid-16th century by his widow, Empress Bega Begum, is one of the earliest examples of Mughal architecture in Delhi. This majestic tomb, set in the midst of a Persian-style charbagh (four-part garden), showcases a harmonious blend of Persian, Turkish, and Indian architectural styles. The use of red sandstone and white marble, the intricate lattice work, and the symmetry of the garden layout all foreshadow the grandeur that would be fully realized in later Mughal constructions.

One of the most significant contributions of the Mughals to Delhi's architectural heritage is the Red Fort, or Lal Qila, constructed by Emperor Shah Jahan in the mid-17th century. This sprawling fortress, built primarily of red sandstone, served as the main residence of the Mughal emperors for nearly two centuries. The Red Fort is a masterpiece of Mughal architecture, featuring a series of grand structures, including the Diwan-i-Aam (Hall of Public Audience), the Diwan-i-Khas (Hall of Private Audience), and the stunning Rang Mahal (Palace of Colors). The fort's massive walls, extending over two kilometers, are punctuated by impressive gates such as the Lahore Gate and the Delhi Gate. The fort complex is also renowned for its beautiful gardens, water channels, and the iconic Naubat Khana (Drum House), where musicians would announce the arrival of the emperor.

Adjacent to the Red Fort is another Mughal marvel, the Jama Masjid, one of the largest mosques in India. Also commissioned by Shah Jahan, this grand mosque was completed in 1656 and remains a vital center of worship and a prominent landmark in Old Delhi. The Jama Masjid's striking architecture features three large domes, two towering minarets, and an expansive courtyard that can accommodate thousands of worshippers. The mosque's façade, adorned with intricate carvings and inlays of white and black marble, exemplifies the elegance and artistic sophistication of Mughal design. The Jama Masjid stands as a testament to the Mughal emperors' devotion to Islam and their patronage of monumental religious architecture.

Shah Jahan's passion for architecture is perhaps most famously exemplified by the Taj Mahal in Agra, but his contributions to Delhi are equally significant. Besides the Red Fort and the Jama Masjid, Shah Jahan also laid out the city's famous Chandni Chowk, a bustling market area that remains a vibrant commercial hub to this day. The design of Chandni Chowk, with its wide streets, canals, and marketplaces, reflects the Mughal emphasis on urban planning and public spaces.

The Mughal emperors were not only patrons of grand architectural projects but also of lush gardens that provided serene retreats from the bustling city. One such garden is the Shalimar Bagh, built by Emperor Shah Jahan in 1653. This Mughal Garden, inspired by the Persian charbagh design, features a central water channel, terraced lawns, and elegant pavilions. Shalimar Bagh was used as a summer retreat by the Mughal emperors and their courtiers, and it exemplifies the Mughal love for nature and horticulture.

Another notable Mughal Garden in Delhi is the Qudsia Bagh, established by Qudsia Begum, the mother of Emperor Ahmad Shah Bahadur, in the mid-18th century. This garden, with its picturesque layout, fountains, and pavilions, reflects the continued influence of Mughal aesthetics in Delhi even during the later years of the empire. The gardens of Delhi, with their emphasis on symmetry, water features, and lush greenery, showcase the Mughals' mastery in creating paradisiacal landscapes that offered respite and rejuvenation.

The Mughal influence on Delhi's architecture extended beyond grand monuments and gardens to include several smaller, yet equally significant, structures. The Zafar Mahal in Mehrauli, built by the later Mughal emperor Bahadur Shah II, is a poignant reminder of the dynasty's final days. This palace, though modest compared to earlier Mughal constructions, features the characteristic Mughal style of arched gateways, intricate carvings, and expansive courtyards. Zafar Mahal served as a summer retreat and a place for the emperor to enjoy the annual Phool Walon Ki Sair festival, reflecting the cultural vibrancy of Mughal Delhi.

The Mughals also left their mark on Delhi's religious landscape through the construction of several mosques and mausoleums. The Sunehri Masjid near the Red Fort, built by Roshan-ud-Daula Zafar Khan in the early 18th century, is a fine example of Mughal religious architecture. This mosque, with its gilded domes and intricate embellishments, stands as a testament to the continued patronage of Islamic art and architecture by the Mughal nobility.

Similarly, the Safdarjung Tomb, built in the mid-18th century, is one of the last monumental tombs of the Mughal era in Delhi. This grand mausoleum, dedicated to Safdarjung, the powerful prime minister of Emperor Muhammad Shah, showcases the declining yet still magnificent Mughal architectural style. The tomb's central dome, arched gateways, and extensive gardens echo the design elements of earlier Mughal masterpieces, though on a slightly smaller scale.

Delhi's Mughal heritage is also evident in the numerous havelis (traditional mansions) that dot the old city. These havelis, built by Mughal nobility and wealthy merchants, reflect the opulent lifestyle and refined tastes of their owners. The Chunnamal Haveli in Chandni Chowk is one of the few remaining examples of these grand residences, with its ornate façade, spacious courtyards, and lavish interiors providing a glimpse into the domestic life of Mughal-era elites.

The Mughal legacy in Delhi extends beyond architecture to encompass the city's cultural, culinary, and artistic traditions. The Mughal emperors were great patrons of the arts, and their courts were centers of cultural exchange and innovation. Persian, Indian, and Central Asian influences merged to create a unique Mughal culture that left a lasting impact on Delhi.

One of the most significant cultural contributions of the Mughals to Delhi is the city's rich culinary heritage. Mughlai cuisine, known for its rich flavors, aromatic spices, and elaborate dishes, continues to be a defining feature of Delhi's food culture. Signature dishes such as biryani, kebabs, and kormas trace their origins to the Mughal kitchens, where royal chefs perfected these recipes. The bustling streets of Old Delhi, particularly around Jama Masjid and Chandni Chowk, are lined with eateries and stalls that serve these delectable Mughal delicacies, offering a culinary journey into the past.

The Mughals also made significant contributions to the arts, particularly in the fields of painting, music, and literature. Mughal miniature paintings, known for their intricate details and vibrant colors, flourished under the patronage of emperors like Akbar, Jahangir, and Shah Jahan. These paintings often depicted court scenes, royal hunts, and floral motifs, reflecting the opulent lifestyle and refined tastes of the Mughal elite. The influence of Mughal art is still visible in Delhi's museums and galleries, which house exquisite collections of these masterpieces.

In the realm of music, the Mughals were instrumental in fostering the development of classical Indian music. The Mughal courts were centers of musical excellence, where renowned musicians and composers such as Tansen and Baiju Bawra performed and created timeless compositions. The fusion of Persian and Indian musical traditions under the Mughals gave rise to new genres and styles that continue to influence Indian classical music today.

Literature also flourished under the Mughals, with the establishment of grand libraries and the patronage of poets, scholars, and writers. Persian was the court language of the Mughal Empire, and many literary works from this period reflect the rich cultural exchange between Persian and Indian traditions. The Mughal emperors themselves were often patrons and connoisseurs of literature, with notable figures like Emperor Akbar commissioning the translation of important texts from Sanskrit to Persian, thereby preserving and promoting India's literary heritage.

Delhi's Mughal marvels are a testament to the dynasty's architectural genius, cultural sophistication, and enduring legacy. The city's skyline, adorned with grand monuments, majestic tombs, and lush gardens, tells the story of an era that transformed Delhi into a center of power, culture, and beauty. The Mughal influence on Delhi extends beyond its physical structures to encompass the city's culinary, artistic, and cultural traditions, making it a living repository of Mughal heritage.

As Delhi continues to evolve as a modern metropolis, the Mughal marvels stand as reminders of a glorious past, inviting residents and visitors alike to explore and appreciate the rich history that has shaped the city's identity. The preservation and celebration of these Mughal legacies ensure that the grandeur and contributions of the Mughal Empire remain an integral part of Delhi's cultural fabric, connecting the past with the present and inspiring future generations.

Chapter 12: Berlin: The Wall's Whisper

Berlin, the capital of Germany, stands as a city deeply scarred by the memories of division and the struggle for freedom and unity. The Berlin Wall, which stood from 1961 to 1989, is one of the most potent symbols of the Cold War, representing not only the physical division of Berlin but also the ideological chasm between East and West. The Wall's whisper is a haunting reminder of the city's tumultuous history, and the stories it tells are woven into the very fabric of Berlin's identity.

The Berlin Wall was erected by the German Democratic Republic (GDR), commonly known as East Germany, in response to the mass defections from East to West Berlin that had been occurring since the end of World War II. In the years leading up to the construction of the Wall, Berlin was a focal point of tension between the Soviet Union and the Western Allies. The city was divided into four sectors, controlled by the United States, the United Kingdom, France, and the Soviet Union. As the ideological divide between the capitalist West and the communist East deepened, Berlin became a symbol of this global struggle.

On the night of August 13, 1961, the GDR began constructing the Berlin Wall. Barbed wire and armed guards were initially deployed to seal off East Berlin from West Berlin, and within days, concrete blocks began to replace the temporary barriers. The Wall eventually evolved into a formidable structure, consisting of concrete segments topped with a smooth pipe to prevent climbing, watchtowers, anti-vehicle trenches, and a wide "death strip" patrolled by armed guards with orders to shoot anyone attempting to escape.

The impact of the Berlin Wall on the city's residents was profound and devastating. Families were torn apart, friends separated, and a once vibrant and interconnected city was split into two isolated halves. The Wall divided not only physical spaces but also lives and futures. Stories of desperate escape attempts, some successful but many tragic, became part of the city's collective memory. The Wall's presence was a daily reminder of the oppression and lack of freedom faced by those in the East.

The construction of the Berlin Wall had significant political and social ramifications. It effectively ended the mass exodus of East Germans to the West, which had been a major embarrassment and economic drain for the GDR. However, it also intensified the Cold War tensions and became a symbol of the broader struggle between the communist and capitalist blocs. The Wall stood as a stark representation of the Iron Curtain that divided Europe, and it became a focal point for protests, propaganda, and international diplomacy.

Life in East Berlin under the shadow of the Wall was marked by strict government control, surveillance, and a lack of political freedom. The Stasi, East Germany's secret police, maintained a pervasive network of informants and monitored almost every aspect of citizens' lives. Despite the oppressive regime, East Berlin also saw cultural and intellectual life thrive in certain areas, with a number of artists, writers, and musicians finding ways to express dissent and creativity within the confines of the system.

West Berlin, on the other hand, became an island of democracy and prosperity surrounded by the communist East. It received substantial support from the Western Allies, particularly the United States, which saw West Berlin as a crucial outpost of freedom in the heart of communist territory. The city became a symbol of resistance against communism and a beacon of hope for those in the East. The vibrant cultural scene in West Berlin, bolstered by its unique status, attracted artists, musicians, and intellectuals from around the world, further emphasizing the stark contrast between the two halves of the city.

The Berlin Wall also became a canvas for political expression. The West Berlin side of the Wall was covered in graffiti, murals, and artworks that reflected the frustrations, hopes, and resistance of those who opposed the division. Artists from around the world came to leave their mark on the Wall, turning it into an evolving piece of political and cultural commentary. The East Berlin side, in contrast, was kept clean and strictly monitored by the authorities, symbolizing the oppressive control of the regime.

The Wall's whisper grew louder as the Cold War progressed, with numerous political and social events highlighting the unsustainable nature of the division. In 1963, U.S. President John F. Kennedy visited West Berlin and delivered his famous "Ich bin ein Berliner" speech, reaffirming American support for West Berlin and freedom. This speech became a powerful symbol of solidarity and resistance against communist oppression.

The 1980s brought significant changes that would ultimately lead to the fall of the Berlin Wall. The policies of glasnost (openness) and perestroika (restructuring) introduced by Soviet leader Mikhail Gorbachev signaled a shift in the Soviet Union's approach to governance and its control over Eastern Europe. These reforms emboldened the populations of East Germany and other Eastern Bloc countries to push for greater political freedoms and economic reforms.

Mass protests began to erupt across East Germany in 1989, with Leipzig becoming a focal point for the peaceful demonstrations demanding political change. The GDR government, facing mounting pressure and an increasingly untenable situation, made a series of concessions, including the relaxation of travel restrictions. On November 9, 1989, a government spokesperson mistakenly announced that travel restrictions would be lifted immediately, leading to a spontaneous and massive gathering of people at the Berlin Wall. In an unprecedented moment, border guards, overwhelmed by the sheer number of people, opened the gates, allowing East and West Berliners to reunite.

The fall of the Berlin Wall was a momentous event that marked the end of an era. The images of jubilant crowds celebrating on top of the Wall, tearing it down piece by piece, became iconic symbols of the triumph of freedom over oppression. The reunification of Berlin and Germany as a whole followed soon after, with official reunification taking place on October 3, 1990.

The legacy of the Berlin Wall continues to resonate in the city today. The remnants of the Wall stand as powerful reminders of the division and suffering endured by Berliners. The East Side Gallery, a preserved section of the Wall, has been transformed into an open-air gallery featuring murals by artists from around the world, celebrating freedom and human rights. The Berlin Wall Memorial and Documentation Center provide a comprehensive historical account of the Wall's impact, offering visitors a poignant and educational experience.

Berlin has embraced its history, using the memory of the Wall to educate future generations and promote the values of freedom, unity, and human rights. The city's transformation from a symbol of division to a beacon of reconciliation and progress is a testament to the resilience and spirit of its people. The reunification of Berlin has led to a vibrant, dynamic metropolis that continues to grow and evolve while honoring its complex past.

The whispers of the Berlin Wall also echo in the personal stories of those who lived through its existence. Memoirs, documentaries, and oral histories capture the experiences of individuals and families affected by the Wall. These narratives, whether of daring escapes, daily struggles, or moments of resistance, add depth and humanity to the historical record. They remind us that behind the political and ideological battles, there were real people whose lives were profoundly shaped by the presence of the Wall.

In contemporary Berlin, the influence of the Wall is evident in the city's architecture, urban planning, and cultural landscape. The once-divided city has undergone significant redevelopment, with former no-man's lands transformed into thriving neighborhoods. The Potsdamer Platz area, which was a desolate wasteland during the division, has been rebuilt into a bustling commercial and cultural hub, symbolizing the city's renewal and unity.

Berlin's cultural scene, enriched by its history, continues to flourish. The city's museums, galleries, and theaters often explore themes related to the Wall and the Cold War, ensuring that the lessons of the past remain relevant. Annual events such as the Festival of Lights, where historical buildings and landmarks are illuminated with art and messages of peace, celebrate Berlin's journey from division to unity.

The Berlin Wall's whisper is a powerful reminder of the fragility of freedom and the importance of vigilance in safeguarding human rights. It serves as a testament to the enduring human spirit and the capacity for change, even in the face of seemingly insurmountable obstacles. Berlin's journey from a city divided by an oppressive regime to a symbol of reconciliation and progress offers hope and inspiration to people around the world.

The Wall's legacy also extends beyond Berlin, influencing global perspectives on freedom, democracy, and human rights. The lessons learned from the Berlin Wall continue to inform discussions on border policies, migration, and the protection of civil liberties. The memory of the Wall underscores the importance of dialogue, diplomacy, and peaceful resolution of conflicts in an interconnected world.

Chapter 13: London: The Empire's Heart

London, the capital of the United Kingdom, has been referred to as "The Empire's Heart" due to its central role in the British Empire, one of the largest and most influential empires in history. The story of London as the heart of the Empire is one of power, wealth, exploration, exploitation, cultural exchange, and profound transformation. Spanning several centuries, this narrative reveals how London evolved from a modest Roman settlement into a global metropolis that influenced and was influenced by its vast colonial domains.

The origins of London can be traced back to its founding by the Romans around 50 AD. Known as Londinium, it served as an important commercial center in Roman Britain. Over the centuries, London grew in importance, particularly during the Middle Ages, when it became the political and economic hub of England. The city's prominence continued to rise, especially after the Norman Conquest in 1066, which brought about significant architectural and administrative developments.

The seeds of the British Empire were sown in the late 16th century during the Elizabethan era. The defeat of the Spanish Armada in 1588 marked the beginning of England's emergence as a formidable naval power. Explorers and privateers like Sir Francis Drake and Sir Walter Raleigh embarked on voyages that expanded England's knowledge of the world and established the first English colonies in the Americas. London, as the nation's capital, was at the forefront of these maritime endeavors, with the city's docks bustling with ships ready to explore and exploit new territories.

The 17th century saw the establishment of the East India Company, a pivotal institution in the expansion of British influence in Asia. Chartered in 1600 by Queen Elizabeth I, the East India Company initially focused on trade in spices, textiles, and other goods from the Indian subcontinent. Over time, it grew into a powerful political and military entity, playing a crucial role in the colonization of India and the establishment of British dominance in the region. The wealth generated from these ventures flowed into London, transforming it into a global financial center.

The 18th century was a period of significant expansion for the British Empire. The Act of Union in 1707 unified England and Scotland, forming the Kingdom of Great Britain and paving the way for a more cohesive and powerful imperial entity. London's prominence as the Empire's heart grew as it became the center of trade, finance, and administration for an ever-expanding realm. The city's ports were the departure points for ships heading to North America, the Caribbean, Africa, and Asia, and its institutions—such as the Bank of England, founded in 1694—underpinned the financial infrastructure necessary to support imperial endeavors.

The Industrial Revolution, which began in the late 18th century, further cemented London's position at the heart of the Empire. The city's population exploded as people moved to urban areas in search of work in the burgeoning factories and industries. London became the world's largest city by the early 19th century, a symbol of industrial might and economic power. The wealth generated from the Empire's colonies, through the exploitation of resources and labor, fueled the city's growth and development. Landmarks such as the British Museum, founded in 1753, and the construction of grand buildings along the Thames, exemplified the cultural and architectural achievements made possible by imperial wealth.

The 19th century was the zenith of the British Empire, and London was the epicenter of its power. The Great Exhibition of 1851, held in the Crystal Palace in Hyde Park, showcased the industrial and cultural achievements of the British Empire to the world. The event was a statement of imperial pride and a demonstration of Britain's dominance in technology, science, and the arts. London's infrastructure and public institutions expanded dramatically during this period. The construction of iconic structures such as the Houses of Parliament, Tower Bridge, and the Victoria and Albert Museum reflected the city's growing status and wealth.

During the Victorian era, London's role as the Empire's heart was evident in its governance and administration. The British Parliament, situated in the Palace of Westminster, was the legislative hub of an empire that spanned continents. Decisions made in London affected millions of people across the globe, from the plains of India to the African savannah. The colonial administration was run from London, with the Colonial Office overseeing the governance of territories around the world. The city was also home to influential figures such as Prime Minister Benjamin Disraeli and explorers like David Livingstone, who played significant roles in shaping the empire's policies and expansion.

The impact of the British Empire on London was not solely economic and political; it was also cultural and demographic. The Empire brought a diverse array of people to London, from colonial administrators and traders to students and laborers. This influx contributed to the city's multicultural character, which remains a defining feature today. Areas such as Limehouse became known for their Chinese communities, while the docks of the East End saw the arrival of sailors and workers from across the Empire. This cultural exchange enriched London's social fabric, introducing new cuisines, traditions, and perspectives.

However, the story of London as the Empire's heart is also one of exploitation and inequality. The wealth that flowed into the city was often derived from the labor and resources of colonized peoples. The transatlantic slave trade, for example, played a significant role in the early economic foundations of the Empire. London merchants and financiers were deeply involved in the trade, and the profits from slavery helped to build and sustain many of the city's institutions and landmarks. The human cost of empire, in terms of lives lost, cultures disrupted, and societies transformed, is a crucial part of this narrative.

The decline of the British Empire in the 20th century brought significant changes to London. The aftermath of World War I and the economic challenges of the interwar period began to erode Britain's global dominance. The independence movements in India, Africa, and other parts of the Empire gained momentum, leading to decolonization in the post-World War II era. The Suez Crisis of 1956 marked a definitive end to Britain's status as a superpower, signaling a shift in the global balance of power.

Despite the decline of the Empire, London remained a global city. The post-war period saw the city transform into a financial and cultural capital, attracting people from around the world. The remnants of the Empire were evident in the multicultural population and the continued influence of British institutions and culture globally. London's museums, galleries, and universities retained their status as world-class institutions, drawing visitors and scholars from former colonies and beyond.

The legacy of the British Empire in London is complex and multifaceted. On one hand, it is a legacy of architectural grandeur, cultural richness, and global influence. On the other, it is a legacy of exploitation, inequality, and historical trauma. Contemporary London grapples with this duality, striving to acknowledge and address the darker aspects of its imperial past while celebrating its diverse and vibrant present.

Today, London's role as the Empire's heart is remembered and reflected upon through various means. Historical tours, exhibitions, and educational programs explore the city's imperial history, offering critical perspectives on the impact of the Empire. Monuments and statues, such as those in Trafalgar Square and along the Thames, serve as reminders of the figures and events that shaped the Empire. The city's diverse neighborhoods, from Brixton to Brick Lane, tell the stories of migration, resilience, and cultural fusion that have defined London in the post-imperial era.

Chapter 14: Buenos Aires: Tango and Turmoil

Buenos Aires, the capital of Argentina, is a city steeped in history, culture, and complexity. It is a city that embodies the spirit of its nation, reflecting both its triumphs and struggles. At the heart of Buenos Aires' cultural identity lies the tango, a passionate and evocative dance that has become synonymous with the city itself. However, Buenos Aires is also a city that has experienced significant political and social turmoil throughout its history. This duality of tango and turmoil provides a rich tapestry through which to explore the essence of Buenos Aires and its role in the broader Argentine narrative.

The origins of Buenos Aires can be traced back to its founding by Spanish explorers in the 16th century. The city was officially established in 1536 by Pedro de Mendoza, but it faced numerous challenges, including attacks by indigenous peoples and a lack of resources. It wasn't until 1580, when Juan de Garay refounded the city, that Buenos Aires began to establish itself as a permanent settlement. Over the next few centuries, Buenos Aires grew steadily, benefiting from its strategic location along the Rio de la Plata, which facilitated trade and commerce.

The 19th century was a period of significant transformation for Buenos Aires and Argentina as a whole. The city played a crucial role in the country's struggle for independence from Spanish rule, which was achieved in 1816. Buenos Aires became the political and economic center of the new nation, attracting immigrants from Europe and other parts of the world. This influx of people brought with it a diversity of cultures, ideas, and traditions that would shape the city's unique character.

One of the most enduring cultural legacies of Buenos Aires is the tango. The tango originated in the late 19th and early 20th centuries in the working-class neighborhoods of Buenos Aires, particularly in the barrios of La Boca and San Telmo. It was a fusion of various musical and dance traditions brought by immigrants, including African, European, and indigenous influences. Initially, the tango was associated with the lower classes and was often performed in brothels and bars. However, it gradually gained acceptance and popularity, eventually becoming a symbol of Argentine identity and pride.

The tango is more than just a dance; it is a reflection of the social and emotional landscape of Buenos Aires. The music and lyrics of tango songs often convey themes of love, longing, and loss, capturing the melancholic and passionate spirit of the city. The dance itself is characterized by its sensual and intricate movements, which require a deep connection between the partners. Famous tango musicians and composers, such as Carlos Gardel and Astor Piazzolla, have left an indelible mark on the genre, contributing to its evolution and international acclaim.

While the tango represents the cultural heartbeat of Buenos Aires, the city has also been shaped by significant political and social upheaval. The early 20th century was marked by periods of economic prosperity and political instability. The rise of populist leaders, most notably Juan Domingo Perón, had a profound impact on the city's development. Perón, who was elected president in 1946, implemented a series of social and economic reforms aimed at improving the lives of the working class. His wife, Eva Perón, became a beloved figure in Argentine society, championing the rights of the poor and marginalized.

However, Perón's presidency was also characterized by authoritarianism and political repression. He was eventually overthrown in a military coup in 1955, leading to a period of political turbulence and military rule. The latter half of the 20th century saw Buenos Aires and Argentina experience some of their darkest moments. The military dictatorship that ruled from 1976 to 1983, known as the National Reorganization Process, was marked by widespread human rights abuses, including the forced disappearance of thousands of people. This period, known as the Dirty War, left deep scars on Argentine society and remains a painful chapter in the nation's history.

Despite these challenges, Buenos Aires continued to evolve and grow. The city has always been a melting pot of cultures and ideas, and this diversity is reflected in its architecture, cuisine, and arts. Buenos Aires boasts a rich architectural heritage, with buildings that showcase a blend of European and Latin American styles. The city's neighborhoods, or barrios, each have their own distinct character and charm. From the colorful streets of La Boca to the elegant avenues of Recoleta, Buenos Aires offers a unique and vibrant urban landscape.

The city's cultural scene is also a testament to its dynamic and creative spirit. Buenos Aires is home to numerous theaters, galleries, and museums, including the iconic Teatro Colón, one of the most renowned opera houses in the world. The city's literary tradition is equally impressive, with Buenos Aires being the birthplace of several influential writers, such as Jorge Luis Borges and Julio Cortázar. The city's love for literature is evident in its numerous bookstores and literary cafes, which continue to be popular gathering spots for intellectuals and artists.

In addition to its cultural offerings, Buenos Aires is known for its culinary delights. The city's cuisine reflects its diverse heritage, with influences from Italy, Spain, and indigenous traditions. Buenos Aires is famous for its asado, or Argentine barbecue, which features a variety of grilled meats, including the beloved beef. The city's cafes, known as "cafés porteños," are a quintessential part of Buenos Aires' social life, where people gather to enjoy coffee, pastries, and conversation.

The late 20th and early 21st centuries have seen Buenos Aires navigate through periods of economic crisis and recovery. The economic turmoil of the late 1990s and early 2000s, culminating in the financial collapse of 2001, had a profound impact on the city and its residents. The crisis led to widespread poverty and unemployment, sparking protests and social movements demanding change. In the years that followed, Buenos Aires has worked to rebuild and rejuvenate its economy, while also addressing the social inequalities that persist.

Today, Buenos Aires continues to be a city of contrasts, where the legacy of tango and the shadows of turmoil coexist. The city's resilience and creativity have allowed it to adapt and thrive, even in the face of adversity. Buenos Aires remains a vibrant and cosmopolitan metropolis, attracting visitors from around the world who come to experience its rich culture, history, and spirit.

The tango, with its passionate rhythms and evocative melodies, continues to be a central part of Buenos Aires' identity. Tango shows, dance clubs, and festivals celebrate this iconic art form, drawing both locals and tourists into its enchanting embrace. The city's historical sites, such as the Casa Rosada, Plaza de Mayo, and the Obelisco, stand as reminders of the tumultuous events that have shaped Buenos Aires and Argentina as a whole.

Buenos Aires is also a city that looks to the future, embracing innovation and progress. The city's tech and startup scene has been growing rapidly, earning Buenos Aires a reputation as a hub for entrepreneurs and innovators in Latin America. Efforts to improve infrastructure, transportation, and public services reflect the city's commitment to enhancing the quality of life for its residents and ensuring sustainable development.

Chapter 15: Lagos: Echoes of Empire

Lagos, Nigeria's largest city and economic powerhouse, is a metropolis that vividly reflects the complex history and enduring legacy of colonialism in Africa. Known as "Echoes of Empire," the narrative of Lagos is deeply intertwined with its colonial past, marked by the imprints of British rule, the impacts of the transatlantic slave trade, and the city's subsequent transformation into a bustling urban center. The story of Lagos is one of resilience, adaptation, and a continuous struggle for identity and progress in the face of historical adversities.

The origins of Lagos can be traced back to the early settlement of the Awori subgroup of the Yoruba people, who established a community on the islands and surrounding mainland of present-day Lagos. The area was originally known as Eko, a name still used by locals. In the 15th century, Portuguese explorers arrived, and Lagos became a key port in the Atlantic slave trade. The Portuguese named the city "Lagos" after a maritime town in Portugal. The strategic location of Lagos made it a significant hub for the trade of enslaved Africans, who were transported to the Americas.

The arrival of the British in the 19th century marked a turning point in the history of Lagos. In 1851, the British Royal Navy bombarded Lagos, leading to the eventual annexation of the city in 1861. Lagos was subsequently declared a British colony. The British aimed to suppress the transatlantic slave trade and promote "legitimate" trade, such as palm oil, cocoa, and other commodities. This shift had profound economic, social, and political implications for Lagos and its inhabitants.

Under British colonial rule, Lagos underwent significant changes. The colonial administration implemented various infrastructural projects, including the construction of roads, railways, and ports, which facilitated trade and the movement of goods. The establishment of Western-style education and missionary activities also began to reshape the social fabric of the city. Christian missionaries played a key role in introducing Western education and religion, which coexisted with traditional African beliefs and practices.

The colonial era brought about the urbanization of Lagos, transforming it into a major commercial center. The influx of migrants from various parts of Nigeria and beyond contributed to the city's rapid growth and diversity. Lagos became a melting pot of cultures, languages, and traditions, reflecting the broader dynamics of colonial Nigeria. The economic opportunities in Lagos attracted people seeking better livelihoods, leading to the expansion of the city's population and the development of new neighborhoods and markets.

Despite these developments, colonial rule was marked by significant inequalities and exploitation. The colonial administration prioritized the interests of the British Empire, often at the expense of the local population. The imposition of taxes, land expropriation, and labor exploitation fueled discontent among the indigenous people. The colonial authorities maintained strict control over political and economic affairs, limiting the participation of Nigerians in governance and decision-making processes.

The struggle for independence in Nigeria gained momentum in the mid-20th century, with Lagos playing a central role in the nationalist movement. Prominent leaders such as Nnamdi Azikiwe, Herbert Macaulay, and Obafemi Awolowo emerged as key figures in the fight against colonial rule. The press, particularly newspapers like the West African Pilot, founded by Azikiwe, became important tools for mobilizing public opinion and advocating for self-governance. The demand for independence was fueled by a growing sense of national identity and the desire to reclaim control over the country's destiny.

In 1960, Nigeria achieved independence from British rule, and Lagos became the capital of the newly independent nation. The post-independence era brought both opportunities and challenges for Lagos. The city continued to grow rapidly, attracting people from all over Nigeria and neighboring countries. Lagos emerged as the economic and cultural hub of Nigeria, with thriving industries, vibrant markets, and a dynamic arts scene. The city became known for its music, particularly the development of Afrobeat, pioneered by Fela Kuti, which blended traditional African rhythms with jazz, funk, and highlife.

However, the post-independence period was also marked by political instability, economic challenges, and social unrest. The Nigerian Civil War (1967-1970) had significant repercussions for Lagos, as the city became a refuge for displaced people and a center of political activity. The war exacerbated existing ethnic and regional tensions, highlighting the fragile nature of Nigeria's unity. Lagos, as the former capital and largest city, played a crucial role in shaping the country's post-war recovery and development.

The oil boom of the 1970s brought unprecedented wealth to Nigeria, and Lagos experienced rapid urbanization and modernization. The city's skyline transformed with the construction of high-rise buildings, highways, and bridges. Lagos became a symbol of Nigeria's aspirations for progress and development. However, the oil boom also brought challenges, including corruption, economic inequality, and environmental degradation. The influx of wealth was not evenly distributed, leading to the growth of informal settlements and slums in various parts of the city.

The late 20th century saw Lagos grappling with the pressures of rapid urbanization. The city's infrastructure struggled to keep pace with its expanding population, resulting in challenges such as traffic congestion, inadequate housing, and insufficient public services. The military coups and political instability that characterized much of Nigeria's post-independence history further complicated governance and development efforts in Lagos.

In 1991, the capital of Nigeria was moved from Lagos to Abuja, a decision aimed at reducing congestion and decentralizing administrative functions. Despite this shift, Lagos remained the economic heart of Nigeria and continued to wield significant influence. The city's resilience and adaptability were evident in its ability to navigate the complexities of urban growth and change.

The 21st century has brought new opportunities and challenges for Lagos. The city has emerged as a global megacity, with a population exceeding 20 million people. Lagos is known for its entrepreneurial spirit, with a burgeoning tech scene and a vibrant creative industry. The city's economy is diverse, encompassing sectors such as finance, telecommunications, entertainment, and manufacturing. Lagos has become a hub for innovation and creativity, attracting investors, entrepreneurs, and artists from around the world.

However, the echoes of empire continue to reverberate in contemporary Lagos. The legacy of colonialism is evident in the city's infrastructure, institutions, and social dynamics. The inequalities and disparities that were entrenched during the colonial period persist, manifesting in issues such as poverty, unemployment, and inadequate public services. The challenges of urbanization, including housing shortages, environmental degradation, and traffic congestion, remain pressing concerns for Lagosians.

Efforts to address these challenges have been multifaceted. The Lagos State government has implemented various initiatives aimed at improving infrastructure, transportation, and public services. Projects such as the Lagos Bus Rapid Transit (BRT) system, the Eko Atlantic City development, and the rehabilitation of roads and bridges are part of ongoing efforts to enhance the city's livability and sustainability. Civil society organizations, community groups, and private sector stakeholders are also playing a crucial role in addressing social and economic issues.

Culturally, Lagos continues to be a beacon of creativity and innovation. The city's arts and entertainment scene are dynamic and influential, with Nollywood, Nigeria's film industry, gaining international recognition. Music, fashion, and visual arts thrive in Lagos, reflecting the city's diverse cultural heritage and contemporary vibrancy. Festivals, concerts, and art exhibitions draw local and international audiences, showcasing Lagos as a cultural capital of Africa.

In recent years, Lagos has also become a focal point for discussions on urban resilience and sustainable development. The city's vulnerability to climate change, particularly rising sea levels and flooding, has prompted efforts to enhance environmental sustainability and disaster preparedness. Initiatives such as the Lagos Resilience Strategy and the Lagos State Climate Action Plan aim to address these challenges and build a more resilient city for the future.

The story of Lagos: Echoes of Empire is one of continuity and change, resilience and adaptation. It is a story that reflects the broader narrative of Nigeria and Africa, where the legacies of colonialism intersect with contemporary struggles for progress and development. Lagos embodies the complexities of a post-colonial society, where the impacts of history are ever-present, yet the potential for innovation and transformation remains boundless.

As Lagos looks to the future, the city's ability to navigate its historical legacies while embracing new opportunities will be crucial. The echoes of empire, both positive and negative, serve as reminders of the city's journey and the challenges that lie ahead. The resilience and creativity of Lagosians, forged in the crucible of history, will continue to shape the city's destiny, ensuring that Lagos remains a vibrant, dynamic, and influential metropolis on the global stage.

Chapter 16: Sydney: Stories from the Harbour

Sydney, the largest city in Australia, is renowned for its stunning harbour, iconic landmarks, and vibrant cultural scene. The history and development of Sydney are deeply intertwined with its harbour, making it a focal point for stories that span centuries. From its origins as an Indigenous settlement to its transformation into a bustling metropolis, Sydney's harbour has played a pivotal role in shaping the city's identity, economy, and culture.

Long before the arrival of European settlers, the area around Sydney Harbour, known as Warrane to the Indigenous Gadigal people, was a thriving center of Aboriginal culture and life. For thousands of years, the Gadigal and other Indigenous groups in the region utilized the harbour's abundant resources for fishing, hunting, and gathering. The harbour was not only a source of sustenance but also a place of spiritual significance and social interaction. The rich Indigenous heritage of Sydney Harbour is evident in the rock carvings, middens, and cultural sites that still exist today, offering a glimpse into the lives and traditions of the original custodians of the land.

The arrival of the First Fleet in 1788 marked a significant turning point in the history of Sydney Harbour. Under the command of Captain Arthur Phillip, the fleet of 11 ships carried convicts, marines, and officials to establish a penal colony in New South Wales. Sydney Cove, located within the harbour, was chosen as the site for the new settlement due to its deep and sheltered waters, which were ideal for anchorage. The founding of Sydney Cove laid the foundations for the city of Sydney, with the harbour serving as the gateway for European exploration, colonization, and expansion.

The early years of the colony were marked by hardship and struggle. The settlers faced numerous challenges, including food shortages, disease, and conflicts with the Indigenous population. Despite these difficulties, the colony gradually began to grow and develop. The harbour played a crucial role in the colony's survival and economic development, facilitating the import of supplies and the export of goods such as wool, wheat, and coal. As the settlement expanded, the harbour became a hub of maritime activity, with ships arriving from and departing to various parts of the world.

The 19th century witnessed significant growth and transformation in Sydney, driven in large part by the harbour's strategic importance. The discovery of gold in New South Wales in the 1850s attracted a surge of immigrants seeking fortune and opportunity, leading to a population boom and economic prosperity. The harbour was a vital conduit for this influx of people and goods, contributing to the rapid expansion of the city. The construction of infrastructure such as wharves, docks, and warehouses around the harbour facilitated trade and commerce, further cementing Sydney's status as a major port city.

During this period, Sydney Harbour also became a focal point for cultural and recreational activities. The picturesque beauty of the harbour and its surrounding landscapes inspired artists, writers, and photographers, who captured its scenic vistas and bustling scenes. Ferries began to operate across the harbour, providing transportation for residents and visitors and fostering the development of waterfront communities. The establishment of public parks and gardens, such as the Royal Botanic Garden, offered spaces for leisure and relaxation, enhancing the harbour's appeal as a social and cultural center.

One of the most iconic landmarks associated with Sydney Harbour is the Sydney Opera House. Designed by Danish architect Jørn Utzon and completed in 1973, the Sydney Opera House is renowned for its distinctive sail-like design and its location on Bennelong Point, a promontory jutting into the harbour. The construction of the Opera House was a monumental engineering and architectural feat, reflecting the ambition and vision of Sydney as a modern and culturally vibrant city. Today, the Sydney Opera House is a UNESCO World Heritage site and a symbol of Australia's artistic and cultural achievements, hosting a wide range of performances and events.

Another architectural marvel that defines Sydney Harbour is the Sydney Harbour Bridge. Completed in 1932, the bridge spans the harbour, connecting the central business district with the North Shore. Known affectionately as the "Coathanger" due to its arch-based design, the Sydney Harbour Bridge is one of the longest steel-arch bridges in the world. The construction of the bridge was a significant engineering achievement, involving thousands of workers and years of labor. The bridge not only facilitated transportation and commerce but also became a beloved landmark and a testament to Sydney's growth and modernization.

The mid-20th century saw Sydney Harbour continue to evolve as a center of commerce, tourism, and recreation. The development of the Circular Quay area transformed it into a major transportation and entertainment hub, with ferry terminals, train stations, and cultural venues such as the Museum of Contemporary Art. The harbour's waters became a playground for sailing, boating, and water sports, attracting enthusiasts from around the world. Iconic events such as the Sydney to Hobart Yacht Race and the annual New Year's Eve fireworks display further solidified the harbour's reputation as a vibrant and dynamic focal point of city life.

Sydney Harbour's significance extends beyond its physical and economic attributes; it is also a site of historical memory and reflection. The harbour witnessed key moments in Australia's history, including the arrival of the First Fleet, the proclamation of

Federation in 1901, and the celebrations of the Sydney 2000 Olympic Games. Commemorative sites and monuments around the harbour, such as the ANZAC War Memorial and the Australian National Maritime Museum, serve as reminders of the nation's heritage and the enduring legacy of those who shaped its history.

The harbour has also been a site of environmental awareness and conservation efforts. Recognizing the ecological importance of the harbour and its diverse marine life, various initiatives have been undertaken to protect and preserve its natural beauty. Programs aimed at reducing pollution, restoring habitats, and promoting sustainable practices have been implemented to ensure the long-term health and vitality of the harbour. The efforts of environmental organizations, government agencies, and community groups have contributed to making Sydney Harbour a cleaner and more resilient ecosystem.

In contemporary times, Sydney Harbour continues to be a dynamic and integral part of the city's identity. The waterfront areas have been revitalized with modern developments, such as Darling Harbour, Barangaroo, and the revitalization of Pyrmont and Walsh Bay. These areas have become vibrant precincts for dining, entertainment, and cultural experiences, attracting locals and tourists alike. The integration of green spaces, public art, and innovative architecture has enhanced the livability and aesthetic appeal of the harbourfront, making it a focal point for urban life.

The cultural diversity of Sydney is also reflected in the activities and events held around the harbour. Festivals such as Vivid Sydney, which features spectacular light installations and projections on the Opera House, celebrate the city's creativity and innovation. Community events, markets, and performances showcase the rich tapestry of cultures that contribute to Sydney's unique character. The harbour serves as a backdrop for celebrations and gatherings, reinforcing its role as a place of connection and community.

The future of Sydney Harbour is shaped by ongoing developments and aspirations for sustainability and inclusivity. Urban planning and development projects aim to balance growth with environmental stewardship, ensuring that the harbour remains a cherished asset for generations to come. Initiatives to enhance public access, improve transportation infrastructure, and promote cultural and recreational activities are central to the vision of a vibrant and inclusive harbour city.

Chapter 17: Tehran: Persia's Pulse

Tehran, the bustling capital of Iran, is a city that embodies the heart and soul of Persia's rich history, culture, and modern aspirations. Known as "Persia's Pulse," Tehran is a metropolis where ancient traditions and contemporary dynamics coexist, reflecting the intricate tapestry of Iran's past and present. This narrative explores the multifaceted history of Tehran, its role as the political and cultural center of Iran, and the profound influences that have shaped its identity over centuries.

The origins of Tehran can be traced back to ancient times, though it was relatively obscure until the early modern period. The area that is now Tehran was part of the vast Persian Empire, which was founded by Cyrus the Great in the 6th century BCE. The region around Tehran was historically overshadowed by the more prominent city of Rey (also known as Rhages), an important settlement that dates back to the Median, Achaemenid, and Sassanian empires. Rey was a significant center of commerce, culture, and governance, and it played a crucial role in the development of the area that would eventually become Tehran.

The turning point for Tehran came in the 18th century during the Qajar dynasty. In 1786, Agha Mohammad Khan, the founder of the Qajar dynasty, chose Tehran as the capital of Persia. The decision to move the capital to Tehran was influenced by its strategic location, defensibility, and proximity to the territories controlled by the Qajars. This marked the beginning of Tehran's transformation from a modest town to a significant political and administrative center.

Under Qajar rule, Tehran began to expand and develop. The city was fortified with walls and gates, and royal palaces and government buildings were constructed. The Golestan Palace, a masterpiece of Qajar architecture, became the royal residence and a symbol of the dynasty's power. The city also saw the establishment of bazaars, mosques, and gardens, reflecting the traditional Persian urban design that emphasized harmony between built environments and nature. Tehran's population grew as people from different parts of Persia migrated to the capital in search of opportunities and a better life.

The 19th century was a period of profound change for Tehran and Persia as a whole. The country faced increasing pressure from foreign powers, particularly Russia and Britain, who sought to expand their influence in the region. This era of geopolitical rivalry, known as the "Great Game," had significant implications for Persia. The Qajar rulers struggled to maintain sovereignty and control over their territories, leading to a series of political and social reforms aimed at modernizing the state and strengthening its institutions.

One of the most notable figures of this period was Amir Kabir, the prime minister under Naser al-Din Shah Qajar. Amir Kabir implemented a series of reforms that sought to modernize Persia's administration, military, and economy. He established the Dar ul-Funun, the first modern institution of higher learning in Persia, which aimed to educate and train a new generation of Persian scholars and professionals. Despite facing resistance from conservative factions and eventually being dismissed and executed, Amir Kabir's legacy left a lasting impact on Tehran and Persia's modernization efforts.

The early 20th century saw further transformation and upheaval in Tehran. The Constitutional Revolution of 1905-1911 was a pivotal moment in Persia's history, as it led to the establishment of a constitution and the formation of a parliamentary system. Tehran was at the heart of this movement, with intellectuals, clerics, merchants, and ordinary citizens demanding greater political participation and the rule of law. The revolution marked a significant shift towards modernity and governance, though it was met with resistance from royalists and foreign powers.

The discovery of oil in Persia in the early 20th century had profound economic and political implications. The Anglo-Persian Oil Company (later British Petroleum) secured concessions for oil exploration and production, leading to increased foreign influence in Persia's affairs. Tehran became a center of political activity and protest as nationalist movements sought to assert control over the country's natural resources and reduce foreign domination. The nationalization of the oil industry in 1951 by Prime Minister Mohammad Mossadegh was a bold move that garnered widespread support but also led to a coup orchestrated by the CIA and MI6, which restored the shah's power.

The reign of Mohammad Reza Shah Pahlavi, the last shah of Iran, was marked by significant modernization and development efforts in Tehran. The city underwent rapid urbanization, with the construction of modern infrastructure, highways, and high-rise buildings. The White Revolution, a series of social and economic reforms initiated by the shah in the 1960s, aimed to modernize Iran's agricultural sector, promote industrialization, and expand education and healthcare. Tehran's population soared as people migrated from rural areas to the capital, seeking employment and better living standards.

However, the shah's modernization efforts were accompanied by political repression and a growing divide between the ruling elite and the general population. Discontent with the regime's authoritarianism, economic inequalities, and perceived Westernization fueled opposition movements. Tehran became a focal point for political activism, with demonstrations, strikes, and protests challenging the shah's rule. The Islamic Revolution of 1979, led by Ayatollah Ruhollah Khomeini, culminated in the overthrow of the monarchy and the establishment of the Islamic Republic of Iran.

The revolution brought about profound changes in Tehran and the entire country. The new Islamic government sought to implement a system based on Islamic principles and values, leading to significant shifts in political, social, and cultural life. Tehran, as the capital of the Islamic Republic, became the center of power and governance. The city's landscape changed with the construction of mosques, religious institutions, and government buildings. The post-revolutionary period also saw efforts to promote social justice, economic self-sufficiency, and resistance to foreign influence.

The Iran-Iraq War (1980-1988) had a significant impact on Tehran. The city faced aerial bombardments and missile attacks, causing loss of life and destruction of infrastructure. Despite the hardships, Tehran's residents demonstrated resilience and solidarity, contributing to the war effort and supporting the nation's defense. The war further shaped Tehran's identity as a city of resistance and determination.

In the decades following the revolution and the war, Tehran has continued to evolve and adapt to changing circumstances. The city has experienced significant population growth, urban expansion, and socio-economic challenges. Traffic congestion, air pollution, and housing shortages are pressing issues that Tehran faces as it navigates the complexities of modern urban life. Efforts to address these challenges include initiatives to improve public transportation, expand green spaces, and promote sustainable development.

Culturally, Tehran remains a vibrant and dynamic city. The city's rich artistic heritage is reflected in its museums, galleries, theaters, and cultural centers. The Tehran Museum of Contemporary Art, home to an impressive collection of modern and contemporary art, showcases both Iranian and international artists. The city's literary scene is also notable, with a thriving community of writers, poets, and intellectuals who contribute to Iran's rich literary tradition.

Tehran is a city of contrasts, where traditional bazaars coexist with modern shopping malls, and historic neighborhoods stand alongside contemporary developments. The Grand Bazaar of Tehran, one of the oldest and largest bazaars in the world, is a bustling center of commerce and trade, offering a glimpse into the city's vibrant economic life. In contrast, the modern districts of northern Tehran, with their upscale shops, cafes, and restaurants, reflect the city's cosmopolitan and globalized character.

The youth of Tehran play a significant role in shaping the city's future. With a large and educated young population, Tehran is a hub of innovation, creativity, and social change. The city's universities, research institutions, and tech startups contribute to a dynamic and forward-looking environment. Young Tehranis are actively engaged in various fields, from technology and entrepreneurship to arts and activism, driving the city's progress and development.

Tehran's political landscape remains complex and multifaceted. The city is the center of Iran's political power, housing the offices of the Supreme Leader, the President, the Parliament, and other key government institutions. Political discourse in Tehran reflects the broader debates and tensions within Iranian society, encompassing issues such as governance, human rights, economic policies, and foreign relations. The city's residents are actively involved in political life, participating in elections, protests, and civic initiatives.

The cultural diversity of Tehran is another defining aspect of the city. As a melting pot of various ethnic, linguistic, and religious groups, Tehran reflects the broader diversity of Iran. The city's neighborhoods are home to people from different backgrounds, including Persians, Azeris, Kurds, Armenians, and others. This diversity is celebrated through cultural festivals, artistic expressions, and community events that highlight the richness of Tehran's multicultural heritage.

In recent years, Tehran has also been a focal point for discussions on urban resilience and sustainability. The city faces challenges related to environmental degradation, climate change, and resource management. Initiatives aimed at promoting green spaces, improving waste management, and enhancing energy efficiency are part of broader efforts to create a more sustainable and livable city. The Tehran Urban Resilience Program and other initiatives reflect the city's commitment to addressing these challenges and building a resilient future.

Chapter 18: New York: The Melting Pot

New York City, often referred to as "The Melting Pot," stands as a quintessential symbol of the United States' cultural diversity and dynamic spirit. This metropolis, known for its towering skyscrapers, bustling streets, and iconic landmarks, is a microcosm of the world, embodying the hopes, dreams, and struggles of countless immigrants who have arrived on its shores over centuries.

The story of New York City begins with its Indigenous inhabitants, the Lenape people, who lived in the region for thousands of years before the arrival of Europeans. The Lenape had a rich culture and society, with a deep connection to the land and its resources. They lived in villages along the rivers and engaged in farming, hunting, and fishing. The area that is now New York City was known as Mannahatta, or "island of many hills," reflecting its varied topography and natural beauty.

The arrival of Europeans in the early 17th century marked a significant turning point in the history of New York. In 1609, English explorer Henry Hudson, sailing under the Dutch flag, navigated the river that now bears his name and laid the groundwork for Dutch colonization. The Dutch established a trading post called New Amsterdam on the southern tip of Manhattan Island in 1624. New Amsterdam quickly grew into a bustling port, serving as a hub for the fur trade and attracting settlers from various parts of Europe.

The Dutch influence on New York City was profound and enduring. The city's grid system, a defining feature of its urban layout, was first implemented by the Dutch. The names of many streets, neighborhoods, and landmarks, such as Harlem (Haarlem), Brooklyn (Breuckelen), and the Bowery (Bouwerij), reflect the city's Dutch heritage. The spirit of religious tolerance and commercial enterprise that characterized New Amsterdam set the stage for the city's future growth and diversity.

In 1664, the English seized control of New Amsterdam and renamed it New York in honor of the Duke of York, the future King James II of England. Under English rule, the city continued to thrive as a center of trade and commerce. The population grew, and New York became increasingly diverse, with immigrants from England, Scotland, Ireland, Germany, and other parts of Europe settling in the city. The English influence brought new institutions and cultural practices, further shaping the city's development.

The American Revolutionary War was a pivotal chapter in New York City's history. The city played a crucial role as both a battleground and a strategic base for the British. The occupation of New York by British forces lasted from 1776 until the end of the war in 1783. Despite the hardships and destruction caused by the war, the city emerged as a symbol of resilience and the pursuit of liberty. After the war, New York became the first capital of the United States, hosting the inauguration of George Washington as the first President in 1789 and the drafting of the Bill of Rights.

The 19th century was a period of rapid growth and transformation for New York City. The construction of the Erie Canal, completed in 1825, was a monumental achievement that connected the Atlantic Ocean to the Great Lakes, facilitating the movement of goods and people. This infrastructure project solidified New York's position as a major port and a gateway to the American interior. The city's population exploded as immigrants from Europe arrived in waves, seeking new opportunities and a better life. The Irish Potato Famine in the 1840s and political upheavals in Germany and Italy led to a surge of immigrants, adding to the city's cultural mosaic.

The influx of immigrants during the 19th century significantly shaped New York City's identity as a melting pot. Neighborhoods such as Little Italy, Chinatown, and the Lower East Side became vibrant enclaves of diverse ethnic communities. These immigrants brought with them their languages, traditions, and cuisines, enriching the city's cultural fabric. The tenements of the Lower East Side, though often crowded and squalid, were a testament to the determination and resilience of those who sought to build new lives in America. The challenges of urban living fostered a sense of community and solidarity among the city's residents.

The turn of the 20th century marked the beginning of New York City's rise as a global metropolis. The construction of iconic skyscrapers such as the Woolworth Building, the Chrysler Building, and the Empire State Building transformed the city's skyline and symbolized its economic might and architectural innovation. The completion of the Brooklyn Bridge in 1883 and the opening of the New York City Subway in 1904 revolutionized transportation, connecting the boroughs and facilitating the movement of millions of people.

The early 20th century also saw the emergence of New York City as a cultural capital. The Harlem Renaissance of the 1920s was a vibrant intellectual and artistic movement that celebrated African American culture and creativity. Harlem became a hub for writers, musicians, and artists, producing luminaries such as Langston Hughes, Zora Neale Hurston, and Duke Ellington. Jazz music, with its roots in African American communities, flourished in the city's clubs and speakeasies, influencing the broader cultural landscape.

The Great Depression of the 1930s brought significant economic challenges to New York City, but it also spurred a wave of public works projects under President Franklin D. Roosevelt's New Deal. Landmarks such as the Triborough Bridge, the Lincoln Tunnel, and the expansion of the subway system were built during this period, providing jobs and modernizing the city's infrastructure. The resilience of New Yorkers during these difficult times underscored the city's enduring spirit of perseverance.

World War II further transformed New York City into a global center of finance, media, and culture. The city's ports and shipyards played a crucial role in the war effort, and the post-war economic boom led to unprecedented growth and prosperity. The United Nations headquarters was established in New York in 1945, solidifying the city's status as a center of international diplomacy and cooperation.

The latter half of the 20th century saw both challenges and triumphs for New York City. The social upheavals of the 1960s, including the civil rights movement and anti-war protests, found a strong voice in the city. The Stonewall Riots of 1969, a pivotal moment in the LGBTQ+ rights movement, took place in Greenwich Village, highlighting New York's role as a center for social change and activism. The city also faced economic decline, rising crime rates, and urban decay during the 1970s, culminating in the near-bankruptcy of the municipal government in 1975. However, New York's leaders and residents worked tirelessly to revitalize the city, leading to a renaissance in the 1980s and 1990s.

The turn of the 21st century brought new challenges and opportunities for New York City. The terrorist attacks of September 11, 2001, were a profound and tragic event that deeply affected the city and the world. The resilience and solidarity displayed by New Yorkers in the aftermath of the attacks underscored the city's enduring strength and unity. The rebuilding of the World Trade Center site, including the construction of the One World Trade Center, became a symbol of recovery and hope.

Today, New York City remains a global icon of diversity, innovation, and cultural dynamism. The city's neighborhoods continue to reflect its rich immigrant heritage, with communities from all over the world contributing to its vibrant mosaic. Times Square, with its dazzling lights and bustling crowds, epitomizes the energy and excitement of the city. Central Park offers a green oasis in the heart of Manhattan, providing a space for recreation and relaxation amidst the urban hustle and bustle.

New York City's cultural institutions are world-renowned, attracting visitors and residents alike. The Metropolitan Museum of Art, the Museum of Modern Art, the American Museum of Natural History, and the Solomon R. Guggenheim Museum are just a few of the city's premier cultural attractions. Broadway, the epicenter of American theater, draws millions of theatergoers each year, showcasing a diverse array of performances from musicals to dramas.

The city's economic and financial influence is unparalleled, with Wall Street serving as the nerve center of global finance. The New York Stock Exchange and Nasdaq are major engines of the global economy, influencing markets and investments worldwide. The city's diverse economy also includes sectors such as technology, media, fashion, and healthcare, making it a hub of innovation and entrepreneurship.

New York City's status as a melting pot is reflected in its culinary scene, which offers a dizzying array of cuisines from around the world. From street vendors selling hot dogs and pretzels to high-end restaurants offering gourmet dining experiences, the city's food culture is a testament to its diversity and creativity. Neighborhoods like Flushing in Queens and Jackson Heights showcase the rich culinary traditions of immigrant communities, offering everything from dim sum to arepas.

The city's educational and research institutions are among the best in the world, attracting students, scholars, and professionals from around the globe. Institutions such as Columbia University, New York University, and the City University of New York contribute to the city's intellectual vibrancy and innovation. The presence of these institutions fosters a dynamic environment for learning, research, and cultural exchange.

New York City's commitment to sustainability and resilience is evident in its efforts to address environmental challenges and promote green initiatives. The city has implemented policies to reduce carbon emissions, improve public transportation, and enhance green spaces. Initiatives such as the High Line, an elevated park built on a former rail line, and the expansion of bike lanes and pedestrian-friendly spaces reflect the city's dedication to creating a sustainable urban environment.

The future of New York City is shaped by its ongoing commitment to diversity, innovation, and resilience. The city's ability to adapt and thrive in the face of challenges is a testament to its enduring spirit and the strength of its residents. As New York continues to evolve, it remains a beacon of opportunity and a symbol of the American dream, embodying the ideals of freedom, creativity, and unity.

Chapter 19: Copenhagen: Viking Vibes

Copenhagen, the capital of Denmark, is a city where ancient Viking history seamlessly blends with modern Scandinavian design and culture. Known for its rich heritage and innovative spirit, Copenhagen embodies the essence of "Viking Vibes," reflecting a unique combination of historical significance and contemporary charm. This narrative explores the multifaceted history of Copenhagen, tracing its development from a Viking fishing village to a bustling metropolis that celebrates its past while embracing the future.

The origins of Copenhagen can be traced back to the early Middle Ages when it was a modest fishing village. Archaeological evidence suggests that the area was inhabited as early as the 6th century, with the first significant settlement emerging around the 10th century during the Viking Age. The Vikings, known for their seafaring prowess and exploration, played a crucial role in the early development of Copenhagen. The city's strategic location along the Øresund Strait made it an ideal spot for trade and commerce, allowing the Vikings to establish a thriving trading post.

The name Copenhagen itself is derived from the Old Danish word "Købmannahavn," which means "merchant's harbor." This reflects the city's early function as a center of trade and commerce. The Vikings were not only fierce warriors but also shrewd traders, engaging in extensive trade networks that spanned Europe and beyond. They traded goods such as furs, amber, and weapons, and in return, they acquired precious metals, spices, and other luxury items. This bustling trade activity laid the foundation for Copenhagen's growth and prosperity.

By the 12th century, Copenhagen had begun to gain prominence as a key port in the Baltic Sea region. The city's development was further accelerated by the construction of fortifications and defensive structures. Bishop Absalon, a Danish cleric and statesman, is often credited with founding Copenhagen in 1167 when he built a fortress on the small island of Slotsholmen, where Christiansborg Palace stands today. This fortress served as a defensive stronghold against pirate attacks and laid the groundwork for the city's expansion.

During the late Middle Ages, Copenhagen continued to grow in importance. It became a vital hub for trade, particularly in the lucrative herring industry. The city's strategic location allowed it to control the entrance to the Baltic Sea, making it a key player in regional politics and commerce. The establishment of the Hanseatic League, a powerful commercial and defensive alliance of merchant guilds and market towns in northern Europe, further boosted Copenhagen's status as a major trading center.

The 15th century marked a period of significant transformation for Copenhagen. King Christian I of Denmark, who ruled from 1448 to 1481, played a pivotal role in shaping the city's development. Under his reign, Copenhagen was officially designated as the capital of Denmark in 1443, solidifying its political and administrative significance. The king's patronage led to the construction of several important buildings and institutions, including the University of Copenhagen, founded in 1479. This prestigious institution of higher learning became a center of education and intellectual activity, attracting scholars and students from across Europe.

The Renaissance period brought further prosperity and cultural enrichment to Copenhagen. The reign of King Christian IV, who ruled from 1588 to 1648, is often considered a golden age for the city. Christian IV was a visionary monarch who embarked on an ambitious building program that transformed Copenhagen's skyline. He commissioned the construction of several iconic structures, including the Round Tower, Rosenborg Castle, and the Stock Exchange (Børsen). These buildings, characterized by their distinctive Renaissance architecture, became symbols of Copenhagen's wealth and sophistication.

Christian IV's reign also saw the expansion of Copenhagen's urban landscape. The king founded the district of Christianshavn, modeled after Amsterdam with its network of canals and narrow streets. This new district became a vibrant hub of trade and industry, attracting merchants, craftsmen, and sailors. The construction of Christiansborg Palace on Slotsholmen further cemented Copenhagen's status as the heart of Danish political power.

The 17th and 18th centuries were marked by both growth and challenges for Copenhagen. The city faced several devastating fires, with the Great Fire of 1728 being particularly destructive. Despite these setbacks, Copenhagen demonstrated remarkable resilience and underwent extensive rebuilding efforts. The city's architecture evolved, with the introduction of Baroque and Rococo styles, exemplified by landmarks such as Amalienborg Palace and the Church of Our Saviour.

The Age of Enlightenment in the 18th century brought about significant intellectual and cultural advancements in Copenhagen. The city became a center for science, philosophy, and the arts, attracting prominent figures such as the astronomer Ole Rømer and the philosopher Søren Kierkegaard. The establishment of institutions like the Royal Danish Academy of Fine Arts and the Royal Danish Theatre contributed to Copenhagen's cultural renaissance, fostering a vibrant artistic community.

The 19th century ushered in a period of modernization and industrialization for Copenhagen. The city's population grew rapidly as people migrated from rural areas in search of employment opportunities. The expansion of infrastructure, including the construction of railways and modern harbors, facilitated economic growth and urban development. The transformation of Tivoli Gardens into a world-famous amusement park in 1843 added to the city's allure, making it a popular destination for both locals and tourists.

The early 20th century was a time of significant political and social change for Copenhagen. Denmark's neutrality during World War I allowed the city to avoid the widespread destruction experienced by other European capitals. However, the economic challenges of the post-war period necessitated reforms and modernization efforts. The rise of the labor movement and the establishment of a welfare state in the 1930s brought about improvements in living conditions and social services for Copenhagen's residents.

World War II had a profound impact on Copenhagen and Denmark as a whole. In 1940, German forces occupied Denmark, and Copenhagen became the center of resistance efforts. The Danish resistance movement, consisting of various underground groups, carried out acts of sabotage and helped to protect Danish Jews from Nazi persecution. The spirit of resilience and solidarity during this dark period left a lasting legacy on the city's identity.

The post-war period saw Copenhagen emerge as a modern and progressive city. The city underwent extensive reconstruction and urban planning to accommodate its growing population. The introduction of modernist architecture and design principles, championed by architects such as Arne Jacobsen and Jørn Utzon, transformed Copenhagen's built environment. Iconic structures like the SAS Royal Hotel and the Sydney Opera House, designed by Jacobsen and Utzon respectively, showcased Danish innovation and design excellence.

Copenhagen's commitment to sustainability and environmental stewardship has become a defining characteristic of the city in recent decades. The city has implemented ambitious initiatives to promote green living, reduce carbon emissions, and enhance urban mobility. The extensive network of cycling lanes and bike-friendly infrastructure has earned Copenhagen the reputation of being one of the most bicycle-friendly cities in the world. The development of eco-friendly neighborhoods, such as the award-winning Ørestad district, reflects the city's dedication to sustainable urban planning.

Copenhagen's cultural scene continues to thrive, with a rich array of museums, galleries, theaters, and festivals. The National Museum of Denmark, the Ny Carlsberg Glyptotek, and the Louisiana Museum of Modern Art are just a few of the city's premier cultural institutions. The Copenhagen Opera House, situated on the waterfront, is a stunning example of modern architecture and a center for world-class performances. The city's culinary landscape has also gained international acclaim, with restaurants like Noma and Geranium setting new standards for Nordic cuisine and innovation.

The city's commitment to education and research is evident in its world-class universities and research institutions. The University of Copenhagen, the Technical University of Denmark, and the Copenhagen Business School attract students and scholars from around the globe, contributing to the city's intellectual vibrancy. Copenhagen's status as a hub for innovation and entrepreneurship is further reinforced by the presence of numerous tech startups and research parks.

Copenhagen's neighborhoods each have their unique character and charm, reflecting the city's diversity and cultural richness. The historic district of Nyhavn, with its colorful waterfront buildings and lively atmosphere, is a beloved landmark and a testament to the city's maritime heritage. The bohemian district of Nørrebro is known for its multicultural vibe, vibrant street art, and eclectic mix of cafes and boutiques. The upscale district of Frederiksberg offers elegant parks, shopping streets, and cultural institutions, providing a contrast to the bustling city center.

Copenhagen's commitment to social equity and inclusivity is evident in its policies and initiatives aimed at fostering a cohesive and harmonious society. The city's welfare system, comprehensive healthcare, and strong emphasis on education and social services contribute to a high quality of life for its residents. Copenhagen's progressive approach to urban development and social policies serves as a model for cities around the world.

The city's dynamic and evolving identity is celebrated through various festivals and cultural events that highlight its rich heritage and contemporary creativity. The annual Copenhagen Jazz Festival, the Roskilde Festival, and the Copenhagen Pride Parade are just a few of the events that showcase the city's vibrant cultural scene and inclusive spirit. The city's role as the host of international conferences and summits, such as the United Nations Climate Change Conference (COP15) in 2009, underscores its global influence and leadership in addressing critical issues.

Chapter 20: Lima: Inca Echoes

Lima, the capital of Peru, is a city that resonates with the echoes of its ancient Inca past while thriving as a modern metropolis. Known for its rich cultural heritage, colonial architecture, and vibrant urban life, Lima stands as a testament to the layers of history that have shaped it.

The history of Lima and its surrounding regions stretches back thousands of years, with evidence of human habitation dating to ancient times. Long before the arrival of the Incas, various indigenous cultures flourished in the coastal areas of Peru. The Lima culture, which thrived between 100 AD and 650 AD, is one of the earliest known civilizations in the region. This culture is noted for its distinctive pottery, textiles, and impressive irrigation systems that supported agriculture in the arid coastal environment.

The rise of the Inca Empire in the 15th century marked a significant turning point in the history of the region. The Incas, originating from the highlands of Cusco, embarked on a series of military campaigns that expanded their empire across much of western South America. By the time of their greatest expansion, the Inca Empire stretched from modern-day Ecuador in the north to Chile in the south, encompassing diverse terrains and cultures. Lima, known as "Itchyma" in the Inca period, was integrated into this vast empire.

The Incas established a sophisticated administrative system to manage their extensive territory. The empire was divided into four regions, or "suyus," each governed by officials appointed by the Inca emperor. The region that included Lima was part of the Chinchaysuyu, the northernmost region of the empire. The Incas implemented advanced agricultural techniques, constructing terraces and irrigation channels to maximize the productivity of the land. The coastal region around Lima became an important agricultural hub, producing crops such as maize, beans, and cotton.

The Incas are perhaps best known for their monumental architecture and engineering achievements. They constructed an extensive network of roads, known as the "Qhapaq Ñan," which connected the far reaches of the empire. These roads facilitated communication, trade, and the movement of armies, ensuring the cohesion of the vast Inca state. Although Lima was not as architecturally prominent as Cusco or Machu Picchu, it played a crucial role in the empire's economic and administrative functions.

The arrival of Spanish conquistadors in the early 16th century heralded a dramatic and tumultuous period in Lima's history. Francisco Pizarro, the Spanish explorer and conqueror, arrived in Peru in 1532 and launched a campaign to overthrow the Inca Empire. The capture and subsequent execution of the Inca emperor Atahualpa marked the beginning of Spanish dominance in the region. In 1535, Pizarro founded the city of Lima, naming it "Ciudad de los Reyes" (City of Kings) in honor of the Spanish monarchs.

Lima quickly became the center of Spanish colonial power in Peru. Its strategic coastal location made it an ideal hub for trade and administration. The Spanish established Lima as the capital of the Viceroyalty of Peru, which encompassed much of Spanish South America. The city's layout followed the Spanish colonial grid pattern, with a central plaza, known as the Plaza Mayor, surrounded by important government and religious buildings. The construction of the Cathedral of Lima and the Archbishop's Palace reflected the centrality of the Catholic Church in colonial society.

The Spanish colonization brought profound changes to the indigenous populations. The encomienda system, under which Spanish settlers were granted control over indigenous communities, led to the exploitation and forced labor of the native people. The introduction of European diseases, to which the indigenous populations had no immunity, resulted in catastrophic population declines. Despite these hardships, indigenous cultures persisted and adapted, contributing to the rich cultural tapestry of colonial Peru.

The colonial period in Lima was marked by economic prosperity driven by the lucrative silver mines of Potosí in present-day Bolivia. Lima became a key port for the export of silver and other goods to Spain. The city's wealth was reflected in the construction of grand mansions, churches, and convents. The University of San Marcos, founded in 1551, became one of the oldest universities in the Americas, fostering intellectual and cultural development in the city.

Throughout the colonial period, Lima experienced periods of social unrest and natural disasters. Earthquakes, such as the devastating quake of 1746, caused significant destruction but also prompted the rebuilding and modernization of the city. Lima's population grew, and its cultural life flourished, with a blend of Spanish, indigenous, and African influences shaping its music, dance, and cuisine.

The early 19th century brought a wave of independence movements across Latin America. Inspired by the ideals of the Enlightenment and the successes of the American and French revolutions, creole leaders in South America sought to overthrow Spanish colonial rule. José de San Martín, an Argentine general and key figure in the struggle for independence, entered Lima in 1821 and declared Peru's independence from Spain. The subsequent battles and political maneuvering culminated in the final defeat of Spanish forces in 1824, solidifying Peru's independence.

The post-independence period in Lima was characterized by political instability and economic challenges. The city grappled with internal conflicts, including civil wars and power struggles between rival factions. However, the late 19th and early 20th centuries brought a period of modernization and urban development. The construction of railways, the expansion of the port, and the introduction of modern infrastructure transformed Lima into a bustling modern city.

Lima's cultural and artistic scene continued to evolve, with influences from Europe and North America blending with indigenous and Afro-Peruvian traditions. The city became a center for literature, music, and the visual arts. Prominent intellectuals and artists, such as the poet César Vallejo and the painter José Sabogal, contributed to the development of a distinct Peruvian cultural identity.

The 20th century brought further changes and challenges to Lima. Rapid urbanization and population growth led to the expansion of the city's boundaries and the development of new neighborhoods. The influx of migrants from rural areas seeking economic opportunities contributed to the city's diversity but also strained its infrastructure and resources. Social and economic inequalities became more pronounced, leading to periods of social unrest and political turmoil.

Despite these challenges, Lima emerged as a vibrant and dynamic metropolis. The city's historical center, with its colonial architecture and cultural landmarks, was recognized as a UNESCO World Heritage site in 1988. Efforts to preserve and restore Lima's historical heritage have been complemented by initiatives to promote sustainable urban development and improve living conditions for its residents.

Today, Lima is a city of contrasts, where the echoes of its Inca and colonial past resonate amidst the bustle of modern life. The city's historic center, with its grand plazas, churches, and colonial mansions, stands in stark contrast to the sprawling urban neighborhoods and modern skyscrapers. The diverse population of Lima, with its mix of indigenous, European, African, and Asian influences, reflects the city's rich cultural mosaic.

Lima's culinary scene has gained international acclaim, earning it the title of the "Gastronomic Capital of the Americas." The city's cuisine is a fusion of indigenous ingredients, Spanish culinary techniques, and influences from other immigrant communities. Dishes such as ceviche, lomo saltado, and anticuchos showcase the creativity and diversity of Lima's culinary traditions. Renowned chefs like Gastón Acurio have played a pivotal role in promoting Peruvian cuisine on the global stage, contributing to Lima's reputation as a food lover's paradise.

The city's cultural life is vibrant and dynamic, with a wide array of festivals, museums, theaters, and music venues. The annual Festival de Lima, an international film festival, and the Gran Teatro Nacional, which hosts performances of opera, ballet, and classical music, are just a few examples of the city's thriving cultural scene. Lima's museums, such as the Larco Museum and the Museum of the Nation, offer insights into the region's rich history and artistic heritage.

Lima's neighborhoods each have their unique character and charm, reflecting the city's diverse and multifaceted identity. The upscale district of Miraflores, with its scenic parks, beaches, and shopping centers, is a popular destination for tourists and locals alike. The bohemian district of Barranco is known for its vibrant arts scene, historic architecture, and lively nightlife. The historic center, or "Centro Histórico," is the heart of colonial Lima, with its grand plazas, churches, and government buildings.

The city's commitment to sustainability and urban development is evident in various initiatives aimed at improving public transportation, green spaces, and infrastructure. Projects such as the Metropolitano bus rapid transit system and the extension of the Lima Metro aim to reduce traffic congestion and improve connectivity within the city. Efforts to create more green spaces and promote environmental awareness reflect Lima's dedication to sustainable urban living.

Lima's educational and research institutions are among the best in the country, attracting students and scholars from across Peru and beyond. The National University of San Marcos, the Pontifical Catholic University of Peru, and other prestigious institutions contribute to the city's intellectual vibrancy and innovation. Lima's role as a center for higher education and research fosters a dynamic environment for learning and cultural exchange.

The city's social and economic challenges continue to be a focus of policy and development efforts. Addressing issues such as poverty, inequality, and access to basic services remains a priority for Lima's leaders and residents. Community organizations, NGOs, and government initiatives work together to improve living conditions and create opportunities for all residents, reflecting a commitment to social equity and inclusion.

Lima's ongoing evolution as a city that honors its past while embracing the future is a testament to its resilience and adaptability. The echoes of the Inca civilization, the legacy of Spanish colonialism, and the influences of diverse cultures all contribute to Lima's unique identity. As the city continues to grow and develop, it remains a vibrant and dynamic metropolis that celebrates its rich history and cultural heritage.

Chapter 21: Bangkok: The Siamese Saga

Bangkok, the capital of Thailand, is a city that embodies the rich cultural heritage and dynamic spirit of the country. Known for its vibrant street life, ornate temples, and bustling markets, Bangkok is a city where the past and present seamlessly intertwine. The story of Bangkok, often referred to as the "Siamese Saga," is a tale of resilience, transformation, and cultural synthesis. From its origins as a small trading post to its emergence as a global metropolis, Bangkok's history is a reflection of Thailand's journey through centuries of change and development.

The origins of Bangkok can be traced back to the early 15th century when it was a small trading post on the west bank of the Chao Phraya River. At that time, the area was known as Bang Makok, which means "place of olive plums." This modest settlement played a crucial role in regional trade, serving as a port for ships traveling between Ayutthaya, the capital of the Siamese Kingdom, and other parts of Southeast Asia. The strategic location of Bangkok along the river made it an ideal spot for commerce and transportation.

The rise of Bangkok as a major city began in the late 18th century during a period of political upheaval in Siam. In 1767, the Burmese army captured and destroyed Ayutthaya, the capital of the Siamese Kingdom, bringing an end to its 417-year reign. This event led to a power vacuum and a period of instability in the region. In the aftermath of Ayutthaya's fall, General Taksin emerged as a key figure in the effort to reunify the kingdom. He established a new capital in Thonburi, located across the river from present-day Bangkok, and declared himself king.

Taksin's reign was short-lived, lasting only 15 years. In 1782, a coup led by General Chao Phraya Chakri resulted in Taksin's overthrow. Chao Phraya Chakri ascended to the throne as King Rama I, founding the Chakri Dynasty, which still reigns in Thailand today. One of his first acts as king was to move the capital from Thonburi to the east bank of the Chao Phraya River, where he established the city of Bangkok. The new capital was named Krung Thep, which means "City of Angels," but it is commonly known as Bangkok in the West.

Under King Rama I, Bangkok underwent significant development and transformation. The king sought to recreate the grandeur of Ayutthaya, and he commissioned the construction of numerous temples, palaces, and fortifications. The Grand Palace, the most iconic landmark of Bangkok, was built during this period. The palace complex includes the Wat Phra Kaew, or Temple of the Emerald Buddha, which houses a revered emerald statue of the Buddha that is considered the palladium of the kingdom. The construction of these monumental structures solidified Bangkok's status as the new capital and a center of political and religious power.

The early 19th century saw continued growth and modernization under the reigns of subsequent kings. King Rama II and King Rama III focused on expanding the city's infrastructure and enhancing its economic prosperity. The construction of canals, known as khlongs, facilitated transportation and trade within the city and with neighboring regions. These canals earned Bangkok the nickname "Venice of the East." The city became a bustling hub of commerce, attracting merchants and traders from China, India, and other parts of Asia.

The mid-19th century marked a period of significant change and adaptation for Bangkok and Siam. The reign of King Mongkut (Rama IV) from 1851 to 1868 was characterized by efforts to modernize the kingdom and establish diplomatic relations with Western powers. King Mongkut recognized the importance of embracing modernization to protect Siam from colonial encroachment. He initiated reforms in education, infrastructure, and the legal system, and he signed treaties with various Western countries, including the United States and the United Kingdom.

King Mongkut's successor, King Chulalongkorn (Rama V), continued the process of modernization and reform. His reign from 1868 to 1910 is often regarded as a golden age for Siam. King Chulalongkorn implemented far-reaching reforms that transformed the kingdom into a modern state. He abolished slavery, reformed the administrative system, and established a modern legal code. The king also focused on improving education, healthcare, and infrastructure. The construction of railways, roads, and telegraph lines facilitated communication and transportation, further integrating Bangkok with the rest of the country.

King Chulalongkorn's efforts to modernize and westernize Siam extended to the cultural and social spheres. He encouraged the adoption of Western dress, customs, and technologies while preserving traditional Thai culture and values. The king's travels to Europe and his interactions with foreign leaders influenced his vision for Siam's development. His commitment to modernization helped Siam avoid colonization and maintain its independence during a period when many neighboring countries fell under colonial rule.

The early 20th century brought further political and social changes to Bangkok and Thailand. The reign of King Vajiravudh (Rama VI) from 1910 to 1925 saw the introduction of Western-style education and the promotion of Thai nationalism. King Vajiravudh established Chulalongkorn University, the first university in Thailand, and encouraged the study of science, literature, and the arts. His reign also witnessed the rise of a new generation of Thai intellectuals and leaders who played a crucial role in shaping the country's future.

The political landscape of Thailand underwent a dramatic transformation in 1932 with the Siamese Revolution, which marked the end of absolute monarchy and the establishment of a constitutional monarchy. The revolution was led by a group of military officers and civilian intellectuals who sought to introduce democratic reforms and reduce the power of the monarchy. The new political system brought significant changes to Bangkok, including the establishment of a parliamentary government and the drafting of a constitution.

The mid-20th century was a period of rapid urbanization and economic growth for Bangkok. The city's population expanded significantly as people from rural areas migrated to the capital in search of better opportunities. The construction of modern buildings, roads, and bridges transformed Bangkok's skyline. The city became a major center for commerce, industry, and culture in Southeast Asia. However, rapid urbanization also brought challenges, including traffic congestion, pollution, and inadequate infrastructure.

The latter half of the 20th century saw Bangkok emerge as a global city with a dynamic economy and a vibrant cultural scene. The city's role as a regional hub for business, tourism, and entertainment attracted people from around the world. Bangkok's diverse population contributed to its cosmopolitan atmosphere, with a mix of traditional Thai culture and international influences. The city became known for its bustling street markets, world-class shopping malls, and thriving nightlife.

One of the defining features of Bangkok is its rich cultural heritage, reflected in its numerous temples, palaces, and historical sites. The city's temples, or wats, are not only places of worship but also architectural masterpieces. Wat Arun, or the Temple of Dawn, is one of Bangkok's most iconic landmarks, known for its stunning spire that rises above the Chao Phraya River. Wat Pho, home to the famous reclining Buddha statue, is another important religious and cultural site. These temples attract millions of visitors each year and play a central role in the city's cultural and spiritual life.

The Grand Palace remains the heart of Bangkok's historical and cultural identity. The complex, with its intricate architecture and lush gardens, continues to serve as the official residence of the Thai king and a venue for important ceremonies and events. The nearby Sanam Luang, a royal field, is used for various state functions and public gatherings. These historic sites are a testament to Bangkok's enduring connection to its royal and cultural heritage.

Bangkok's cultural scene extends beyond its historical landmarks. The city is home to a thriving arts community, with numerous galleries, theaters, and performance venues. The Bangkok Art and Culture Centre (BACC) is a focal point for contemporary art and cultural activities, hosting exhibitions, workshops, and performances that showcase the creativity and talent of local and international artists. The city's music and dance traditions, including classical Thai dance and music, are celebrated and preserved through performances and festivals.

The culinary landscape of Bangkok is another highlight of the city's cultural richness. Thai cuisine, known for its bold flavors and aromatic spices, is a major attraction for both locals and tourists. The city's street food scene is legendary, with vendors offering a wide variety of dishes, from spicy som tam (papaya salad) to savory pad Thai (stir-fried noodles). Bangkok's markets, such as Chatuchak Weekend Market and Or Tor Kor Market, are famous for their fresh produce, exotic ingredients, and delicious street food. The city's dining scene also includes high-end restaurants that blend traditional Thai flavors with modern culinary techniques, earning Bangkok a reputation as a global food destination.

Bangkok's role as a regional and global hub has been further enhanced by its modern infrastructure and connectivity. Suvarnabhumi Airport, one of the largest and busiest airports in

Southeast Asia, serves as a gateway to Thailand and a major transit point for international travelers. The city's public transportation system, including the BTS Skytrain and MRT subway, provides efficient and convenient options for navigating the bustling metropolis. These developments have made Bangkok a major center for business, tourism, and international conferences.

The city's economic growth has been driven by a diverse range of industries, including manufacturing, finance, technology, and tourism. Bangkok's central business district is home to numerous multinational corporations, financial institutions, and commercial enterprises. The city's vibrant startup ecosystem has also fostered innovation and entrepreneurship, attracting investment and talent from around the world. Bangkok's economic dynamism has contributed to its status as a leading city in Southeast Asia.

Despite its rapid modernization and economic success, Bangkok faces ongoing challenges related to urbanization, environmental sustainability, and social equity. Traffic congestion, air pollution, and flooding are persistent issues that require innovative solutions and effective governance. Efforts to address these challenges include the development of green spaces, improvements in public transportation, and initiatives to promote sustainable urban planning. Community engagement and collaboration between government, private sector, and civil society are crucial to creating a more livable and resilient city.

Bangkok's future is shaped by its ability to balance tradition and modernity, preserving its rich cultural heritage while embracing innovation and progress. The city's dynamic and diverse population is a source of strength and creativity, driving its continued evolution as a global metropolis. As Bangkok navigates the complexities of the 21st century, it remains a city of contrasts and possibilities, where the past and present coexist in a vibrant and ever-changing tapestry.

Chapter 22: Riyadh: Desert Secrets

Riyadh, the capital of Saudi Arabia, stands as a modern marvel amidst the vast expanse of the Arabian Desert. Its journey from a small, fortified village to a bustling metropolis encapsulates the transformative power of vision, resilience, and ambition. Riyadh's story is deeply intertwined with the broader narrative of Saudi Arabia's history, marked by ancient trade routes, Islamic heritage, tribal dynamics, and the profound impact of oil discovery.

The history of Riyadh can be traced back to ancient times when the Arabian Peninsula was home to a variety of tribal communities. The region that would become Riyadh was part of the broader area known as Najd, a central plateau in the heart of the peninsula. Najd was characterized by its harsh desert environment, but it was also a crossroads for various trade routes that connected the Arabian Peninsula with the rest of the Middle East. These trade routes facilitated the exchange of goods, ideas, and cultural practices, contributing to the development of early settlements in the region.

The name "Riyadh" is derived from the Arabic word "rawḍa," meaning "gardens" or "meadows," reflecting the area's fertile land where water sources were available. The earliest known reference to Riyadh dates back to the pre-Islamic era when it was a small agricultural settlement. The region's inhabitants were primarily engaged in farming, herding, and trade. The harsh desert climate necessitated a lifestyle that was adaptive and resilient, with communities relying on oases and seasonal rains to sustain their livelihoods.

The advent of Islam in the 7th century brought significant changes to the Arabian Peninsula, including the region of Najd. The spread of Islam unified the disparate tribes of Arabia under a common religious and political framework. Najd, including Riyadh, became part of the early Islamic caliphates, which brought increased stability and prosperity to the region. However, Riyadh remained relatively obscure compared to other major cities in the Islamic world, such as Mecca and Medina.

Riyadh's fortunes began to change in the 18th century with the rise of the Al Saud family and the establishment of the First Saudi State. In 1744, Muhammad ibn Abd al-Wahhab, a religious reformer, formed an alliance with Muhammad ibn Saud, the leader of the Al Saud family. This alliance aimed to purify Islamic practices in the region and establish a state based on strict adherence to Islamic principles. The Al Saud-Wahhabi alliance proved to be a powerful force, and they rapidly expanded their control over much of the Arabian Peninsula.

Riyadh played a pivotal role in the early years of the Saudi state. In 1824, Turki ibn Abdullah, a descendant of Muhammad ibn Saud, captured Riyadh and made it the capital of the Second Saudi State. Under his leadership, Riyadh grew in importance as a political and military center. The city's strategic location and fortified structures made it a key stronghold in the ongoing conflicts with rival tribes and external powers. The Al Saud family's ability to maintain control over Riyadh was crucial to their efforts to consolidate power and expand their influence.

The Second Saudi State faced numerous challenges, including internal divisions and external threats. In the late 19th century, the Al Saud family was temporarily ousted from Riyadh by their rivals, the Al Rashid family of Ha'il. However, the resilience and determination of the Al Saud family would soon lead to a dramatic turn of events. In 1902, Abdulaziz ibn Abdul Rahman Al Saud, also known as Ibn Saud, led a daring raid to recapture Riyadh from the Al Rashid. This bold move marked the beginning of the modern Saudi state and the establishment of Riyadh as its enduring capital.

Ibn Saud's recapture of Riyadh was a turning point in the history of the Arabian Peninsula. With Riyadh as his base, Ibn Saud embarked on a series of military campaigns to unify the disparate regions of Arabia under his rule. By 1932, he had successfully united the majority of the Arabian Peninsula, founding the Kingdom of Saudi Arabia. Riyadh, now the capital of a unified kingdom, began to transform from a modest desert town into a burgeoning city.

The discovery of oil in Saudi Arabia in the 1930s had a profound impact on Riyadh and the entire kingdom. The vast oil reserves brought unprecedented wealth and economic development to the region. Riyadh, as the political and administrative center, became the focal point for this transformation. The influx of oil revenue enabled massive infrastructure projects, including the construction of modern roads, buildings, and utilities. The city's population began to grow rapidly as people from across the kingdom and beyond were drawn to Riyadh by the promise of economic opportunities and improved living standards.

The rapid modernization of Riyadh accelerated in the latter half of the 20th century under the leadership of successive Saudi kings. King Faisal, who ruled from 1964 to 1975, implemented a series of reforms aimed at modernizing the kingdom while maintaining its Islamic heritage. His efforts included improvements in education, healthcare, and infrastructure. Riyadh benefited from these reforms, with the establishment of modern schools, hospitals, and universities. The city's skyline began to change with the construction of new government buildings, commercial centers, and residential areas.

King Khalid, who succeeded King Faisal, continued the process of modernization. His reign saw the development of key institutions such as King Saud University and King Khalid International Airport, which further enhanced Riyadh's status as a major urban center. The city's growth was guided by comprehensive urban planning efforts that aimed to balance modernization with the preservation of cultural and historical heritage.

The 1980s and 1990s were marked by continued expansion and diversification of Riyadh's economy. The Saudi government invested heavily in industries beyond oil, including finance, telecommunications, and manufacturing. Riyadh's financial district, with its modern skyscrapers and corporate offices, became a symbol of the city's economic dynamism. The development of industrial zones and technology parks attracted businesses and investors from around the world, positioning Riyadh as a regional hub for commerce and innovation.

The turn of the 21st century brought new challenges and opportunities for Riyadh. The city's population had grown significantly, leading to increased demands on infrastructure, housing, and public services. The Saudi government launched ambitious projects to address these challenges and further enhance the city's global standing. Vision 2030, an economic and social reform plan introduced by Crown Prince Mohammed bin Salman, aims to diversify the economy, reduce dependence on oil, and promote sustainable development. Riyadh is at the heart of these efforts, with initiatives focused on improving quality of life, fostering innovation, and attracting international investment.

One of the key components of Vision 2030 is the development of Riyadh as a global city. Major projects such as the Riyadh Metro, a state-of-the-art public transportation system, are designed to improve mobility and reduce traffic congestion. The King Abdullah Financial District, a major business and financial hub, aims to position Riyadh as a leading center for finance and commerce in the Middle East. The city is also investing in cultural and recreational facilities, including museums, theaters, and parks, to enhance the quality of life for residents and visitors.

Riyadh's cultural heritage is a vital aspect of its identity and appeal. The city is home to numerous historical sites and landmarks that reflect its rich history and Islamic heritage. The Masmak

Fortress, a 19th-century mud-brick fort, is a symbol of Riyadh's historical significance and the Al Saud family's legacy. The National Museum of Saudi Arabia, located in the King Abdulaziz Historical Center, offers a comprehensive overview of the kingdom's history, culture, and achievements. The Diriyah district, the ancestral home of the Al Saud family, is being developed into a cultural and heritage destination that celebrates the city's origins and historical importance.

The city's cultural scene is complemented by a vibrant arts and entertainment sector. Riyadh hosts a variety of events and festivals that showcase Saudi culture, music, and cuisine. The annual Riyadh Season, a major entertainment and cultural festival, attracts millions of visitors with its diverse program of concerts, performances, and exhibitions. The city's dining scene has also flourished, with a wide range of restaurants offering both traditional Saudi dishes and international cuisine.

Riyadh's role as the political and administrative center of Saudi Arabia underscores its importance in the kingdom's governance and international relations. The city is home to key government institutions, including the Royal Court, the Council of Ministers, and various ministries and agencies. Diplomatic missions and international organizations have established their presence in Riyadh, reflecting the city's status as a hub for regional and global diplomacy.

Riyadh's future is shaped by its commitment to sustainable development and innovation. The city's leadership is focused on creating a smart and sustainable urban environment that meets the needs of its growing population while preserving its cultural and historical heritage. Efforts to promote green spaces, renewable energy, and efficient public transportation are integral to Riyadh's vision for a sustainable and livable city.

Chapter 23: Lisbon: Age of Exploration

Lisbon, the capital city of Portugal, is steeped in a rich history that prominently features the Age of Exploration, a period spanning the 15th and 16th centuries when Portuguese explorers embarked on unprecedented maritime expeditions. This era, often referred to as the Age of Discoveries, marked Lisbon as a central hub of global navigation and exploration. The city's strategic location at the mouth of the Tagus River provided an ideal launching point for ships setting out to explore the uncharted waters of the Atlantic and beyond.

The impetus for Portugal's explorations stemmed from a combination of economic, political, and scientific motivations. The desire to find new trade routes to Asia, bypassing the overland routes controlled by Ottoman and Venetian intermediaries, played a crucial role. Additionally, the spirit of the Renaissance, with its emphasis on human curiosity and the quest for knowledge, further fueled these ventures. Under the leadership of Prince Henry the Navigator, who established a school of navigation at Sagres, Portugal became a pioneer in maritime exploration. Although Prince Henry himself did not sail, his patronage of explorers and innovations in navigation significantly advanced the nation's capabilities.

Lisbon's shipyards became bustling centers of activity as shipbuilders constructed the advanced vessels known as caravels. These ships, with their innovative design and capability to sail closer to the wind, were instrumental in the success of the Portuguese explorers. The city's docks witnessed the departure of numerous expeditions that would forever alter the course of history. One of the earliest and most notable expeditions was led by Bartolomeu Dias, who in 1488 became the first European to sail around the southern tip of Africa, later named the Cape of Good Hope. This monumental achievement opened the sea route to the Indian Ocean and laid the groundwork for future expeditions to Asia.

In 1497, Vasco da Gama embarked from Lisbon on a historic voyage that would establish a direct sea route to India. After navigating around the Cape of Good Hope, da Gama's fleet reached the shores of Calicut (present-day Kozhikode) in India, thus securing a direct maritime link between Europe and Asia. This breakthrough had profound implications for global trade, as it allowed Portugal to establish a lucrative spice trade monopoly, significantly enhancing the nation's wealth and influence. Lisbon's docks overflowed with exotic goods, such as spices, silks, and precious stones, transforming the city into a bustling center of commerce and cultural exchange.

The wealth generated from these explorations financed the construction of grand monuments and buildings in Lisbon, many of which still stand today. The Belém Tower, a UNESCO World Heritage site, is a prominent example of Manueline architecture, a style that flourished during the reign of King Manuel I. This architectural style, characterized by intricate detailing and maritime motifs, symbolized Portugal's global maritime dominance. The Jerónimos Monastery, another masterpiece of Manueline architecture, was commissioned by King Manuel I to commemorate Vasco da Gama's successful voyage to India. The monastery not only serves as a testament to Portugal's navigational prowess but also as a final resting place for da Gama himself.

Lisbon's role in the Age of Exploration also had significant cultural and intellectual ramifications. The city's libraries and academies became repositories of newfound knowledge, with maps, charts, and navigational instruments reflecting the expanding horizons of European understanding. The influx of foreign goods and ideas stimulated a vibrant cultural exchange, influencing Portuguese art, cuisine, and daily life. The navigational achievements of the Portuguese also had a lasting impact on global cartography. The meticulous maps and charts produced by Portuguese cartographers during this period were highly prized and used by explorers from other European nations. These advancements in cartography not only facilitated further explorations but also contributed to a more accurate and comprehensive understanding of the world's geography.

However, the Age of Exploration also had darker consequences, particularly in the context of colonialism and the transatlantic slave trade. As Portuguese explorers established trading posts and colonies in Africa, Asia, and the Americas, they often exploited local populations and resources. The establishment of the Atlantic slave trade, in which Lisbon played a significant role, had devastating effects on African societies, leading to the forced displacement and suffering of millions of people. This legacy of exploitation and violence is an integral part of the history of the Age of Exploration and continues to shape contemporary discussions about colonialism and its impacts.

Chapter 24: Casablanca: A Tangier Tale

Casablanca, Morocco's largest city and economic hub, boasts a rich and diverse history that extends far beyond its modern reputation as a bustling metropolis. Although Casablanca might be better known today for its economic prowess and cinematic fame, its history is deeply intertwined with the broader historical narrative of Morocco and North Africa. A particularly intriguing aspect of this history is the city's connection to Tangier, another of Morocco's iconic cities, which adds layers of complexity and richness to Casablanca's tale.

The relationship between Casablanca and Tangier dates back centuries, rooted in their shared strategic significance as coastal cities along Morocco's Atlantic and Mediterranean shores. Both cities have served as key points of contact between Morocco and the wider world, influencing each other's development through commerce, culture, and politics. During the Phoenician and Carthaginian periods, coastal settlements in the region, including what would become Casablanca, were integral to maritime trade routes that connected North Africa with Europe and the Near East. These early interactions set the stage for the cities' future roles as gateways between continents.

In the early Islamic period, the Umayyad and later the Almoravid and Almohad dynasties expanded their influence across North Africa, establishing trade networks and fostering the spread of Islam. Tangier, due to its strategic location at the entrance to the Mediterranean, became a significant center of commerce and cultural exchange. The influence of these dynasties extended to the region that would become Casablanca, contributing to its growth and development. By the 14th century, under the Marinid dynasty, both Tangier and the burgeoning settlement of Anfa (modern-day Casablanca) had developed into important urban centers.

The fortunes of Casablanca and Tangier continued to evolve in parallel, shaped by the ebb and flow of regional and global power dynamics. The 15th century saw the rise of Portuguese influence along the Moroccan coast, leading to the capture of several key ports, including Tangier in 1471 and Anfa in 1468. The Portuguese transformed Anfa into a fortified trading post, renaming it Casa Branca (White House), a name that would eventually evolve into Casablanca. This period of Portuguese control left a lasting imprint on the architectural and urban development of both cities, with fortifications and European-style buildings becoming prominent features.

By the early 16th century, the Portuguese faced increasing resistance from Moroccan forces, culminating in the recapture of Anfa by the Wattasid dynasty. This marked the beginning of a new era for Casablanca, as the city was rebuilt and repopulated under Moroccan rule. Meanwhile, Tangier remained under Portuguese control until 1661, when it was ceded to England as part of the dowry of Catherine of Braganza, who married King Charles II. The English, however, struggled to maintain their hold on Tangier, facing persistent resistance from Moroccan forces led by the Alaouite dynasty. In 1684, the English abandoned Tangier, which was then retaken by the Moroccans.

The 18th and 19th centuries saw both Casablanca and Tangier experiencing significant growth and transformation. Tangier, with its strategic location, became an international city of intrigue and diplomacy. It was during this period that Tangier began to develop its reputation as a haven for expatriates, artists, and spies, a status that would endure well into the 20th century. Casablanca, on the other hand, continued to grow as a commercial hub, attracting merchants and settlers from various parts of Morocco and beyond.

The turn of the 20th century brought profound changes to Morocco, including the establishment of the French and Spanish protectorates. In 1912, Casablanca was incorporated into the French protectorate, while Tangier retained a unique international status, governed by multiple foreign powers. The French administration embarked on an ambitious plan to modernize Casablanca, transforming it into a showcase of colonial urban planning and architecture. Wide boulevards, grand public buildings, and European-style neighborhoods were constructed, giving Casablanca a distinct cosmopolitan character.

During the early 20th century, Casablanca's growth was fueled by its strategic importance as a port and commercial center. The city's port became one of the busiest in North Africa, facilitating trade and attracting investment. Meanwhile, Tangier's status as an international zone made it a magnet for a diverse array of residents, including diplomats, businessmen, and artists. The unique blend of Moroccan and international influences in Tangier created a vibrant cultural milieu that would inspire writers such as Paul Bowles and William S. Burroughs.

The mid-20th century was a period of great change and upheaval for both cities. World War II brought Casablanca into the global spotlight as a key strategic location for Allied forces. The 1942 Allied landings in North Africa, known as Operation Torch, included Casablanca as a major objective, leading to the city's occupation by Allied troops. This event highlighted Casablanca's geopolitical significance and reinforced its role as a critical hub in the region. Tangier, meanwhile, continued to be a center of intrigue during the war, with its international status making it a hotbed of espionage and diplomatic activity.

The post-war period saw the rise of nationalist movements across North Africa, culminating in Morocco's independence from French and Spanish rule in 1956. Casablanca and Tangier, now fully integrated into the newly independent Kingdom of Morocco, embarked on paths of modernization and development. Casablanca, in particular, experienced rapid urbanization and economic growth, becoming the country's leading industrial and financial center. The city's population surged as rural migrants flocked to Casablanca in search of opportunities, transforming it into a sprawling metropolis.

Tangier, while also growing and modernizing, retained much of its unique character as a cosmopolitan city with a rich cultural heritage. The influx of international residents continued, contributing to Tangier's vibrant artistic and intellectual scene. The city's historical medina, with its narrow winding streets and traditional Moroccan architecture, remained a focal point of Tangier's identity, attracting tourists and expatriates alike.

In contemporary times, Casablanca and Tangier continue to play vital roles in Morocco's economy and cultural landscape. Casablanca, as the economic powerhouse of the country, hosts major corporations, financial institutions, and a bustling port that connects Morocco to global markets. The city's skyline is dotted with modern skyscrapers, and its urban landscape reflects the dynamic and diverse nature of its population. Tangier, with its strategic location and historical significance, has emerged as a key gateway between Africa and Europe. The development of the Tanger-Med port, one of the largest in Africa, has further enhanced the city's economic importance.

The cultural and historical connections between Casablanca and Tangier remain strong, with both cities continuing to influence each other in various ways. Casablanca's modernity and Tangier's cosmopolitanism represent two facets of Morocco's identity, reflecting the country's rich and diverse heritage. As Morocco continues to navigate the challenges and opportunities of the 21st century, the intertwined histories of Casablanca and Tangier serve as a testament to the enduring legacy of these remarkable cities.

Chapter 25: Seoul: Shadows of Dynasties

Seoul, the capital of South Korea, is a city where ancient history and modernity coexist in a remarkable blend. The city's history is deeply rooted in the legacies of several dynasties that have ruled over Korea, each leaving indelible marks on Seoul's cultural, architectural, and political landscape. The shadows of these dynasties provide a rich tapestry of stories that have shaped the city's identity over the centuries.

The history of Seoul as a significant settlement dates back to the early Three Kingdoms period, around the 4th century CE. During this time, the area that is now Seoul was part of the Baekje Kingdom. Baekje, one of the Three Kingdoms along with Goguryeo and Silla, was known for its advanced culture and trade networks. The Han River, which flows through Seoul, was a crucial waterway that facilitated commerce and communication. The region's fertile land and strategic location made it an attractive area for settlement and development. The establishment of Wiryeseong, Baekje's capital, in present-day Seoul, marked the beginning of the city's long history as a political and cultural center.

As the Three Kingdoms period progressed, the city came under the control of the Goguryeo Kingdom in the late 5th century and then the Silla Kingdom in the 7th century. Silla's unification of the Korean Peninsula in 668 CE under the Unified Silla dynasty further cemented Seoul's importance. The Unified Silla period was marked by significant cultural and economic development, and Seoul benefited from its central location within the unified kingdom. The construction of Buddhist temples and other cultural institutions during this time contributed to the city's growing prominence.

The subsequent Goryeo Dynasty (918-1392) saw Seoul, then known as "Namgyeong" (Southern Capital), continue to thrive as a secondary capital. The Goryeo rulers valued the city for its strategic location and economic potential. During this period, Seoul became a center of Confucian learning and Buddhist culture, with the construction of numerous temples and the establishment of educational institutions. The dynasty's focus on centralization and bureaucracy also led to the development of administrative structures that would later influence Seoul's governance.

The most significant transformation of Seoul began with the rise of the Joseon Dynasty in 1392. King Taejo, the founder of the Joseon Dynasty, established Seoul, then known as "Hanyang," as the capital of the newly founded kingdom. The decision to make Hanyang the capital was based on its favorable geographical features, including the natural protection offered by surrounding mountains and its access to the Han River. Under the Joseon Dynasty, Seoul was meticulously planned and developed according to Confucian principles. The construction of Gyeongbokgung Palace, the main royal palace, symbolized the central authority and cultural aspirations of the Joseon rulers.

The Joseon Dynasty's reign, which lasted for over five centuries, left an indelible mark on Seoul's cultural and architectural heritage. The city was divided into different sectors, each serving specific functions such as residential areas, marketplaces, and government offices. The layout of the city reflected Confucian ideals of order and hierarchy, with the palace and government buildings located in the northern part of the city, signifying their importance. The construction of city walls and gates, such as Sungnyemun (Namdaemun), served both defensive and administrative purposes, controlling access to the city and symbolizing its status as the heart of the kingdom.

Throughout the Joseon period, Seoul became a vibrant center of Confucian scholarship, art, and commerce. The establishment of the Confucian academy, Sungkyunkwan, in 1398, further solidified the city's role as an intellectual hub. Scholars from across the kingdom traveled to Seoul to study and take part in the civil service examinations, which were the primary means of entering government service. The city's markets, such as the famous Dongdaemun Market, thrived as centers of trade and commerce, attracting merchants and artisans from various regions.

The late Joseon period, however, was marked by internal strife, external invasions, and social upheaval. The Imjin War (1592-1598), also known as the Japanese invasions of Korea, brought significant destruction to Seoul. Japanese forces captured and occupied the city, causing extensive damage to palaces, temples, and other structures. The invasion left a lasting impact on the city, leading to efforts to rebuild and restore its cultural heritage in the subsequent years. The Manchu invasions in the early 17th century further destabilized the kingdom, exacerbating the challenges faced by the Joseon rulers.

Despite these challenges, Seoul continued to evolve and adapt. The city's recovery and reconstruction efforts included the rebuilding of Gyeongbokgung Palace and other significant structures. The development of new technologies and the introduction of Western ideas during the 19th century brought additional changes to the city's landscape and culture. The opening of Korea to foreign trade and diplomatic relations in the late 19th century led to the establishment of foreign legations and the introduction of modern infrastructure, such as electric streetcars and telegraph lines.

The end of the Joseon Dynasty came with the annexation of Korea by Japan in 1910. The Japanese colonial period (1910-1945) brought profound changes to Seoul, as the city was renamed "Keijo" and underwent extensive modernization efforts. The Japanese authorities implemented urban planning projects that included the construction of new roads, buildings, and public facilities. While these developments modernized the city, they also led to the displacement of Korean cultural and historical landmarks. The demolition of parts of Gyeongbokgung Palace to make way for the Japanese Governor-General's Office was a particularly symbolic and painful event for Koreans.

The liberation of Korea from Japanese rule in 1945 marked a new chapter in Seoul's history. The city became the capital of the Republic of Korea (South Korea) in 1948, and efforts to restore and preserve its cultural heritage gained momentum. The Korean War (1950-1953), however, brought significant devastation to Seoul, as the city changed hands multiple times during the conflict. The war left much of the city in ruins, necessitating extensive rebuilding and rehabilitation efforts in the post-war years.

The decades following the Korean War witnessed Seoul's rapid transformation into a modern metropolis. The city's reconstruction efforts were fueled by economic development and industrialization, leading to the emergence of high-rise buildings, modern infrastructure, and expanded urban areas. The Miracle on the Han River, a period of rapid economic growth from the 1960s to the 1990s, saw Seoul becoming a global city and a major economic center. The city's population surged, and its skyline was transformed with the construction of skyscrapers and modern commercial districts.

Amidst this rapid modernization, efforts to preserve and celebrate Seoul's historical and cultural heritage continued. The restoration of Gyeongbokgung Palace and other historical sites became a priority, reflecting a growing recognition of the importance of preserving the city's past. Cultural festivals, museums, and heritage sites in Seoul offer glimpses into the city's rich history, attracting both locals and tourists. The Jongmyo Shrine, a UNESCO

World Heritage site, serves as a testament to the city's enduring connection to its Confucian heritage and the ancestral rites of the Joseon Dynasty.

In contemporary times, Seoul seamlessly blends its ancient traditions with cutting-edge technology and innovation. The city's neighborhoods, such as Bukchon Hanok Village, preserve traditional Korean architecture amidst the bustling urban environment. Modern landmarks like the Namsan Seoul Tower and the Dongdaemun Design Plaza coexist with historical sites, creating a unique juxtaposition of old and new. The Cheonggyecheon Stream, a restored urban waterway, exemplifies Seoul's commitment to sustainable urban development while honoring its historical significance.

Seoul's cultural vibrancy is further reflected in its dynamic arts and entertainment scene. The city is a global hub for K-pop, fashion, and contemporary art, attracting creative talents from around the world. Cultural districts such as Hongdae and Gangnam are renowned for their nightlife, shopping, and entertainment options, showcasing the city's youthful energy and creativity. The annual Seoul Lantern Festival and various cultural events celebrate the city's rich heritage and diverse cultural expressions.

Chapter 26: Johannesburg: Gold Rush Ghosts

Johannesburg, South Africa's largest city and economic powerhouse, has a history intricately linked to the discovery of gold in the late 19th century. The gold rush that began in the Witwatersrand region in 1886 transformed Johannesburg from a modest settlement into a sprawling metropolis. The legacy of the gold rush, with its boomtown fervor and subsequent decline, has left an enduring impact on the city's landscape and culture, giving rise to what can be termed as "gold rush ghosts."

The story of Johannesburg's gold rush begins in 1886 when an Australian prospector named George Harrison discovered a gold reef on the Langlaagte farm. This discovery set off a frenzy as prospectors, entrepreneurs, and adventurers flocked to the region, hoping to strike it rich. The promise of vast wealth attracted people from all over the world, leading to a rapid influx of settlers and the establishment of numerous mining camps. These camps soon coalesced into a burgeoning settlement, which was named Johannesburg after Johann Rissik and Christiaan Johannes Joubert, officials in the Transvaal government.

The initial gold finds were alluvial, meaning they were found in riverbeds and required relatively simple extraction methods. However, it soon became apparent that the true wealth lay in the deep underground reefs of the Witwatersrand basin. The mining of these deep-level reefs required significant investment in technology and infrastructure, leading to the establishment of large mining companies. The most prominent of these was the Randlords, a group of wealthy entrepreneurs who controlled the majority of the gold mining industry. Figures like Cecil Rhodes and Barney Barnato amassed enormous fortunes, further fueling the growth of Johannesburg.

As the gold mining industry expanded, so did Johannesburg. The city quickly developed from a makeshift collection of tents and shacks into a bustling urban center. Infrastructure projects, such as the construction of railways, roads, and buildings, were undertaken to support the growing population and facilitate the transportation of gold. The establishment of banks, businesses, and trading posts created a vibrant commercial environment, attracting further investment and immigration. By the turn of the 20th century, Johannesburg had become the largest city in South Africa and a major financial hub.

However, the rapid growth and prosperity brought by the gold rush were accompanied by significant social and environmental challenges. The influx of people from diverse backgrounds led to overcrowding, inadequate housing, and poor sanitation conditions. The mining industry itself was fraught with dangers, including hazardous working conditions and frequent accidents. The deep-level mines required extensive labor, and the majority of this labor was provided by African workers who were subjected to harsh and exploitative conditions. The segregation and discrimination inherent in the colonial system were exacerbated by the economic disparities of the gold rush, laying the groundwork for the institutionalized racism of apartheid.

The environmental impact of the gold rush was also profound. The extraction and processing of gold generated large amounts of waste, including toxic chemicals such as cyanide and mercury, which polluted the soil and water sources. The landscape of the Witwatersrand was transformed by the excavation of vast open-pit mines and the creation of mine dumps, which are still visible today. These dumps, composed of crushed rock and other mining byproducts, are a stark reminder of the environmental costs of the gold rush.

The early 20th century saw Johannesburg continue to grow and modernize, with the construction of new buildings, roads, and public services. The city's architecture reflected its cosmopolitan character, with influences from European, American, and local styles. The iconic Carlton Centre, once the tallest building in Africa, symbolized Johannesburg's status as a leading commercial and financial center. Despite its progress, the city remained deeply divided along racial and economic lines, with affluent neighborhoods and business districts juxtaposed against impoverished townships and informal settlements.

The legacy of the gold rush also includes the development of a rich cultural heritage. Johannesburg became a melting pot of cultures, languages, and traditions, as people from different backgrounds converged in the city. The vibrant arts scene, including music, theater, and literature, flourished, reflecting the diverse experiences and aspirations of its inhabitants. Jazz, in particular, found a strong foothold in Johannesburg, with the city becoming a hub for renowned musicians and performers. The stories of the gold rush, with its tales of fortune, hardship, and adventure, became an integral part of Johannesburg's cultural narrative.

The economic boom of the gold rush was not sustainable indefinitely. As the easily accessible gold deposits were exhausted, mining operations had to delve deeper and deeper, increasing costs and reducing profitability. The Great Depression of the 1930s further strained the industry, leading to closures and layoffs. Despite these challenges, gold mining remained a crucial part of Johannesburg's economy, with new technologies and methods being developed to extract gold from deeper and more difficult deposits. The establishment of the Chamber of Mines in 1889 and the Rand

Refinery in 1920 were significant milestones in the industry's evolution.

The mid-20th century was a period of significant political and social change in South Africa. The rise of the apartheid regime in 1948 institutionalized racial segregation and discrimination, profoundly affecting Johannesburg. The city's neighborhoods were segregated by law, with non-white populations forcibly relocated to designated areas such as Soweto (South Western Townships). The apartheid policies exacerbated the economic disparities and social injustices that had been entrenched during the gold rush era. The struggle against apartheid became a defining feature of Johannesburg's history, with the city serving as a focal point for resistance and activism.

The eventual dismantling of apartheid in the early 1990s marked the beginning of a new era for Johannesburg. The city embarked on a journey of transformation and reconciliation, seeking to address the legacies of inequality and injustice. The Truth and Reconciliation Commission, established in 1995, aimed to uncover the atrocities of the apartheid era and promote healing and unity. Johannesburg's skyline continued to evolve, with new developments and urban renewal projects aimed at revitalizing the city and making it more inclusive.

Today, Johannesburg is a dynamic and diverse metropolis that continues to grapple with the ghosts of its gold rush past. The city's economy has diversified, with sectors such as finance, technology, and manufacturing playing significant roles alongside the mining industry. Johannesburg remains a major financial center, home to the Johannesburg Stock Exchange and numerous multinational corporations. The city's universities and research institutions contribute to its status as an educational and intellectual hub.

The cultural legacy of the gold rush is still evident in Johannesburg's vibrant arts and entertainment scene. The city's theaters, galleries, and music venues showcase a rich tapestry of artistic expression, reflecting both its historical heritage and contemporary creativity. The annual Johannesburg Arts Alive Festival, for example, celebrates the city's cultural diversity and artistic talent, attracting performers and audiences from around the world. The Apartheid Museum, Constitution Hill, and other historical sites provide important insights into the city's complex history and the ongoing journey towards social justice.

Environmental challenges remain a significant concern for Johannesburg. The legacy of the gold rush has left the city with numerous mine dumps and contaminated sites that pose risks to public health and the environment. Efforts to rehabilitate these areas and mitigate their impacts are ongoing, with initiatives aimed at promoting sustainable urban development and green spaces. The city's commitment to addressing its environmental issues is reflected in projects such as the rehabilitation of the Jukskei River and the development of eco-friendly infrastructure.

Chapter 27: Hanoi: Tales of Resistance

Hanoi, the capital of Vietnam, is a city rich in history and culture, marked by its tales of resistance against foreign domination and internal strife. The city's history spans over a thousand years, during which it has served as the heart of Vietnamese political, cultural, and military life. Its story is one of resilience and determination, shaped by its strategic importance and the indomitable spirit of its people.

The origins of Hanoi can be traced back to the early days of the Vietnamese civilization. The city was originally known as Thăng Long, meaning "Ascending Dragon," a name given by Emperor Lý Thái Tổ in 1010 when he moved the capital of the Đại Việt (Great Viet) kingdom to this location. The choice of Thăng Long as the capital was influenced by its favorable geographical position, with the Red River providing essential resources and a natural defense against invasions. The Lý Dynasty's establishment of Thăng Long as the capital marked the beginning of a new era of prosperity and cultural development.

The Lý Dynasty (1009-1225) laid the foundations for the city's growth, constructing significant infrastructure, including palaces, temples, and the famous One Pillar Pagoda. Thăng Long flourished as a political and cultural center, attracting scholars, artists, and traders. The city's layout, characterized by its grid pattern and central citadel, reflected the Confucian ideals of order and hierarchy. During this period, Thăng Long became a symbol of Vietnamese identity and sovereignty, embodying the nation's aspirations for independence and unity.

The subsequent Trần Dynasty (1225-1400) continued to develop Thăng Long, but this era was also marked by significant challenges, including the Mongol invasions of the late 13th century. The Mongol Empire, under Kublai Khan, launched multiple invasions of Đại Việt, seeking to expand their dominion. The

Vietnamese, led by the Trần Dynasty, mounted fierce resistance against the invaders. The most notable figure in this resistance was General Trần Hưng Đạo, who orchestrated successful military campaigns that ultimately repelled the Mongol forces. The Battle of Bạch Đằng in 1288 was a decisive victory for the Vietnamese, showcasing their strategic prowess and determination to defend their homeland.

The resilience of Thăng Long during the Mongol invasions solidified its status as a bastion of Vietnamese resistance. The city's ability to withstand such formidable foes became a source of national pride and inspiration. The Trần Dynasty's successful defense against the Mongols not only preserved Thăng Long but also reinforced the Vietnamese spirit of independence and resistance against foreign domination. This legacy of resistance would continue to shape the city's history in the centuries to come.

The early 15th century brought another period of foreign domination, this time by the Ming Dynasty of China. The Ming occupation (1407-1427) was marked by harsh rule and efforts to assimilate Vietnamese culture into the Chinese imperial system. The Vietnamese resistance movement, led by Lê Lợi, culminated in the Lam Sơn Uprising. Lê Lợi, a charismatic leader, rallied the Vietnamese people and waged a protracted guerrilla war against the Ming forces. The resistance movement ultimately succeeded in driving out the Ming occupiers, and Lê Lợi established the Lê Dynasty, restoring Vietnamese sovereignty.

Under the Lê Dynasty (1428-1789), Thăng Long, now renamed Đông Kinh (Eastern Capital), continued to prosper as a political, cultural, and economic hub. The dynasty's efforts to strengthen central authority and promote Confucian values contributed to the city's development. Đông Kinh became a center of learning and culture, attracting scholars and artists from across the kingdom. The construction of the Temple of Literature, dedicated to Confucius, symbolized the city's status as a bastion of Confucian scholarship and education.

The 16th and 17th centuries saw Đông Kinh embroiled in internal conflicts, particularly the rivalry between the Trịnh and Nguyễn families, who vied for control over the northern and southern regions of Vietnam, respectively. Despite the political turmoil, the city remained a vibrant center of commerce and culture. The rise of the Tây Sơn Dynasty in the late 18th century brought further upheaval, but it also set the stage for the emergence of a new era in Vietnamese history.

The Tây Sơn Dynasty's overthrow of the Lê Dynasty and subsequent unification of Vietnam under Emperor Quang Trung marked a brief but significant period of consolidation. Quang Trung's victory over the Chinese Qing forces at the Battle of Ngọc Hồi-Đống Đa in 1789 was another testament to the resilience and martial prowess of the Vietnamese people. Thăng Long, once again, played a central role in these events, serving as the focal point of resistance and national revival.

The 19th century introduced a new phase of foreign intervention, this time from European powers. The French colonization of Vietnam began in the mid-19th century, with Hanoi becoming the administrative center of French Indochina in 1887. The French colonial period brought significant changes to the city's architecture, infrastructure, and social fabric. French colonial buildings, wide boulevards, and modern amenities transformed Hanoi into a cosmopolitan city. However, the colonial rule was also marked by exploitation, repression, and resistance.

The early 20th century saw the rise of nationalist movements in Vietnam, with Hanoi at the forefront of the struggle for independence. The city became a hotbed of political activity, with intellectuals, students, and workers organizing protests and resistance against French colonial rule. The founding of the

Indochinese Communist Party by Hồ Chí Minh in 1930 galvanized the nationalist movement, leading to increased efforts to mobilize the population and fight for independence.

World War II and the Japanese occupation of Vietnam further destabilized French colonial rule, creating an opportunity for the Vietnamese independence movement to gain momentum. The August Revolution of 1945, led by the Viet Minh, resulted in the declaration of independence by Hồ Chí Minh in Hanoi's Ba Đình Square. The establishment of the Democratic Republic of Vietnam marked the beginning of a new chapter in Hanoi's history, but it also set the stage for further conflict.

The First Indochina War (1946-1954) between the Viet Minh and French forces culminated in the decisive Battle of Điện Biên Phủ. The Viet Minh's victory forced the French to negotiate a ceasefire, leading to the Geneva Accords and the division of Vietnam into North and South. Hanoi became the capital of North Vietnam, while Saigon (now Ho Chi Minh City) served as the capital of South Vietnam. The division of the country set the stage for the Vietnam War (1955-1975), a protracted and brutal conflict that would have a profound impact on Hanoi and the entire nation.

During the Vietnam War, Hanoi was the political and military center of North Vietnam. The city endured extensive bombing campaigns by the United States, particularly during Operation Rolling Thunder and the Christmas Bombing of 1972. Despite the devastation, the resilience and determination of the Vietnamese people remained unbroken. The war ultimately ended with the fall of Saigon in 1975, leading to the reunification of Vietnam under communist rule. Hanoi became the capital of the unified Socialist Republic of Vietnam.

The post-war years were marked by efforts to rebuild and recover from the ravages of conflict. Hanoi underwent significant reconstruction and modernization, with investments in infrastructure, industry, and education. The city's historical sites and cultural heritage were preserved and restored, reflecting a renewed focus on national identity and pride. The Đổi Mới (Renovation) reforms of the late 1980s and 1990s brought about significant economic liberalization, leading to rapid urbanization and development in Hanoi.

Today, Hanoi is a vibrant and dynamic city that embodies the spirit of resilience and resistance that has defined its history. The city's landscape is a blend of ancient temples, colonial architecture, and modern skyscrapers, reflecting its diverse cultural heritage and ongoing transformation. Historical sites such as the Thăng Long Imperial Citadel, the Ho Chi Minh Mausoleum, and the Hoa Lo Prison Museum offer glimpses into the city's storied past and the struggles that have shaped its identity.

Hanoi's cultural scene is equally rich and diverse, with traditional arts, music, and theater thriving alongside contemporary expressions. The city's festivals, such as the Tet Lunar New Year celebration and the Mid-Autumn Festival, showcase the vibrant traditions and communal spirit of the Vietnamese people. The Old Quarter, with its narrow streets and bustling markets, remains a living testament to Hanoi's historical continuity and cultural vitality.

Chapter 28: Dublin: Celtic Crossroads

Dublin, the capital of Ireland, stands as a testament to centuries of history, culture, and resilience. Known as "Celtic Crossroads," Dublin has evolved from its ancient Celtic roots into a vibrant modern city, embodying the spirit and complexity of Ireland itself. The city's history is marked by a series of transformative events, cultural shifts, and moments of profound significance that have shaped its identity and left an indelible mark on its landscape.

The origins of Dublin can be traced back to the early Celtic settlements in the region. The area around Dublin Bay was inhabited by Celtic tribes as early as 140 AD. These early settlers established small communities and engaged in agriculture, trade, and craftsmanship. The Celts, known for their rich mythology, artistry, and warrior culture, laid the foundations for Dublin's future development. The city's name, Dublin, derives from the Gaelic "Dubh Linn," meaning "Black Pool," a reference to a dark tidal pool where the River Poddle met the River Liffey.

The arrival of the Vikings in the 9th century marked a significant turning point in Dublin's history. In 841 AD, Viking raiders established a fortified settlement along the River Liffey, which they called Dyflin. The Vikings transformed Dublin into a thriving trade hub, engaging in commerce with other parts of Europe and beyond. They introduced advanced shipbuilding techniques, fortified structures, and a network of trade routes that would become crucial to Dublin's economic development. The Viking legacy is still evident in Dublin's streets, place names, and archaeological sites, such as Dublinia, an interactive museum that explores Viking and medieval Dublin.

By the 11th century, the influence of the Vikings began to wane, and Dublin came under the control of the native Irish kingdom of Leinster. This period of relative stability allowed Dublin to grow as a political and economic center. However, the arrival of the Anglo-Normans in the 12th century once again altered the course of Dublin's history. In 1170, the Anglo-Norman invasion, led by Strongbow (Richard de Clare), resulted in the capture of Dublin. The Anglo-Normans established a stronghold in the city and began to reshape its urban landscape.

Under Anglo-Norman rule, Dublin saw significant architectural and administrative developments. The construction of Dublin Castle, initially a Viking fortress, was expanded and fortified to serve as the seat of English power in Ireland. The castle became the center of governance, administration, and military operations. The Anglo-Normans also established religious institutions, including Christ Church Cathedral and St. Patrick's Cathedral, which remain iconic landmarks in Dublin today. These developments cemented Dublin's status as a key political and religious center.

The subsequent centuries were marked by fluctuating fortunes for Dublin, as it navigated periods of prosperity, conflict, and cultural change. The city continued to grow, and by the 14th century, it had become a vibrant medieval town with a diverse population. However, the political landscape was often turbulent, with power struggles between native Irish clans, Anglo-Norman lords, and the English crown. The Black Death in the mid-14th century also had a devastating impact on Dublin's population and economy.

The Tudor conquest of Ireland in the 16th century brought Dublin firmly under English control. The establishment of the Kingdom of Ireland in 1541 by Henry VIII marked the beginning of direct English rule. Dublin became the center of English administration and governance in Ireland, with the construction of new civic buildings, fortifications, and infrastructure. The city's strategic importance as a military and administrative hub was reinforced by the construction of new walls and defenses.

The 17th century saw Dublin experience significant social, economic, and cultural changes. The Plantation of Ulster and the subsequent influx of English and Scottish settlers brought new influences to the city. Dublin's population grew, and its economy diversified, with the expansion of trade, manufacturing, and commerce. The city also witnessed the establishment of Trinity College in 1592, an institution that would become a cornerstone of Irish education and intellectual life.

The 18th century is often regarded as Dublin's "Golden Age," a period of remarkable growth, prosperity, and cultural flourishing. The city underwent extensive urban development, with the construction of Georgian-style buildings, grand squares, and elegant streets. The development of areas such as St. Stephen's Green, Merrion Square, and Fitzwilliam Square transformed Dublin into one of the most architecturally distinguished cities in Europe. The completion of the Custom House and the Four Courts further enhanced the city's status as a center of commerce and governance.

During this period, Dublin became a hub of intellectual and artistic activity. The city's literary and cultural scene thrived, with figures such as Jonathan Swift, Oliver Goldsmith, and Richard Brinsley Sheridan making significant contributions to literature and the arts. The establishment of institutions such as the Royal Dublin Society and the Royal Irish Academy fostered scientific, artistic, and scholarly pursuits. Theaters, galleries, and salons became vibrant centers of cultural exchange and creativity.

However, Dublin's prosperity was not without its challenges. The city was also a site of political unrest and social inequality. The tensions between the Anglo-Irish ascendancy and the native Irish population were palpable, and movements for political and social reform gained momentum. The Irish Volunteers, formed in 1778, advocated for greater political autonomy and rights for the Irish people. The period culminated in the 1798 Rebellion, a significant uprising against British rule, which, although ultimately unsuccessful, left a lasting impact on Dublin and Ireland's quest for independence.

The 19th century brought both progress and hardship to Dublin. The Act of Union in 1801, which merged the Kingdom of Ireland with the Kingdom of Great Britain, had profound implications for the city. Dublin, which had been the seat of the Irish Parliament, experienced a decline in political influence as power shifted to London. The city's economy was also affected, and many of its grand Georgian houses fell into disrepair.

Despite these challenges, Dublin remained a center of cultural and intellectual activity. The city's literary tradition continued to flourish, with writers such as James Joyce, W.B. Yeats, and Oscar Wilde emerging as key figures in the Irish Literary Revival. Joyce's "Ulysses," set in Dublin, captured the essence of the city's streets, characters, and spirit, cementing its place in literary history. The Abbey Theatre, founded by Yeats and Lady Gregory, became a focal point for the development of Irish drama and national identity.

The struggle for Irish independence reached its zenith in the early 20th century, with Dublin playing a central role in the events that led to the establishment of the Irish Free State. The 1916 Easter Rising, a pivotal moment in the fight for independence, saw Dublin's streets become the battleground for a week-long insurrection against British rule. Key locations such as the General Post Office (GPO) and O'Connell Street witnessed intense fighting and destruction. Although the rebellion was suppressed, it galvanized support for the independence movement and paved the way for the subsequent War of Independence (1919-1921).

The signing of the Anglo-Irish Treaty in 1921 led to the establishment of the Irish Free State, with Dublin as its capital. The city faced the challenges of rebuilding and recovering from the war, but it also embarked on a new chapter of self-determination and development. The 20th century saw Dublin evolve into a modern European capital, with investments in infrastructure, industry, and education. The city's population grew, and its cultural and social life continued to thrive.

Dublin's cultural renaissance in the mid-20th century was marked by the emergence of new voices in literature, music, and the arts. The city's vibrant literary scene produced acclaimed writers such as Samuel Beckett, Brendan Behan, and Roddy Doyle. Dublin also became a center for traditional Irish music, with venues such as O'Donoghue's Pub and the Gaiety Theatre hosting legendary performances. The city's arts festivals, including the Dublin Theatre Festival and the Dublin International Film Festival, attracted international attention and celebrated Dublin's creative spirit.

The latter part of the 20th century and the early 21st century witnessed significant economic and social transformations in Dublin. The city's economy diversified, with the growth of the technology, finance, and tourism sectors. The "Celtic Tiger" period of the 1990s and early 2000s brought unprecedented economic growth, leading to urban development, job creation, and increased prosperity. Dublin's skyline transformed with the construction of modern buildings, shopping centers, and cultural institutions.

Despite the economic boom, Dublin also faced challenges related to housing, infrastructure, and social inequality. The global financial crisis of 2008 had a profound impact on the city, leading to economic downturns and austerity measures. However, Dublin's resilience and adaptability allowed it to recover and continue its growth trajectory. The city's commitment to innovation, education, and cultural preservation has positioned it as a dynamic and forward-looking European capital.

Today, Dublin is a city that seamlessly blends its rich historical heritage with modern vibrancy. The city's architectural landscape is a testament to its diverse history, with medieval castles, Georgian townhouses, and contemporary structures coexisting harmoniously. Dublin's cultural scene remains as dynamic as ever, with a thriving arts community, world-class museums, and a bustling music and nightlife scene. The city's festivals, including St. Patrick's Day celebrations, Bloomsday, and the Dublin Fringe Festival, attract visitors from around the world and showcase Dublin's unique character and creativity.

Dublin's educational institutions, such as Trinity College Dublin and University College Dublin, continue to be centers of excellence and innovation, attracting students and scholars from across the globe. The city's commitment to research, technology, and entrepreneurship has fostered a vibrant startup ecosystem, earning Dublin the nickname "Silicon Docks" for its concentration of tech companies and startups along the Grand Canal.

Chapter 29: Toronto: Northern Narratives

Toronto, the largest city in Canada, is a vibrant metropolis known for its cultural diversity, economic dynamism, and historical significance. The story of Toronto, often referred to as "Northern Narratives," is a rich tapestry woven from the threads of indigenous heritage, colonial development, waves of immigration, and modern urbanization. From its origins as a settlement inhabited by indigenous peoples to its current status as a global city, Toronto's history is marked by transformation, resilience, and a continuous influx of new narratives.

Long before European settlers arrived, the area now known as Toronto was inhabited by indigenous peoples, including the Huron-Wendat, Haudenosaunee (Iroquois), and Mississauga nations. These indigenous communities thrived along the shores of Lake Ontario, utilizing the region's abundant natural resources for hunting, fishing, and agriculture. The name "Toronto" itself is believed to have originated from the Mohawk word "Tkaronto," meaning "place where trees stand in the water," referring to the narrows between Lake Simcoe and Lake Couchiching.

The arrival of European explorers in the early 17th century marked the beginning of a new chapter in Toronto's history. French explorers such as Étienne Brûlé and Samuel de Champlain ventured into the region, establishing fur trading posts and forging alliances with indigenous communities. The French influence waned with the British conquest of New France in 1763, leading to the region's incorporation into British North America.

The late 18th century saw the establishment of the settlement of York, the precursor to modern Toronto. In 1793, John Graves Simcoe, the first Lieutenant Governor of Upper Canada, selected the site for its strategic location along the northern shore of Lake Ontario. Simcoe envisioned York as a military and administrative center that would secure British interests in the region and provide a counterbalance to American expansionism. Fort York was constructed to defend the settlement, and the town quickly grew as settlers arrived, attracted by land grants and economic opportunities.

York's early years were marked by hardship and struggle. The War of 1812 between the United States and Britain brought conflict to the region, with York being attacked and burned by American forces in 1813. Despite the devastation, the settlement was rebuilt, and its resilience laid the foundation for its future growth. By the mid-19th century, York had transformed into the City of Toronto, reflecting its expanding population and economic significance.

The 19th century was a period of rapid growth and development for Toronto. The city became a vital transportation hub with the construction of railways and the expansion of its port facilities. The Grand Trunk Railway, completed in the 1850s, connected Toronto to other major cities in Canada and the United States, facilitating the movement of goods and people. The city's industrial base expanded, with factories, mills, and workshops springing up to produce a wide range of goods, from textiles to machinery.

Toronto's population grew rapidly during this period, fueled by waves of immigration. The city became a destination for immigrants from the British Isles, Europe, and beyond, each group contributing to the city's cultural mosaic. Irish immigrants, fleeing the Great Famine of the 1840s, settled in significant numbers, shaping the social and cultural fabric of the city. The construction of St. Michael's Cathedral and other landmarks reflected the growing influence of the Irish Catholic community.

The late 19th and early 20th centuries saw further diversification of Toronto's population. Immigrants from Italy, Eastern Europe, China, and other regions arrived, each group establishing vibrant communities and contributing to the city's economic and cultural life. The Jewish community, in particular, played a significant role in the city's development, with Jewish immigrants establishing businesses, cultural institutions, and places of worship.

Toronto's growth was not without its challenges. The city grappled with issues such as poverty, labor unrest, and political corruption. The Great Fire of 1904, which destroyed a significant portion of downtown Toronto, highlighted the need for improved urban planning and infrastructure. In response, the city undertook significant rebuilding efforts, modernizing its streets, buildings, and services.

The early 20th century also saw the rise of social and political movements that would shape Toronto's future. The labor movement gained momentum, with workers organizing strikes and protests to demand better wages and working conditions. Women's suffrage and social reform movements also emerged, advocating for gender equality and social justice. These movements laid the groundwork for the progressive changes that would come in the latter half of the century.

The post-World War II era brought unprecedented growth and transformation to Toronto. The city experienced a population boom, driven by a new wave of immigration and economic prosperity. Immigrants from southern Europe, the Caribbean, South Asia, and East Asia arrived, further enriching the city's cultural diversity. The construction of modern high-rise buildings, highways, and suburban developments transformed Toronto's skyline and urban landscape.

The 1960s and 1970s were a period of significant social change and activism in Toronto. The city became a center of countercultural movements, with youth advocating for civil rights, environmentalism, and anti-war causes. The establishment of community organizations and cultural institutions reflected the growing influence of diverse ethnic and cultural groups. The rise of multiculturalism as a national policy in Canada further reinforced Toronto's identity as a multicultural metropolis.

The late 20th century saw Toronto emerge as a global city, with a dynamic economy and a vibrant cultural scene. The city became a major center for finance, technology, and education, attracting businesses and talent from around the world. The Toronto Stock Exchange became one of the largest in the world, and the city's universities and research institutions gained international recognition.

Culturally, Toronto flourished with a thriving arts and entertainment scene. The Toronto International Film Festival, founded in 1976, grew to become one of the most prestigious film festivals globally, attracting filmmakers, actors, and audiences from around the world. The city's theaters, galleries, and music venues showcased a diverse array of artistic expression, from classical performances to contemporary art and music.

Toronto's neighborhoods became microcosms of global cultures, with areas such as Chinatown, Little Italy, Greektown, and Little India offering unique cultural experiences. The city's culinary scene reflected its multicultural makeup, with restaurants and food markets offering a wide range of international cuisines. Festivals celebrating different cultures, such as Caribana, the Toronto Caribbean Carnival, and the Taste of the Danforth, became integral parts of the city's cultural calendar.

The turn of the 21st century brought new challenges and opportunities for Toronto. The city continued to grow, with ongoing immigration and urban development. Issues such as affordable housing, public transportation, and environmental sustainability became pressing concerns for policymakers and residents. The city's efforts to address these challenges included initiatives to promote green spaces, improve public transit, and support affordable housing projects.

Toronto's role as a global city was further solidified by its participation in international events and organizations. The city hosted major international conferences, sports events, and cultural exhibitions, showcasing its capabilities on the world stage. Toronto's reputation as a welcoming and inclusive city attracted tourists, students, and professionals from around the globe.

The COVID-19 pandemic, which began in 2019, posed unprecedented challenges for Toronto. The city faced public health crises, economic disruptions, and social inequalities exacerbated by the pandemic. However, Toronto's resilience and community spirit shone through as residents, businesses, and government agencies came together to support one another. The city's response to the pandemic highlighted the importance of healthcare, social services, and community solidarity in navigating crises.

Today, Toronto stands as a dynamic and diverse metropolis, reflecting the narratives of its past and the aspirations of its future. The city's skyline, with its iconic CN Tower, modern skyscrapers, and historic buildings, symbolizes its blend of tradition and innovation. Toronto's neighborhoods, parks, and cultural institutions continue to thrive, offering residents and visitors a rich tapestry of experiences.

The indigenous heritage of the region remains an integral part of Toronto's identity, with efforts to acknowledge and celebrate the contributions of indigenous peoples. Initiatives such as the creation of indigenous cultural centers, land acknowledgments, and the inclusion of indigenous perspectives in education and public discourse reflect a commitment to reconciliation and respect for indigenous cultures.

Toronto's cultural scene continues to evolve, with new generations of artists, writers, musicians, and performers pushing the boundaries of creativity and expression. The city's commitment to inclusivity and diversity is evident in its support for marginalized communities and its celebration of different cultural traditions. Toronto's vibrant LGBTQ+ community, for example, is celebrated through events such as Pride Toronto, one of the largest pride festivals in the world.

Economically, Toronto remains a powerhouse, with a robust and diversified economy. The city's financial district, technology sector, and innovation hubs continue to attract investment and talent. Toronto's role as a gateway to North America and its strategic location within the Great Lakes region position it as a key player in global trade and commerce.

Chapter 30: Brasília: A Modernist Dream

Brasília, the capital of Brazil, stands as one of the most remarkable urban planning and architectural achievements of the 20th century. Conceived as a symbol of Brazil's progress and modernization, Brasília was envisioned as a utopian city that would embody the ideals of modernism and provide a blueprint for future urban development. Its creation was a bold experiment in urban design and a testament to the ambition and vision of its creators. The story of Brasília is one of innovation, aspiration, and the quest to create a modernist dream in the heart of Brazil.

The idea of creating a new capital city for Brazil was not a novel one. As early as the 18th century, Brazilian leaders recognized the strategic importance of relocating the capital from the coastal city of Rio de Janeiro to a more central location. The goal was to promote the development of the interior regions of the country and reduce the concentration of political and economic power along the coast. However, it wasn't until the mid-20th century that this vision began to take shape.

In 1956, Juscelino Kubitschek, a visionary and dynamic leader, assumed the presidency of Brazil. Kubitschek was committed to modernizing the country and accelerating its economic and social development. One of his most ambitious initiatives was the construction of a new capital city in the central highlands of Brazil, a project that would come to be known as Brasília. Kubitschek believed that building Brasília would symbolize a new era of progress and unity for Brazil, and he made it a cornerstone of his administration's developmental agenda.

The task of designing the new city was entrusted to two of Brazil's most prominent modernists: the architect Oscar Niemeyer and the urban planner Lúcio Costa. Niemeyer, known for his innovative and expressive use of reinforced concrete, and Costa, with his expertise in urban planning, were ideal choices for the project. Together, they set out to create a city that would be both functional and aesthetically groundbreaking.

Lúcio Costa's master plan for Brasília, known as the Plano Piloto, was chosen from a national competition. Costa's design was inspired by the principles of modernist urbanism and the ideas of the Congrès Internationaux d'Architecture Moderne (CIAM), which emphasized functional zoning, the separation of pedestrian and vehicular traffic, and the creation of open, green spaces. Costa's plan took the form of an airplane or bird, with the "wings" representing residential and commercial areas and the "fuselage" serving as the administrative and governmental center.

The design of Brasília was revolutionary in its departure from traditional urban planning concepts. Costa's plan divided the city into distinct zones, each with a specific function. The Residential Axis, or Eixo Residencial, comprised superquadras (superblocks), each containing apartment buildings, schools, shops, and recreational facilities. These superquadras were designed to provide residents with all necessary amenities within walking distance, promoting a sense of community and reducing the need for long commutes.

The Monumental Axis, or Eixo Monumental, was the central spine of the city and housed the major governmental and administrative buildings. This grand boulevard was lined with iconic structures designed by Oscar Niemeyer, including the National Congress, the Presidential Palace (Palácio do Planalto), the Supreme Federal Court, and the Cathedral of Brasília. Niemeyer's architectural designs were characterized by their bold, sweeping forms, fluid lines, and innovative use of concrete, reflecting the spirit of modernism and the optimism of the era.

Construction of Brasília began in 1956 and proceeded at a rapid pace, driven by Kubitschek's determination to complete the project within his five-year term. The construction site, located in a remote and sparsely populated region, presented significant logistical challenges. Thousands of workers, known as candangos, were recruited from all over Brazil to work on the project. Despite the harsh conditions and the monumental scale of the undertaking, the construction of Brasília progressed swiftly.

On April 21, 1960, Brasília was officially inaugurated as the capital of Brazil. The city's inauguration was a moment of national pride and a testament to Brazil's capacity for innovation and achievement. Brasília's completion marked the culmination of an extraordinary effort to create a new city from scratch, a city that would symbolize Brazil's aspirations for the future.

Brasília's design and architecture were met with international acclaim and admiration. The city's modernist aesthetic, with its sleek lines, open spaces, and striking buildings, represented a bold departure from traditional urban forms. Niemeyer's buildings, in particular, were celebrated for their artistic and sculptural qualities, blending form and function in ways that were both innovative and visually stunning.

However, the realization of Brasília as a modernist dream was not without its challenges and criticisms. While the city was designed to be a model of efficiency and functionality, some aspects of its planning and execution faced scrutiny. One of the primary criticisms was the city's lack of human scale and its emphasis on monumental spaces. The vast open areas and wide boulevards, while impressive, often felt impersonal and disconnected from the daily lives of residents. The separation of residential, commercial, and administrative zones also led to a sense of isolation and compartmentalization.

Another significant issue was the social and economic disparity that emerged in Brasília. The original vision of the city included housing for all social classes, but in practice, the affluent and influential occupied the prime residential areas, while the working-class population was relegated to satellite cities and peripheral regions. This segregation exacerbated social inequalities and created challenges in terms of access to services and opportunities.

Despite these challenges, Brasília continued to evolve and develop over the decades. The city's status as the political and administrative center of Brazil attracted government officials, diplomats, and professionals, contributing to its growth and diversification. The influx of people and the expansion of infrastructure and services gradually helped address some of the initial shortcomings of the city's design.

Brasília's cultural and artistic scene also flourished, reflecting the city's unique identity and heritage. The city became a hub for modernist art, architecture, and design, with institutions such as the Brasília National Museum and the Cultural Complex of the Republic showcasing contemporary Brazilian art and culture. The city's music scene, particularly the genre of Brazilian popular music known as MPB (Música Popular Brasileira), thrived, with Brasília serving as a creative incubator for musicians and artists.

In 1987, Brasília was designated a UNESCO World Heritage Site, recognizing its exceptional value as a modernist urban and architectural masterpiece. The designation acknowledged the city's significance as a pioneering example of 20th-century urban planning and design, as well as its cultural and historical importance. Brasília's inclusion on the World Heritage list further cemented its status as a symbol of Brazil's modernist legacy and its contributions to global architectural and urbanistic discourse.

In recent years, Brasília has continued to grow and adapt to the changing needs and aspirations of its residents. The city has seen efforts to address urban challenges such as traffic congestion, environmental sustainability, and social inclusion. Projects to enhance public transportation, create green spaces, and promote affordable housing have been implemented to improve the quality of life in the city and make it more accessible and equitable.

Brasília's modernist dream remains a source of inspiration and reflection for urban planners, architects, and scholars worldwide. The city's ambitious vision, innovative design, and bold execution offer valuable lessons in the possibilities and limitations of modernist urbanism. While Brasília's creation was a monumental achievement, it also serves as a reminder of the complexities and challenges inherent in designing and building cities that seek to embody idealistic visions of progress and modernity.

Chapter 31: Helsinki: Baltic Tales

Helsinki, the capital of Finland, stands at the crossroads of Scandinavian, Russian, and Baltic influences, boasting a rich and layered history that often goes unnoticed in the shadow of its more famous neighbors like Stockholm and St. Petersburg. The city, established in 1550 by King Gustav I of Sweden, was initially intended to be a trading rival to the Hanseatic city of Reval (now Tallinn, Estonia). However, it struggled to grow due to the superior trading infrastructure of its competitors and the swampy, malaria-ridden terrain on which it was built.

The initial growth of Helsinki was sluggish, and for many years, it remained a small, relatively insignificant settlement. It wasn't until the 18th century, with the construction of the formidable Sveaborg (Suomenlinna) fortress by the Swedes, that Helsinki began to gain strategic importance. Sveaborg was a massive naval base and defense structure designed to protect against Russian expansionism. It played a crucial role during the Russo-Swedish wars, symbolizing a bastion of Swedish power in the region. Despite its intended purpose, Sveaborg fell to Russian forces in 1808, marking a significant turning point in Helsinki's history.

In 1809, Finland was ceded to Russia as a Grand Duchy, and in 1812, the Russian Tsar Alexander I moved the Finnish capital from Turku to Helsinki. This move was partly strategic, aimed at reducing Swedish influence and establishing a closer connection between Finland and Russia. The shift marked the beginning of Helsinki's transformation into a major city. Under Russian rule, Helsinki experienced rapid modernization. The city's layout was re-designed by the German-born architect Carl Ludvig Engel, who created a neoclassical city center, with broad streets and grand buildings, including the iconic Helsinki Cathedral, Senate Square, and the University of Helsinki. This new architectural style gave Helsinki a distinctly European appearance, setting it apart from other cities in the Nordic region.

Helsinki's development continued throughout the 19th century, fueled by industrialization and an influx of people from rural areas seeking work in the city. The growth of the railway network further connected Helsinki with the rest of Finland and other parts of Europe, promoting trade and commerce. By the turn of the 20th century, Helsinki had become the cultural and economic heart of Finland. This period also saw a burgeoning sense of Finnish national identity, with Helsinki playing a central role in the country's push for independence from Russia.

The early 20th century was a turbulent time for Helsinki. In 1917, Finland declared independence from Russia, a move that was followed by a brutal civil war in 1918. Helsinki was a significant battleground during the conflict, with the city witnessing intense fighting between the Red Guards (aligned with the Russian Bolsheviks) and the White Guards (supported by the German Empire). The Whites eventually emerged victorious, and Helsinki became the capital of an independent Finland. The interwar period saw Helsinki continue to grow, with significant investment in infrastructure and public services.

World War II brought further challenges to Helsinki. The city was bombed by Soviet forces during the Winter War (1939-1940) and the Continuation War (1941-1944), but it managed to escape the widespread destruction that many other European cities faced. After the war, Helsinki experienced a period of rapid reconstruction and expansion. The 1952 Summer Olympics, hosted by Helsinki, marked Finland's post-war re-entry onto the world stage and spurred significant development in the city.

The latter half of the 20th century saw Helsinki evolve into a modern, cosmopolitan city. The city's architecture reflects this transition, blending historical buildings with cutting-edge modern designs. Notable examples include Alvar Aalto's Finlandia Hall and the contemporary Kiasma Museum of Contemporary Art. Helsinki's cultural scene flourished, with the city becoming known for its vibrant arts, music, and design sectors. The Design District in Helsinki is a testament to the city's commitment to creativity and innovation, showcasing a mix of traditional Finnish craftsmanship and modern design.

Helsinki's location on the Baltic Sea has always been a defining feature of the city, influencing its economy, culture, and identity. The city's harbors have been key to its economic development, serving as vital links to the rest of the world. Over the centuries, Helsinki has been a melting pot of different cultures and influences, from Swedish and Russian to more recent waves of immigrants from around the globe. This diversity is reflected in the city's architecture, cuisine, and cultural life, making Helsinki a dynamic and multicultural city.

One of the lesser-known aspects of Helsinki's history is its relationship with the sea. The city's archipelago, comprising over 300 islands, has played a crucial role in its development. These islands have been used for various purposes over the centuries, from military fortifications to leisure and recreation. Today, they are popular destinations for both locals and tourists, offering a unique glimpse into Helsinki's maritime heritage.

Helsinki's hidden histories are not limited to its political and architectural developments. The city has also been a center of scientific and technological innovation. The University of Helsinki, established in 1640, is one of the oldest and most prestigious institutions in Finland, contributing significantly to the country's intellectual and cultural life. The city has also been at the forefront of medical research and technology, with institutions like the Helsinki University Hospital leading advancements in healthcare.

In recent years, Helsinki has emerged as a leader in sustainable urban development and technology. The city's commitment to environmental sustainability is evident in its ambitious goals to reduce carbon emissions and promote green energy. Helsinki has been recognized internationally for its efforts to create a livable, sustainable city that balances economic growth with environmental responsibility.

Helsinki's history is a tapestry of diverse influences, from its Swedish and Russian past to its emergence as a modern, independent capital. The city's hidden histories, from its strategic military significance to its role as a center of innovation and culture, offer a fascinating glimpse into the complexities of its development. Today, Helsinki stands as a testament to the resilience and creativity of its people, a city that has continually reinvented itself while preserving its unique character and heritage.

Chapter 32: Kuala Lumpur: Colonial Echoes

Kuala Lumpur, the vibrant capital of Malaysia, is a city that encapsulates a fascinating blend of cultural, historical, and architectural influences. Its hidden histories, especially those pertaining to its colonial past, offer a rich tapestry of narratives that reflect the complexities and transformations experienced by the city over the centuries. The roots of Kuala Lumpur, often abbreviated as KL, can be traced back to the mid-19th century, when it was founded as a tin mining settlement. However, its rise from a swampy, malaria-ridden jungle outpost to a bustling metropolis is deeply intertwined with the broader colonial dynamics of the region.

The story of Kuala Lumpur began in earnest in 1857, when Chinese tin prospectors, led by Raja Abdullah, ventured into the area at the confluence of the Klang and Gombak rivers. The name "Kuala Lumpur" itself, meaning "muddy confluence" in Malay, is a testament to the geographical features of its origins. The Chinese miners, primarily from the Hakka and Cantonese communities, played a pivotal role in establishing the early economy of the region, which was centered around the extraction of tin. This commodity was in high demand globally, fueling the early growth of the settlement. However, the burgeoning mining activities also attracted conflicts and power struggles among the local chieftains and miners, leading to frequent outbreaks of violence and instability.

The strategic importance of Kuala Lumpur grew during the late 19th century, particularly under British colonial rule. In 1874, the British established their control over the Malay Peninsula through the Pangkor Treaty, which marked the beginning of their significant political and economic influence in the region. The British saw the potential of Kuala Lumpur as a commercial and administrative hub, given its strategic location and burgeoning economy driven by the tin trade. Sir Frank Swettenham, the first Resident-General of the Federated Malay States, played a crucial role in the development of Kuala Lumpur, transforming it into a well-organized administrative center. He was instrumental in the establishment of the city's infrastructure, including roads, government buildings, and public services, which laid the foundation for its future growth.

One of the defining features of Kuala Lumpur's colonial period was the influx of diverse ethnic communities, particularly the Chinese and Indians, who were brought in by the British to work in the tin mines and rubber plantations. This migration significantly altered the demographic composition of the city, creating a multicultural society that remains a hallmark of Kuala Lumpur today. The Chinese community, in particular, established themselves in the trading and business sectors, while the Indian community, many of whom were brought in as laborers, contributed to the development of the city's infrastructure and economy. The interaction and coexistence of these different ethnic groups have profoundly influenced the cultural and social fabric of Kuala Lumpur, making it a melting pot of cultures and traditions.

The architectural landscape of Kuala Lumpur during the colonial era also reflects its diverse influences and the British vision of urban development. The city's architecture from this period is a fascinating blend of British, Moorish, and local styles, creating a unique aesthetic that still defines parts of the city today. Notable examples include the Sultan Abdul Samad Building, an iconic structure that combines Gothic, Moorish, and Western design elements, and the Kuala Lumpur Railway Station, which showcases the Indo-Saracenic style. These buildings were not only functional but also symbolic of the British colonial power and its aspirations for the region. The construction of such grand structures in Kuala Lumpur was part of the broader British colonial policy of creating administrative and commercial hubs that reflected their control and vision for development.

Kuala Lumpur's colonial history is also marked by significant socio-political changes and resistance. The early 20th century saw the rise of nationalist movements in Malaya, driven by growing discontent with British colonial rule and the desire for self-determination. The Japanese occupation during World War II (1942-1945) further intensified nationalist sentiments, as the brutal occupation exposed the vulnerabilities and limitations of British colonial authority. The Japanese occupation had a profound impact on Kuala Lumpur, as it disrupted the city's economy and brought about significant hardship and suffering for its residents. The end of the war and the subsequent return of British control did little to quell the rising tide of nationalism.

The post-war period was a time of significant political upheaval and transformation for Kuala Lumpur. The Malayan Emergency (1948-1960), a guerrilla war fought between Commonwealth armed forces and the Malayan National Liberation Army (MNLA), significantly affected Kuala Lumpur and the surrounding regions. The conflict, rooted in the struggle for independence and the fight against communist insurgents, led to widespread violence and insecurity. Kuala Lumpur became a focal point of military and political activity during this period, with the British implementing measures such as curfews and resettlement programs to combat the insurgents. The emergency period left an indelible mark on the city, shaping its political landscape and accelerating the push for independence.

Kuala Lumpur's journey towards independence was marked by significant milestones, including the establishment of the Federation of Malaya in 1948 and the eventual declaration of independence on August 31, 1957. The proclamation of independence, which took place at the newly constructed Merdeka Stadium in Kuala Lumpur, was a momentous event that marked the end of British colonial rule and the beginning of a new era for the city and the country. Kuala Lumpur's role as the capital of the newly independent nation cemented its status as the political and economic center of Malaysia.

The post-independence era brought about rapid urbanization and modernization for Kuala Lumpur. The city experienced significant economic growth, driven by industrialization and the expansion of the service sector. The construction of new infrastructure, including highways, bridges, and skyscrapers, transformed the city's skyline and laid the foundation for its future development. The Petronas Twin Towers, completed in 1998, symbolize Kuala Lumpur's emergence as a global city and its aspirations for economic and technological advancement. The city's transformation from a colonial outpost to a modern metropolis is a testament to its resilience and adaptability.

Despite the rapid modernization, Kuala Lumpur's colonial echoes remain an integral part of its identity. The city's historical buildings and neighborhoods, such as the colonial-era shop houses in Chinatown and the British-style bungalows in the suburbs, serve as reminders of its colonial past and the diverse influences that have shaped its development. The preservation of these historical sites and the recognition of their cultural significance reflect the city's commitment to honoring its heritage while embracing the future.

Kuala Lumpur's colonial history is not just a story of economic and architectural development but also a narrative of cultural exchange and transformation. The city's unique blend of Malay, Chinese, Indian, and Western influences has created a rich cultural mosaic that is reflected in its cuisine, festivals, and everyday life. This cultural diversity, rooted in the city's colonial past, continues to define Kuala Lumpur and contribute to its vibrant and dynamic character.

Today, Kuala Lumpur stands as a testament to the complexities and contradictions of its colonial past. It is a city that has emerged from the shadows of colonialism to become a symbol of Malaysia's growth and development. The hidden histories of Kuala Lumpur, with their tales of migration, conflict, and transformation, offer a fascinating glimpse into the city's journey from a humble mining settlement to a modern, cosmopolitan capital. These stories, often overshadowed by the city's rapid modernization, are an integral part of Kuala Lumpur's identity and provide a deeper understanding of the forces that have shaped its past and continue to influence its present and future.

Chapter 33: Vienna: Imperial Reflections

Vienna, the grand capital of Austria, is a city steeped in history and culture, a place where the past resonates through its imperial architecture, art, and music. The city is often associated with grandeur and opulence, reflecting its central role in the Habsburg Empire. The hidden histories of Vienna, filled with tales of imperial power, cultural flourishing, and political intrigue, offer a rich tapestry of narratives that illuminate the city's evolution from a Roman outpost to the heart of a vast European empire.

The roots of Vienna stretch back to Roman times when it was known as Vindobona, a military outpost established around the first century AD. This strategic location on the banks of the Danube River was crucial for controlling trade routes and repelling invasions from Germanic tribes. The remnants of this period, including Roman walls and artifacts, are still visible in the city today, providing a glimpse into its ancient past. However, it was during the Middle Ages that Vienna began to emerge as a significant center of power and culture.

The rise of Vienna as an imperial city began in earnest with the ascendancy of the Habsburgs in the late Middle Ages. The Habsburgs, originally from Switzerland, became one of the most powerful dynasties in Europe through a combination of strategic marriages, political alliances, and military conquests. In 1278, Rudolf I of Habsburg defeated Ottokar II of Bohemia, securing the Austrian territories for his family. This victory laid the foundation for Vienna's development as the capital of the Habsburg Empire. The Habsburgs chose Vienna as their seat of power due to its strategic location at the crossroads of Central Europe, which made it an ideal center for administration, trade, and diplomacy.

Under Habsburg rule, Vienna experienced a period of significant growth and transformation. The city became the administrative and cultural heart of the empire, attracting artists, scholars, and merchants from across Europe. The medieval city, with its narrow streets and Gothic architecture, began to expand beyond its original boundaries. The construction of the Hofburg Palace, the Habsburgs' principal residence, symbolized Vienna's emerging status as an imperial capital. The palace complex, which grew over the centuries to include numerous buildings and courtyards, became the center of political power and a focal point of imperial grandeur.

The Renaissance and Baroque periods were particularly significant in shaping Vienna's cultural and architectural heritage. The 16th and 17th centuries saw the city transform into a hub of artistic and intellectual activity, driven by the patronage of the Habsburg court. The construction of magnificent Baroque buildings, such as St. Charles's Church (Karlskirche) and the Belvedere Palace, reflected the wealth and power of the Habsburgs and their desire to create a city that rivaled the great capitals of Europe. These buildings, with their intricate facades and lavish interiors, remain iconic symbols of Vienna's imperial past and its commitment to the arts and culture.

Vienna's role as a cultural capital was further enhanced by the flourishing of music and art during the 18th and 19th centuries. The city became synonymous with classical music, producing some of the most renowned composers in history, including Wolfgang Amadeus Mozart, Ludwig van Beethoven, and Franz Schubert. These composers found patronage and inspiration in Vienna, which became a center of musical innovation and performance. The city's grand concert halls, such as the Musikverein and the Vienna State Opera, continue to be celebrated venues for classical music, attracting performers and audiences from around the world.

The 19th century was a period of significant change for Vienna, as the city underwent rapid industrialization and modernization. The Habsburg Empire, under the rule of Emperor Franz Joseph I, embarked on a series of ambitious projects to transform Vienna into a modern metropolis. The construction of the Ringstrasse, a grand boulevard encircling the old city, symbolized this transformation. The Ringstrasse was lined with monumental buildings, including the Vienna State Opera, the Parliament, the University of Vienna, and the Kunsthistorisches Museum, each reflecting the architectural styles and cultural aspirations of the time. These buildings not only served as centers of political, cultural, and academic life but also showcased the wealth and power of the empire.

The late 19th and early 20th centuries were also marked by significant political and social changes in Vienna. The city became a center of intellectual and cultural activity, attracting thinkers and artists who would leave a lasting impact on European culture. Figures such as Sigmund Freud, Gustav Klimt, and Egon Schiele were part of Vienna's vibrant cultural scene, contributing to the city's reputation as a hub of innovation and creativity. The Vienna Secession, an art movement founded by artists who sought to break away from traditional styles, reflected the dynamic and evolving nature of the city's cultural life.

However, Vienna's imperial grandeur and cultural flourishing were overshadowed by the political upheavals of the early 20th century. The assassination of Archduke Franz Ferdinand in 1914, an event that triggered World War I, marked the beginning of the end for the Habsburg Empire. The war brought significant hardship and suffering to Vienna, as the city faced food shortages, political unrest, and economic decline. The collapse of the Habsburg Empire in 1918 and the subsequent establishment of the Republic of Austria marked a profound transformation for Vienna, as the city transitioned from being the capital of a vast empire to a smaller, independent nation.

The interwar period was a time of significant political and social change for Vienna. The city faced economic challenges and political instability, as it grappled with the legacy of the war and the collapse of the empire. The rise of fascism in Europe and the annexation of Austria by Nazi Germany in 1938 brought further turmoil to Vienna. The city became a focal point of Nazi ideology and policies, leading to the persecution and deportation of its Jewish population and other minorities. The impact of World War II on Vienna was devastating, as the city suffered significant damage from bombings and the brutal fighting that took place during the final days of the war.

The post-war period marked a time of reconstruction and renewal for Vienna. The city, divided into four occupation zones by the Allied powers, faced the daunting task of rebuilding its infrastructure and economy. Despite these challenges, Vienna emerged as a center of diplomacy and international cooperation, hosting organizations such as the United Nations and the International Atomic Energy Agency. The city's commitment to neutrality and its role as a bridge between East and West during the Cold War further enhanced its status as a center of international relations.

Today, Vienna stands as a testament to its imperial past and its resilience in the face of adversity. The city's rich architectural heritage, including the Hofburg Palace, Schönbrunn Palace, and the numerous Baroque and Gothic churches, serves as a reminder of its grand imperial history. The preservation and restoration of these historical sites reflect Vienna's commitment to honoring its past while embracing the future.

Vienna's cultural legacy, rooted in its imperial history, continues to thrive in its vibrant arts and music scene. The city's museums, galleries, and concert halls attract visitors from around the world, offering a glimpse into its rich cultural heritage and its ongoing contributions to the arts. The Vienna Philharmonic Orchestra and the Vienna State Opera remain world-renowned institutions, continuing the city's tradition of excellence in classical music.

The hidden histories of Vienna, from its Roman origins to its role as the heart of the Habsburg Empire, offer a fascinating narrative of a city that has continually evolved and adapted to the changing tides of history. Vienna's imperial reflections are not just about grand buildings and cultural achievements but also about the resilience and creativity of its people. The city, with its rich history and dynamic present, continues to inspire and captivate those who visit and those who call it home.

Chapter 34: Jakarta: Archipelago Adventures

Jakarta, the sprawling and dynamic capital of Indonesia, embodies a unique blend of history, culture, and modernity, serving as a microcosm of the country's rich and diverse heritage. As the heart of the largest archipelago in the world, Jakarta's history is intertwined with the ebb and flow of maritime trade, colonial encounters, and cultural exchanges. The city's evolution from a small port town into a bustling metropolis reflects the broader historical and cultural narratives of Indonesia, offering a fascinating lens through which to explore the archipelago's adventures.

The story of Jakarta begins long before it became the capital of Indonesia. Archaeological evidence suggests that the area around Jakarta, then known as Sunda Kelapa, was inhabited as early as the 5th century AD by the Sundanese people. The port of Sunda Kelapa, strategically located at the mouth of the Ciliwung River on the northwest coast of Java, became an important hub for trade and commerce in the region. It was part of the Tarumanagara Kingdom, one of the earliest Hindu-Buddhist polities in the Indonesian archipelago. The kingdom's inscriptions, dating from the 5th century, indicate a sophisticated society with connections to the Indian subcontinent, highlighting the early influence of Hindu and Buddhist cultures in the region.

Sunda Kelapa's strategic location made it a coveted prize for various regional powers. By the 14th century, it had become a significant trading port for the Hindu Kingdom of Pajajaran, which controlled much of West Java. The port's importance grew due to its role in the regional spice trade, with merchants from China, India, and the Middle East frequenting its shores. The arrival of Islam in the Indonesian archipelago in the 13th century brought significant cultural and religious changes, with Sunda Kelapa becoming a focal point for the spread of Islam in Java. The port's conversion to Islam was solidified when it fell under the control of the Sultanate of Demak in 1527, leading to the renaming of the city to Jayakarta, meaning "victorious deed" or "complete victory."

The transformation of Jayakarta into a significant urban center took a dramatic turn with the arrival of European powers in the 16th century. The Portuguese were among the first Europeans to establish a presence in the region, seeking to control the lucrative spice trade. However, it was the Dutch who would leave a lasting impact on Jakarta's history. In 1619, the Dutch East India Company (VOC), led by Jan Pieterszoon Coen, captured and razed Jayakarta, establishing a new settlement named Batavia on its ruins. The establishment of Batavia marked the beginning of over three centuries of Dutch colonial rule in the region, profoundly shaping the city's development and its role in the global trade network.

Under Dutch rule, Batavia became the administrative and economic center of the Dutch East Indies, serving as the hub for the VOC's vast trading empire. The city was designed according to European urban planning principles, with a grid layout and fortified walls. The Dutch built canals, which earned Batavia the nickname "The Queen of the East" or "The Venice of Asia." These canals, initially intended to facilitate trade and transportation, soon became a symbol of Batavia's colonial splendor and its integration into the global maritime economy. The city's architecture reflected its colonial heritage, with grand buildings such as the Stadhuis (city hall) and the Dutch East India Company's headquarters showcasing Dutch architectural styles and serving as reminders of the colonial authorities' power.

Batavia's role as a center of trade and administration attracted a diverse population, including Dutch settlers, Chinese merchants, Indian laborers, and indigenous Javanese. This multicultural population contributed to a vibrant and dynamic society, where different cultures, religions, and traditions coexisted and influenced each other. The Chinese community, in particular, played a crucial role in Batavia's economic life, dominating the trade and retail sectors. The city's Chinatown, known as Glodok, became a bustling commercial district, reflecting the significant contributions of the Chinese diaspora to the city's development.

The Dutch colonial period in Batavia was marked by significant economic growth and development, but it was also a time of exploitation and oppression. The colonial authorities imposed harsh labor conditions on the indigenous population, using forced labor to build infrastructure and extract resources. The social and economic inequalities between the European colonizers and the indigenous population led to frequent tensions and uprisings. One of the most notable uprisings was the Chinese massacre of 1740, when thousands of Chinese residents were killed by Dutch forces in response to a rebellion against the oppressive colonial policies. This event left a lasting scar on the city's history and underscored the brutal realities of colonial rule.

The late 19th and early 20th centuries brought significant changes to Batavia and the wider Dutch East Indies. The Industrial Revolution and the expansion of the global economy led to increased economic activity and urbanization in Batavia. The city saw the construction of new infrastructure, including roads, railways, and ports, to support its growing role as a commercial hub. The development of new industries, such as oil and rubber, further boosted the city's economy and attracted a new wave of immigrants and settlers. Batavia's population grew rapidly, and the city expanded beyond its colonial core to accommodate new residential and commercial districts.

The early 20th century was also a time of growing nationalist sentiment in Indonesia, driven by the desire for independence and the rejection of colonial rule. Batavia became a center of political and intellectual activity, with the establishment of nationalist organizations and the rise of prominent figures such as Sukarno and Hatta, who would later play key roles in the struggle for independence. The city was a hotbed of political activism, with newspapers, educational institutions, and social organizations fostering a sense of national identity and unity among Indonesians. The Japanese occupation during World War II (1942-1945) further fueled nationalist sentiments, as the brutal occupation exposed the weaknesses of colonial powers and galvanized the Indonesian independence movement.

The end of World War II marked a turning point in Batavia's history, as the city became a focal point in the struggle for Indonesian independence. In 1945, following the Japanese surrender, Sukarno and Hatta declared Indonesia's independence in Jakarta, as the city was renamed. The declaration of independence set off a four-year struggle against Dutch attempts to re-establish colonial control. Jakarta was at the center of this conflict, witnessing significant political and military activity as Indonesian nationalists fought to secure their country's sovereignty. The struggle culminated in 1949 with the Dutch recognition of Indonesian independence, marking the end of colonial rule and the beginning of a new era for Jakarta and Indonesia.

The post-independence period brought significant challenges and opportunities for Jakarta as the capital of the newly independent Indonesia. The city faced the daunting task of rebuilding its infrastructure and economy after years of war and colonial exploitation. Jakarta's role as the political and administrative center of Indonesia required significant investments in infrastructure and public services to support its growing population and its role as the seat of government. The city's rapid urbanization and industrialization attracted migrants from across the archipelago, leading to significant demographic changes and the expansion of the city's boundaries.

Jakarta's transformation into a modern metropolis has been marked by both successes and challenges. The city's economic growth has driven significant development, with the construction of skyscrapers, shopping malls, and modern residential areas transforming its skyline. Jakarta has become a major economic hub in Southeast Asia, attracting investment and businesses from around the world. The city's diverse population and cultural heritage are reflected in its vibrant arts and cultural scene, with numerous festivals, museums, and cultural institutions celebrating Indonesia's rich traditions and history.

However, Jakarta's rapid development has also brought significant challenges, including environmental degradation, traffic congestion, and social inequalities. The city's infrastructure has struggled to keep pace with its growth, leading to issues such as flooding, pollution, and inadequate public services. The challenges of urbanization have also highlighted the social and economic disparities within the city, with many residents living in informal settlements and lacking access to basic services. The city's leaders have faced the difficult task of balancing economic development with the need to address these social and environmental challenges, seeking to create a more sustainable and inclusive future for Jakarta.

Jakarta's history is a reflection of the broader narratives of the Indonesian archipelago, a story of cultural diversity, political struggles, and economic transformation. The city's evolution from a small port town to a bustling metropolis mirrors the broader historical and cultural currents that have shaped Indonesia's development. Jakarta's hidden histories, from its early days as a trading hub to its role in the struggle for independence and its transformation into a modern capital, offer a fascinating lens through which to explore the complexities and dynamics of Indonesia's past and present.

Today, Jakarta stands as a testament to the resilience and dynamism of the Indonesian people, a city that embodies the spirit of the archipelago and its rich and diverse heritage. The city's vibrant culture, dynamic economy, and complex history make it a unique and fascinating place, reflecting the broader narratives of the Indonesian archipelago and offering a window into the adventures and challenges that have shaped its development. As Jakarta continues to grow and evolve, it remains a symbol of Indonesia's past, present, and future, a city that encapsulates the spirit and diversity of the world's largest archipelago.

Chapter 35: Oslo: Nordic Sagas

Oslo, the capital of Norway, is a city that embodies a rich tapestry of history, culture, and tradition, rooted deeply in the Nordic sagas and the storied past of Scandinavia. From its Viking heritage to its role as a center of modern governance and culture, Oslo offers a captivating narrative that spans over a millennium. The city's evolution is closely intertwined with the broader historical developments of Norway and the Nordic region, reflecting a unique blend of ancient traditions, maritime prowess, and contemporary vibrancy.

The history of Oslo can be traced back to the Viking Age, a period that began around the late 8th century and lasted until the early 11th century. This era is often romanticized for its adventurous seafaring and exploration, but it also laid the foundations for the cultural and political development of Norway. The Vikings, known for their impressive naval capabilities and expeditions across Europe and beyond, established Oslo as a vital center for trade and settlement. The area that would become Oslo was strategically located at the head of the Oslofjord, providing access to the North Sea and making it an ideal hub for maritime activities.

The earliest recorded mention of Oslo dates to around 1040 AD, when it was founded by King Harald Hardrada, a formidable figure in Norwegian history. Harald, who had a storied career as a mercenary and later as a king, saw the potential of Oslo's location and established it as a royal residence and a center for trade and commerce. The city quickly grew in importance, serving as a focal point for the kingdom's political and economic activities. The proximity to the sea facilitated trade with other regions, including England, the Baltic states, and the rest of Scandinavia, further enhancing Oslo's significance in the Viking world.

The transition from the Viking Age to the Middle Ages marked a significant transformation for Oslo and Norway as a whole. The introduction of Christianity in the 11th century brought about profound changes in society, culture, and governance. The conversion to Christianity was largely driven by political leaders, such as King Olaf II (St. Olaf), who sought to consolidate their power and integrate Norway more closely with the rest of Europe. The establishment of churches and the spread of Christian institutions helped to unify the kingdom and provided a new cultural and religious framework that would shape the future of Oslo.

During the medieval period, Oslo continued to develop as a key administrative and economic center. The construction of the Akershus Fortress in the late 13th century by King Haakon V was a significant milestone in the city's history. The fortress, strategically located on a promontory overlooking the Oslofjord, served as a defensive stronghold and a royal residence. It became a symbol of the kingdom's power and a focal point for political and military activities. The medieval city of Oslo, with its cobblestone streets and timber buildings, was a bustling center of trade, culture, and governance, reflecting the growing importance of the city within the kingdom.

The 14th century was a period of significant turmoil for Oslo and Norway, marked by the devastating impact of the Black Death and political instability. The plague, which swept through Europe in the mid-14th century, had a catastrophic effect on Norway, leading to a significant decline in the population and a collapse of the economy. The political landscape was further complicated by the union of Norway, Sweden, and Denmark under the Kalmar Union in 1397. This union, intended to consolidate the Scandinavian kingdoms under a single monarch, resulted in a complex and often contentious relationship between the member states. For Oslo, the union meant a loss of political autonomy and a decline in its status as a royal capital, as the center of power shifted to Copenhagen.

Despite these challenges, Oslo remained an important regional center, maintaining its role as a hub for trade and commerce. The city's strategic location and its access to maritime routes continued to make it a vital link in the Nordic trade network. The 16th and 17th centuries saw a gradual recovery and resurgence for Oslo, as the city rebuilt its economy and infrastructure. The timber trade, in particular, played a crucial role in revitalizing the city's economy, with timber from Norway's vast forests being exported to other parts of Europe. This period also saw the construction of new buildings and the expansion of the city's infrastructure, reflecting a renewed sense of growth and development.

The 17th century brought about significant changes for Oslo with the ascension of Christian IV of Denmark-Norway to the throne. In 1624, a devastating fire ravaged Oslo, destroying much of the medieval city. King Christian IV seized the opportunity to rebuild the city according to modern urban planning principles. He relocated the city closer to the Akershus Fortress and renamed it Christiania (later spelled Kristiania), in his honor. The new city was designed with a grid layout, wide streets, and more durable stone buildings, marking a significant departure from the medieval city's narrow, timber-framed structures. This reconstruction laid the foundation for the modern city of Oslo and set the stage for its future growth and development.

The 18th and 19th centuries were a time of significant change and modernization for Christiania. The city continued to grow as a center of trade and industry, benefiting from Norway's abundant natural resources, including timber, fish, and minerals. The rise of the industrial revolution in the 19th century brought about rapid urbanization and economic expansion, with new factories, railways, and infrastructure transforming the cityscape. Christiania became a vibrant center of commerce and industry, attracting migrants from rural areas and contributing to the city's growing population and diversity.

The 19th century also saw a resurgence of Norwegian nationalism and a growing movement for independence from Denmark. The cultural and intellectual life of Christiania played a crucial role in this movement, with figures such as Henrik Ibsen and Edvard Grieg contributing to a renewed sense of national identity and pride. The city's theaters, universities, and cultural institutions became centers of intellectual and artistic activity, fostering a sense of cultural renaissance that laid the groundwork for Norway's eventual independence.

The dissolution of the union with Denmark in 1814 and the subsequent union with Sweden marked a new chapter in Christiania's history. Although Norway remained in a union with Sweden, it gained significant autonomy and established its own constitution and parliament. Christiania, as the capital of Norway, became the center of political life, with the construction of new government buildings and institutions reflecting the city's growing importance as a center of governance and administration. The independence movement continued to gain momentum, culminating in the peaceful dissolution of the union with Sweden in 1905 and the establishment of Norway as an independent kingdom.

The early 20th century was a period of significant growth and modernization for Christiania, which was officially renamed Oslo in 1925, reverting to its original name. The city continued to expand, with new neighborhoods, parks, and public buildings reflecting the aspirations of a modern, independent Norway. The interwar period saw significant investments in infrastructure and public services, including the construction of the Oslo City Hall, a symbol of the city's democratic governance and civic pride.

The impact of World War II on Oslo was profound, as the city was occupied by Nazi Germany from 1940 to 1945. The occupation brought significant hardship and suffering to the people of Oslo, with restrictions on freedoms, economic challenges, and the persecution of Jewish residents and other minorities. The resistance movement in Norway, including in Oslo, played a crucial role in opposing the occupation and supporting the Allied efforts. The liberation of Norway in 1945 marked a new beginning for Oslo, as the city and the country embarked on the process of rebuilding and recovery.

The post-war period was a time of significant transformation for Oslo, as the city embraced a new era of growth and modernization. The discovery of oil in the North Sea in the 1960s brought significant economic benefits to Norway, transforming the country into one of the wealthiest in the world. Oslo, as the capital, benefited from this economic boom, with investments in infrastructure, education, and public services contributing to the city's development. The construction of new buildings, including modernist architecture and cultural institutions, reflected Oslo's aspirations as a center of innovation and culture.

Today, Oslo is a vibrant and dynamic city that reflects the rich tapestry of its history and the diverse influences that have shaped its development. The city's architecture, from the medieval Akershus Fortress to the modernist Opera House, showcases a blend of tradition and modernity that defines Oslo's unique character. The city's museums, including the Viking Ship Museum and the National Gallery, offer a window into its rich cultural heritage, while its theaters, concert halls, and festivals celebrate its vibrant arts scene.

Oslo's role as a center of governance and diplomacy is also significant, with institutions such as the Nobel Peace Center highlighting its commitment to peace and international cooperation. The city's commitment to sustainability and green initiatives reflects its role as a leader in environmental stewardship and urban innovation, with projects such as the Fjord City development transforming Oslo's waterfront into a model of sustainable urban living.

The hidden histories of Oslo, from its Viking origins to its modern role as a global city, offer a fascinating narrative of a city that has continually evolved and adapted to the changing tides of history. The city's rich cultural heritage, dynamic economy, and vibrant arts scene make it a unique and captivating place, reflecting the broader narratives of Norway and the Nordic region. As Oslo continues to grow and develop, it remains a testament to the resilience and creativity of its people, a city that embodies the spirit of the Nordic sagas and the rich traditions of Scandinavia.

Chapter 36: Caracas: Bolivarian Beginnings

Caracas, the capital city of Venezuela, stands as a testament to a rich and turbulent history deeply intertwined with the legacy of Simón Bolívar and the broader narrative of South America's struggle for independence from Spanish colonial rule. Nestled in the coastal mountain range of northern Venezuela, Caracas has evolved from a modest colonial settlement into a bustling metropolis, serving as a focal point for political, economic, and cultural developments in the region. The city's story, particularly its role in the birth of the Bolivarian revolution, offers a compelling exploration of the complexities and aspirations of a nation striving for sovereignty and self-determination.

The history of Caracas begins with its foundation in 1567 by Spanish explorer Diego de Losada. The city was established as Santiago de León de Caracas in the fertile Caracas Valley, an area inhabited by indigenous peoples, primarily the Caracas tribe, before the arrival of the Spaniards. The location was strategically chosen for its relatively temperate climate and defensible terrain, which offered protection from coastal raiders and provided a base for further colonial expansion into the interior of South America. The early settlement of Caracas quickly became a vital center for the Spanish colonial administration and a hub for agricultural production, particularly cocoa, which became a major export commodity.

Throughout the 16th and 17th centuries, Caracas experienced steady growth as an important colonial outpost. The city's economy was primarily agrarian, with plantations producing cocoa, coffee, and other crops that were exported to Europe. The wealth generated from these exports contributed to the development of a prosperous colonial elite, who built grand estates and invested in the city's infrastructure. Despite its economic success, Caracas and its inhabitants were subject to the rigid social hierarchy and exploitative practices characteristic of Spanish colonial rule, which created significant social and economic inequalities.

The 18th century was a period of increasing tension and unrest in Caracas, driven by a combination of economic hardship, social inequalities, and the influence of Enlightenment ideas. The decline of the Spanish Empire and the growing discontent among the colonial population set the stage for a series of uprisings and revolts against the colonial authorities. The economic challenges faced by Caracas, including the declining profitability of its agricultural exports and the restrictive trade policies imposed by the Spanish Crown, exacerbated the grievances of the local population. The rigid social structure, which marginalized the indigenous peoples, enslaved Africans, and mixed-race populations, further fueled the desire for change and liberation.

One of the pivotal figures in the history of Caracas and Venezuela is Simón Bolívar, a visionary leader whose efforts were instrumental in the struggle for independence from Spanish colonial rule. Born in Caracas in 1783 into a wealthy and influential Creole family, Bolívar was exposed to Enlightenment ideas and the revolutionary movements that were sweeping across Europe and the Americas. The early death of his parents and his subsequent travels to Europe provided him with a unique perspective on the political and social dynamics of the time, shaping his vision for an independent and unified South America.

Bolívar's return to Caracas in 1807 coincided with a period of significant political upheaval. The Napoleonic invasion of Spain in 1808 weakened the authority of the Spanish Crown and created an opportunity for the colonies to seek greater autonomy and independence. In 1810, a revolutionary junta in Caracas declared the city's independence from Spain, marking the beginning of a prolonged and bloody struggle for Venezuelan independence. Bolívar emerged as a key leader in this movement, advocating for the liberation of South America from Spanish rule and the establishment of a republic based on the principles of equality and justice.

The struggle for independence was marked by a series of military campaigns and political upheavals, with Caracas playing a central role as a base for revolutionary activities and a symbol of the broader aspirations for freedom and self-determination. Bolívar's leadership and his vision for a united South America inspired countless individuals to join the cause, leading to significant victories and the eventual liberation of Venezuela in 1821. The declaration of independence and the subsequent establishment of the Republic of Gran Colombia, which included present-day Venezuela, Colombia, Ecuador, and Panama, represented the fulfillment of Bolívar's dream for a unified and independent South America.

Despite the initial successes of the independence movement, the post-colonial period was marked by significant challenges and internal conflicts. The dissolution of Gran Colombia in 1831 and the subsequent political fragmentation of the region highlighted the difficulties of achieving lasting unity and stability in the face of diverse regional interests and external pressures. Caracas, as the capital of the newly independent Venezuela, faced significant challenges in building a stable and prosperous nation. The city's leaders grappled with issues such as political corruption, economic instability, and social inequalities, which continued to shape the development of Caracas and Venezuela throughout the 19th and 20th centuries.

The 20th century was a period of significant transformation for Caracas, as the discovery of oil in Venezuela in the early 20th century brought unprecedented economic growth and development. The city experienced rapid urbanization and modernization, with the construction of new infrastructure, skyscrapers, and residential areas transforming its skyline. The influx of wealth from the oil industry contributed to the development of a modern and cosmopolitan city, attracting migrants from rural areas and other countries. Caracas became a vibrant center of culture, commerce, and politics, reflecting the broader economic and social changes taking place in Venezuela.

Despite the economic boom, the wealth generated from the oil industry was unevenly distributed, leading to significant social inequalities and political instability. The rapid urbanization of Caracas also brought challenges such as inadequate housing, infrastructure, and public services, creating significant disparities between the affluent and impoverished areas of the city. The political landscape was marked by frequent changes in government, with periods of authoritarian rule and democratic governance reflecting the ongoing struggle to establish a stable and inclusive political system.

The late 20th and early 21st centuries saw a resurgence of the Bolivarian ideals and a renewed focus on social justice and equality, driven by the rise of Hugo Chávez and his Bolivarian Revolution. Chávez, who was elected president in 1998, sought to transform Venezuela through a series of social and economic reforms aimed at addressing the deep-rooted inequalities and injustices that had characterized the country's history. The Bolivarian Revolution, named in honor of Simón Bolívar, sought to redistribute wealth, expand social programs, and promote participatory democracy, reflecting a commitment to the principles of equality and justice that had inspired the original struggle for independence.

The impact of the Bolivarian Revolution on Caracas has been profound, with significant investments in social programs, housing, education, and healthcare transforming the lives of many residents. The city has seen the construction of new public infrastructure, including transportation networks, cultural institutions, and public spaces, aimed at improving the quality of life for its inhabitants. The emphasis on participatory democracy and community involvement has also fostered a sense of empowerment and agency among the city's residents, reflecting the broader aspirations for a more inclusive and equitable society.

However, the Bolivarian Revolution has also faced significant challenges and criticisms, including economic instability, political polarization, and issues related to governance and corruption. The economic policies implemented by the Chávez government, including the nationalization of key industries and the redistribution of wealth, have been controversial and have contributed to significant economic challenges, including hyperinflation, shortages of basic goods, and a decline in oil production. The political landscape has been marked by intense polarization and conflict, with frequent protests, demonstrations, and clashes between supporters and opponents of the government.

Despite these challenges, the legacy of the Bolivarian Revolution and the broader narrative of Caracas as a city of Bolivarian beginnings continues to resonate deeply with the people of Venezuela and beyond. The ideals of independence, equality, and justice that inspired the original struggle for liberation continue to shape the aspirations and struggles of the city and the country, reflecting a commitment to the principles that have defined its history.

Today, Caracas remains a city of contrasts and complexities, embodying the rich tapestry of its historical and cultural heritage. The city's architecture, from the colonial-era buildings in the historic center to the modernist skyscrapers and public spaces, reflects the diverse influences that have shaped its development. The vibrant cultural scene, including music, theater, and visual arts, showcases the creativity and resilience of its people, while the bustling markets, cafes, and public squares reflect the dynamic and diverse nature of the city.

Caracas's role as the political and cultural heart of Venezuela continues to be significant, with the city's institutions, universities, and cultural centers playing a crucial role in shaping the country's future. The ongoing challenges and opportunities faced by Caracas reflect the broader dynamics of Venezuelan society, offering a window into the aspirations, struggles, and resilience of a nation committed to the principles of freedom, equality, and justice.

The hidden histories of Caracas, from its colonial beginnings to its role in the Bolivarian revolution and its ongoing journey toward a more inclusive and equitable society, offer a compelling narrative of a city that has continually evolved and adapted to the changing tides of history. The city's rich cultural heritage, dynamic political landscape, and vibrant social life make it a unique and captivating place, reflecting the broader narratives of Venezuela and the Latin American region. As Caracas continues to grow and develop, it remains a testament to the resilience and creativity of its people, a city that embodies the spirit of the Bolivarian ideals and the rich traditions of South America's struggle for independence and self-determination.

Chapter 37: Nairobi: The Great Rift's Secrets

Nairobi, the capital city of Kenya, stands as a dynamic testament to the complex interplay of natural beauty, colonial legacy, cultural diversity, and rapid urbanization. Nestled in the highlands of the Great Rift Valley, Nairobi is a city where the ancient geological forces that shaped the landscape converge with the modern aspirations of a nation striving for development and progress. The city's history, culture, and identity are deeply intertwined with the secrets of the Great Rift Valley, a geological marvel that has played a significant role in the development of human civilization and continues to influence the city's trajectory in myriad ways.

The Great Rift Valley, stretching over 6,000 kilometers from the Middle East to Mozambique, is one of the most significant geological formations on Earth. It is a place of immense beauty and geological diversity, characterized by a series of rift valleys, escarpments, and volcanic features. This immense fissure in the Earth's crust has been a crucible for the evolution of human ancestors, with some of the earliest known hominid fossils discovered in the region. The Rift Valley's rich archaeological and paleoanthropological sites have provided invaluable insights into human evolution, making it a key area of study for scientists and researchers.

Nairobi's location in the highlands adjacent to the Rift Valley has played a pivotal role in its development and significance. The area's fertile soils, temperate climate, and abundant water sources made it an attractive location for early human settlement and agricultural activities. The Maasai people, a semi-nomadic ethnic group known for their pastoralist lifestyle, were among the early inhabitants of the region. The Maasai established a strong presence in the highlands, using the fertile grasslands for grazing their cattle and maintaining a way of life that was closely connected to the land and its natural resources.

The arrival of the British colonialists in the late 19th century marked a significant turning point in the history of Nairobi and the broader region. The British, motivated by strategic and economic interests, sought to establish control over the East African territories and create a network of colonies that would facilitate trade and resource extraction. The construction of the Uganda Railway, which began in 1896, was a key component of this strategy, aimed at connecting the interior of East Africa with the port of Mombasa on the Indian Ocean.

Nairobi, originally a small Maasai watering hole known as Enkare Nairobi, meaning "cool waters," was chosen as a key railway depot due to its strategic location halfway between Mombasa and Lake Victoria. The construction of the railway brought significant changes to the area, transforming it from a sparsely populated region into a bustling hub of activity. The establishment of Nairobi as a railway depot in 1899 marked the birth of the city as we know it today, with the influx of workers, traders, and settlers contributing to its rapid growth and development.

The colonial era was a period of significant transformation for Nairobi, as the city grew into a major administrative and commercial center for British East Africa. The construction of colonial infrastructure, including government buildings, roads, and residential areas, reflected the aspirations of the British to create a modern and efficient colonial capital. The colonial authorities implemented policies aimed at segregating the population along racial lines, with distinct areas designated for Europeans, Asians, and Africans. This segregation created a divided city, with significant disparities in access to resources, services, and opportunities based on race and ethnicity.

Despite these challenges, Nairobi's diverse population contributed to the city's vibrant cultural and social life. The presence of different ethnic groups, including the Kikuyu, Luo, Luhya, and Somali, among others, created a rich tapestry of cultural practices, languages, and traditions. The Indian community, brought to Kenya by the British to work on the railway, played a significant role in the city's economic and commercial activities, contributing to the development of Nairobi as a major center of trade and commerce. The city's diverse cultural heritage is reflected in its cuisine, music, and festivals, which showcase the rich traditions and customs of its inhabitants.

The struggle for independence in the mid-20th century was a period of significant political and social upheaval for Nairobi and Kenya as a whole. The growing discontent with colonial rule, driven by issues such as land dispossession, racial discrimination, and economic inequality, culminated in the Mau Mau uprising in the 1950s. The Mau Mau movement, primarily composed of Kikuyu militants, sought to challenge British authority and demand greater rights and freedoms for the indigenous population. The uprising was met with brutal repression by the colonial authorities, resulting in significant loss of life and widespread displacement.

The attainment of independence in 1963 marked a new chapter in the history of Nairobi and Kenya. The city, now the capital of an independent nation, became a symbol of the aspirations and hopes of the Kenyan people for a better and more equitable future. The post-independence period was characterized by significant efforts to address the legacy of colonialism, including the implementation of policies aimed at promoting economic development, social justice, and national unity. The construction of new infrastructure, the expansion of educational and healthcare services, and the establishment of national institutions reflected the ambitions of the newly independent state to build a modern and prosperous nation.

Nairobi's role as a center of political and economic activity continued to grow in the post-independence period, with the city emerging as a major hub for regional and international organizations. The establishment of the United Nations Environment Programme (UNEP) headquarters in Nairobi in 1972 underscored the city's growing significance on the global stage, positioning it as a key player in international efforts to address environmental challenges. The presence of numerous international organizations, diplomatic missions, and multinational corporations has contributed to Nairobi's status as a leading center of commerce, diplomacy, and development in East Africa.

The rapid growth and urbanization of Nairobi in the late 20th and early 21st centuries have brought significant challenges and opportunities. The city's population has grown exponentially, driven by rural-to-urban migration and the expansion of economic activities. This rapid urbanization has led to the development of new residential and commercial areas, transforming the city's landscape and creating a vibrant and dynamic urban environment. However, the rapid growth has also placed significant pressure on infrastructure, services, and resources, leading to challenges such as inadequate housing, traffic congestion, and environmental degradation.

Nairobi's informal settlements, or slums, such as Kibera and Mathare, highlight the significant disparities in access to resources and services that continue to characterize the city. These areas are home to a large portion of the city's population, who often live in precarious conditions with limited access to basic amenities such as clean water, sanitation, and healthcare. The challenges faced by residents of informal settlements underscore the broader issues of social inequality and exclusion that need to be addressed to ensure a more inclusive and equitable urban development.

Despite these challenges, Nairobi remains a city of immense potential and opportunity. The city's dynamic economy, driven by sectors such as finance, technology, and tourism, has positioned it as a leading center of innovation and entrepreneurship in Africa. The rise of the technology sector, in particular, has transformed Nairobi into a major hub for tech startups and innovation, earning it the nickname "Silicon Savannah." The growth of the digital economy has created new opportunities for employment, investment, and economic development, contributing to the city's vibrant and forward-looking character.

Nairobi's rich cultural heritage and vibrant arts scene continue to be significant aspects of the city's identity. The city is home to numerous cultural institutions, including museums, theaters, and art galleries, which showcase the diverse traditions and artistic expressions of its inhabitants. The annual Nairobi International Film Festival, the Nairobi Fashion Week, and various music and cultural festivals highlight the city's dynamic and creative spirit, reflecting the rich tapestry of its cultural heritage.

The natural beauty of the Great Rift Valley and its surrounding landscapes remains a significant draw for residents and visitors alike. Nairobi's proximity to national parks and nature reserves, such as Nairobi National Park and the Great Rift Valley itself, offers unique opportunities for wildlife viewing and outdoor activities. The presence of wildlife within the city limits, including lions, giraffes, and rhinos, underscores Nairobi's unique character as a city where the natural and urban worlds intersect in fascinating ways.

The hidden secrets of the Great Rift Valley, from its ancient geological formations to its rich archaeological and cultural heritage, continue to shape the identity and development of Nairobi. The valley's unique landscapes, including volcanic craters, escarpments, and lakes, provide a stunning backdrop for the city and offer a wealth of opportunities for scientific research, tourism, and conservation.

The discovery of early human fossils in the Rift Valley has provided invaluable insights into the origins and evolution of our species, highlighting the region's significance as a cradle of human civilization.

Today, Nairobi stands as a testament to the resilience and creativity of its people, a city that embodies the aspirations and hopes of a nation striving for development and progress. The city's dynamic economy, diverse cultural heritage, and vibrant social life make it a unique and captivating place, reflecting the broader narratives of Kenya and the African continent. As Nairobi continues to grow and develop, it remains a city of contrasts and complexities, where the secrets of the Great Rift Valley continue to shape its past, present, and future.

Chapter 38: Zagreb: Balkan Chronicles

Zagreb, the capital city of Croatia, stands as a fascinating testament to the complex and tumultuous history of the Balkan Peninsula. Nestled at the crossroads of Central Europe and the Mediterranean, Zagreb is a city where diverse cultural influences and historical legacies converge, creating a rich tapestry that reflects the broader narratives of the Balkans. The story of Zagreb, from its ancient origins to its modern-day status as a vibrant cultural and political hub, offers a compelling exploration of the region's dynamic history and the enduring spirit of its people.

The history of Zagreb dates back to Roman times when the area was part of the Roman province of Pannonia. Archaeological evidence suggests that the region was inhabited by the Illyrians and later by the Celts before becoming part of the Roman Empire. The Romans established a settlement known as Andautonia, located near present-day Zagreb, which served as an important administrative and military center. The remnants of Roman architecture and artifacts, such as mosaics and pottery, provide a glimpse into the early history of the region and its integration into the Roman world.

The early medieval period saw significant changes in the region, with the arrival of the Slavs in the 6th and 7th centuries. The Slavic tribes settled in the area and established small communities, laying the foundations for the future development of Zagreb. The city itself traces its origins to two medieval settlements: Kaptol and Gradec. Kaptol, established in 1094 with the founding of the Zagreb Diocese by King Ladislaus I of Hungary, became an ecclesiastical center, while Gradec, which received a royal charter from King Béla IV of Hungary in 1242, developed as a fortified town on the opposite hill.

The medieval period was marked by the rivalry and occasional conflicts between Kaptol and Gradec, reflecting the broader dynamics of power and influence in the region. Despite these tensions, the two settlements gradually grew and prospered, benefiting from their strategic location on important trade routes connecting the Adriatic Sea with the interior of Europe. The establishment of the Zagreb Diocese and the construction of the Zagreb Cathedral in Kaptol played a crucial role in the religious and cultural development of the city, while Gradec's status as a free royal town facilitated its growth as a center of commerce and trade.

The union of Kaptol and Gradec into a single city, known as Zagreb, in the 19th century marked a significant milestone in the city's history. The unification reflected broader trends of political and social change in the region, as the Habsburg Empire, which had dominated the area for centuries, began to experience internal pressures and calls for reform. The 19th century was a period of significant transformation for Zagreb, as the city underwent rapid modernization and development. The construction of new infrastructure, including roads, railways, and public buildings, transformed Zagreb into a modern European city, reflecting the aspirations of its inhabitants for progress and development.

The 19th century also saw the rise of the Croatian national revival, a movement aimed at promoting Croatian language, culture, and identity. Figures such as Ljudevit Gaj and Bishop Josip Juraj Strossmayer played a crucial role in this movement, advocating for the preservation and promotion of Croatian heritage in the face of increasing Germanization and Hungarian influence. The establishment of cultural institutions, such as the Croatian National Theatre and the University of Zagreb, and the publication of important literary works, such as the "Illyrian Letters," reflected the growing sense of national consciousness and pride among the Croatian people.

The early 20th century was a period of significant political and social upheaval for Zagreb and the broader region. The collapse of the Austro-Hungarian Empire at the end of World War I led to the creation of the Kingdom of Serbs, Croats, and Slovenes, later known as Yugoslavia. The new state, which sought to unite the South Slavic peoples under a single political entity, faced significant challenges and internal tensions, reflecting the diverse and often conflicting interests of its constituent regions and ethnic groups. Zagreb, as the capital of the Croatian region, became a center of political and cultural activity, playing a crucial role in the debates and struggles over the future of the region.

The interwar period was marked by significant economic and social challenges, as the region grappled with the effects of the Great Depression and the political instability of the Yugoslav state. The rise of nationalist movements and the increasing tensions between different ethnic and political groups created a volatile and unstable environment, setting the stage for the conflicts and upheavals that would characterize the region in the following decades. Despite these challenges, Zagreb continued to develop as a major cultural and economic center, with the construction of new public buildings, the expansion of educational institutions, and the growth of the city's industrial base.

World War II brought significant turmoil and devastation to Zagreb and the broader region. The invasion and occupation of Yugoslavia by Axis powers in 1941 led to the establishment of the Independent State of Croatia (NDH), a puppet state under the control of the fascist Ustaše regime. The Ustaše, led by Ante Pavelić, implemented brutal policies of repression and ethnic cleansing, targeting Jews, Serbs, Roma, and political opponents. The period was marked by widespread violence and atrocities, with the city of Zagreb becoming a center of resistance and opposition to the fascist regime. The activities of the Partisan resistance movement, led by Josip Broz Tito, played a crucial role in the liberation of the region and the eventual defeat of the Axis powers.

The post-war period saw the establishment of the Socialist Federal Republic of Yugoslavia under the leadership of Tito. The new socialist state sought to create a unified and modern society, based on principles of social justice, equality, and economic development. Zagreb, as the capital of the Socialist Republic of Croatia, played a crucial role in the reconstruction and development of the region, with significant investments in infrastructure, industry, and education. The city's cultural and artistic life flourished, with the establishment of new cultural institutions, the promotion of arts and literature, and the organization of major cultural events and festivals.

The late 20th century was a period of significant political and social change for Zagreb and Croatia, as the collapse of the socialist state and the disintegration of Yugoslavia led to the emergence of new independent states. The Croatian War of Independence, which began in 1991, was a period of intense conflict and upheaval, as Croatia sought to assert its independence and sovereignty in the face of opposition from Serbian forces and the Yugoslav People's Army. The war brought significant devastation and loss of life, with widespread destruction of infrastructure and displacement of populations. Despite the challenges, Zagreb emerged as a symbol of resilience and determination, playing a crucial role in the struggle for independence and the reconstruction of the nation.

The post-independence period has been marked by significant efforts to rebuild and modernize Zagreb and the broader region. The city's economy has undergone significant transformation, with the growth of new industries, the expansion of the service sector, and the development of a vibrant cultural and creative economy. The construction of new infrastructure, the renovation of historic buildings, and the development of new residential and commercial areas have transformed Zagreb into a modern European city, reflecting the aspirations and hopes of its inhabitants for a prosperous and sustainable future.

Zagreb's cultural heritage and vibrant arts scene continue to be significant aspects of the city's identity. The city is home to numerous cultural institutions, including museums, theaters, and galleries, which showcase the diverse traditions and artistic expressions of its inhabitants. The Zagreb Film Festival, the International Folklore Festival, and various music and cultural events highlight the city's dynamic and creative spirit, reflecting the rich tapestry of its cultural heritage. The city's historic center, with its charming streets, historic buildings, and vibrant public spaces, offers a glimpse into the rich history and cultural heritage of Zagreb, reflecting the diverse influences and traditions that have shaped its development.

The natural beauty of the surrounding landscapes, including the Medvednica mountain and the Sava River, offers unique opportunities for outdoor activities and recreation, contributing to the quality of life for the city's residents and visitors. The presence of parks, gardens, and green spaces within the city provides a tranquil and scenic environment, reflecting the city's commitment to sustainability and environmental conservation. The integration of natural and urban elements in Zagreb's landscape underscores the city's unique character as a place where the natural and cultural worlds intersect in fascinating ways.

The hidden histories and complex narratives of Zagreb, from its ancient origins to its modern-day status as a vibrant cultural and political hub, offer a compelling exploration of the broader dynamics of the Balkan region. The city's rich cultural heritage, dynamic economy, and vibrant social life make it a unique and captivating place, reflecting the broader narratives of Croatia and the Balkan Peninsula. As Zagreb continues to grow and develop, it remains a city of contrasts and complexities, where the secrets of the Balkans continue to shape its past, present, and future. The city's ongoing journey towards a more inclusive, equitable, and sustainable future reflects the aspirations and hopes of its inhabitants, as they navigate the challenges and opportunities of a rapidly changing world.

Chapter 39: Kuwait City: Oil's Odyssey

Kuwait City, the capital of Kuwait, serves as a dynamic example of transformation and growth driven by the discovery and exploitation of oil. This bustling metropolis, perched on the northwestern shore of the Persian Gulf, is a testament to the profound impact that oil wealth has had on shaping a nation's economy, culture, and geopolitical stature. The journey of Kuwait City from a modest fishing village to a global economic powerhouse is a compelling narrative of resilience, ambition, and strategic foresight, intricately linked to the rise of the oil industry in the region.

Kuwait's history, like much of the Arabian Peninsula, is deeply rooted in its strategic geographical location and the natural resources that have shaped its development. Before the discovery of oil, Kuwait's economy was primarily based on maritime activities such as fishing, pearl diving, and trade. The city of Kuwait was established in the early 18th century by the Bani Utub tribe, who migrated from central Arabia. They settled in the area due to its advantageous position for trade and its access to the sea. The early economy of Kuwait was heavily reliant on the maritime trade routes that connected the Indian Ocean with the Mediterranean, making it a significant hub for commerce and interaction between different cultures.

The first significant shift in Kuwait's economic landscape occurred in the early 20th century with the decline of the pearl industry. The advent of cultured pearls in Japan and the Great Depression led to a collapse in demand for natural pearls, which had been a major source of income for Kuwait. This economic downturn prompted the ruling Al-Sabah family to seek new sources of revenue to sustain the emirate's economy. The turning point came in 1938 with the discovery of oil in the Burgan field, one of the largest oil fields in the world. This discovery marked the beginning of a new era for Kuwait, transforming it from a small, economically vulnerable sheikhdom into a nation with significant economic potential.

The first commercial shipment of Kuwaiti crude oil in 1946 signaled the start of Kuwait's oil-driven economic boom. The revenues generated from oil exports provided the financial foundation for rapid development and modernization. The Al-Sabah family, particularly Emir Abdullah Al-Salem Al-Sabah, who ruled from 1950 to 1965, played a crucial role in guiding this transformation. Under his leadership, Kuwait embarked on an ambitious program of infrastructure development, including the construction of roads, hospitals, schools, and housing projects. These initiatives were aimed at improving the quality of life for Kuwaiti citizens and laying the groundwork for a modern, prosperous state.

The wealth generated by oil exports also enabled Kuwait to pursue an active and influential foreign policy. During the mid-20th century, Kuwait played a significant role in regional politics, leveraging its oil wealth to support various political causes and provide financial assistance to other Arab nations. Kuwait's newfound economic power allowed it to assert greater autonomy and influence on the international stage, particularly within the framework of the Organization of the Petroleum Exporting Countries (OPEC), which was founded in 1960. Kuwait's role in OPEC was instrumental in shaping global oil markets and ensuring that the interests of oil-producing nations were represented in international negotiations.

The rapid urbanization of Kuwait City during the second half of the 20th century was a direct consequence of the oil boom. The city's population grew rapidly as people from rural areas and neighboring countries moved to the capital in search of better economic opportunities. The influx of foreign workers, particularly from South Asia, the Middle East, and North Africa, played a crucial role in the development of Kuwait's oil industry and broader economy. This diverse and cosmopolitan population contributed to the city's dynamic cultural landscape, blending traditional Kuwaiti customs with influences from across the globe.

The architectural landscape of Kuwait City underwent a dramatic transformation during this period of rapid growth. The traditional mud-brick houses and narrow streets of the old town gave way to modern skyscrapers, luxury hotels, and sprawling residential complexes. Landmark projects such as the Kuwait Towers, the National Assembly Building, and the Liberation Tower became symbols of Kuwait's modernization and economic prosperity. The city's skyline, characterized by a mix of traditional Islamic architecture and cutting-edge modern design, reflects the unique fusion of heritage and innovation that defines Kuwait's approach to development.

Despite the significant progress made during the oil boom, Kuwait faced a number of challenges and setbacks. The most significant of these was the Iraqi invasion of Kuwait in 1990, which led to a seven-month occupation and widespread devastation. The invasion, prompted by disputes over oil production and territorial claims, had a profound impact on Kuwait's economy and infrastructure. The liberation of Kuwait in 1991, led by a coalition of international forces, marked the beginning of a difficult and costly process of reconstruction and recovery. The Kuwaiti government, with substantial financial support from the international community, undertook extensive efforts to rebuild the nation's infrastructure, restore public services, and revive the economy.

The post-invasion period also prompted a reevaluation of Kuwait's economic strategy and a renewed focus on diversification. The Kuwaiti government recognized the need to reduce the nation's dependence on oil revenues and to develop other sectors of the economy. Initiatives to promote investment in industries such as finance, tourism, and information technology were launched, aimed at creating a more sustainable and resilient economic model. The establishment of free trade zones, the promotion of foreign investment, and the development of a more dynamic private sector were key components of this strategy.

Kuwait's commitment to economic diversification is reflected in its ambitious Vision 2035 development plan, which aims to transform the nation into a leading regional trade and financial hub. The plan includes major infrastructure projects such as the construction of new ports, airports, and industrial zones, as well as investments in education, healthcare, and social services. The development of the Silk City project, a massive urban development initiative aimed at creating a new economic and cultural center in the north of the country, is a key component of this vision. These efforts are intended to position Kuwait as a major player in the global economy and to ensure long-term economic stability and prosperity.

Kuwait City's cultural scene has also flourished in recent decades, reflecting the nation's rich heritage and its commitment to promoting cultural exchange and innovation. The city is home to a number of important cultural institutions, including the Kuwait National Museum, the Dar al-Athar al-Islamiyyah, and the Sheikh Jaber Al-Ahmad Cultural Centre. These institutions play a crucial role in preserving Kuwait's cultural heritage, promoting the arts, and fostering a greater understanding of the nation's history and traditions. The annual Kuwait International Book Fair, the Kuwait Film Festival, and various art exhibitions and cultural events highlight the city's vibrant cultural landscape and its role as a center of creativity and intellectual exchange.

The impact of oil wealth on Kuwait City's social and cultural dynamics has been profound. The rapid economic development and modernization brought about by the oil boom have led to significant changes in the nation's social fabric. The traditional tribal structures and customs that once dominated Kuwaiti society have been complemented by a more diverse and cosmopolitan cultural landscape, influenced by the influx of foreign workers and the exposure to global trends and ideas. The city's population is characterized by a mix of native Kuwaitis, expatriates, and migrant workers, creating a multicultural environment that is reflected in the city's diverse culinary scene, artistic expressions, and social interactions.

Despite the benefits of economic development, Kuwait faces ongoing challenges related to social inequality, environmental sustainability, and political reform. The nation's reliance on foreign labor has created significant disparities in wealth and access to services, with many migrant workers facing difficult living and working conditions. Efforts to address these issues, including the implementation of labor reforms and the promotion of social inclusion and equity, are crucial for ensuring the long-term sustainability of Kuwait's economic and social development.

Environmental sustainability is another critical challenge for Kuwait, particularly given the nation's reliance on oil production and its impact on the environment. The Kuwaiti government has recognized the importance of addressing environmental issues, including air pollution, water scarcity, and climate change, and has launched a number of initiatives aimed at promoting sustainable development and environmental conservation. The development of renewable energy sources, such as solar and wind power, and the promotion of energy efficiency and conservation are key components of Kuwait's environmental strategy.

Political reform is also an important aspect of Kuwait's future development. The nation has a unique political system that combines elements of traditional tribal governance with modern democratic institutions. The Kuwaiti National Assembly, established in 1963, is one of the oldest parliamentary bodies in the region and plays a crucial role in the nation's political life. Efforts to promote greater political participation, transparency, and accountability are essential for ensuring that Kuwait's political system remains responsive to the needs and aspirations of its citizens.

Kuwait City's journey from a modest fishing village to a modern metropolis is a compelling narrative of transformation and growth, driven by the discovery and exploitation of oil. The city's development has been shaped by a complex interplay of historical, economic, and cultural factors, reflecting the broader dynamics of the region and the challenges and opportunities that come with rapid modernization and globalization. As Kuwait City continues to evolve, it remains a dynamic and vibrant center of economic, cultural, and political activity, embodying the aspirations and hopes of a nation striving for a prosperous and sustainable future. The city's ongoing journey, shaped by its rich heritage and its strategic vision for the future, offers a fascinating glimpse into the broader narratives of the Gulf region and the global economy.

Chapter 40: Budapest: Thermal Tales

Budapest, the capital of Hungary, is famously known as the "City of Spas" due to its rich thermal water resources and historic baths. The city's unique location on a geological fault line has blessed it with an abundance of thermal springs, which have been utilized for therapeutic and recreational purposes for centuries. The thermal waters of Budapest are renowned for their healing properties, containing various minerals such as calcium, magnesium, sulfate, and bicarbonate, which are beneficial for treating ailments like arthritis, circulatory problems, and respiratory issues.

The history of Budapest's thermal baths dates back to ancient times. The Romans were the first to recognize the healing potential of the city's thermal springs, establishing the Aquincum settlement around the 1st century AD. Aquincum, located in what is now the Óbuda district of Budapest, was a thriving Roman city with a network of public baths that served as centers for socializing, relaxation, and medical treatments. The remains of these ancient Roman baths can still be seen today, offering a glimpse into the city's deep-rooted spa culture.

After the fall of the Roman Empire, the significance of the thermal springs continued through the Middle Ages. However, it was during the Ottoman occupation of Hungary in the 16th and 17th centuries that the thermal bath culture in Budapest truly flourished. The Ottomans, who had a strong tradition of bathing and hydrotherapy, built several stunning bathhouses that are still in use today. One of the most famous Ottoman-era baths is the Rudas Bath, constructed in 1550. The Rudas Bath features a beautiful octagonal pool, a large dome with colored glass windows, and intricate tilework that reflects the architectural style of the period. Another notable Ottoman bath is the Király Bath, which was built in 1565 and has retained much of its original structure and ambiance, offering a unique historical bathing experience.

In the 19th century, during the Austro-Hungarian Empire, Budapest's reputation as a spa destination grew even further. The development of grand bath complexes, such as the Széchenyi Thermal Bath, marked this period. Opened in 1913, the Széchenyi Bath is one of the largest spa complexes in Europe and a prime example of Neo-Baroque architecture. It boasts 15 indoor pools and 3 large outdoor pools, along with a range of saunas, steam rooms, and treatment facilities. The Széchenyi Bath is renowned for its hot spring waters, which are drawn from a depth of over 1,200 meters and have a temperature of around 76°C (169°F). The outdoor pools, surrounded by elegant colonnades and statues, are particularly popular, offering a delightful contrast of warm waters and crisp air, especially in the winter months.

Another iconic thermal bath in Budapest is the Gellért Bath, located at the foot of Gellért Hill. The Gellért Bath, part of the luxurious Gellért Hotel, opened in 1918 and is celebrated for its Art Nouveau design. The bath complex features beautiful mosaics, stained glass windows, and marble columns, creating an atmosphere of opulence and relaxation. The thermal waters of the Gellért Bath are sourced from natural springs in the nearby hill, and the bath offers a variety of pools, including a wave pool, a sun terrace, and therapeutic pools with different temperatures and mineral compositions.

The Lukács Bath, another prominent thermal spa, has a rich history dating back to the 12th century when it was used by knights of the Order of Saint John. The current structure, built in the 19th century, has been a popular spot for locals and tourists alike. The Lukács Bath is particularly famous for its "Healing Water Gallery," where visitors can drink the mineral-rich thermal water believed to aid in digestive and metabolic disorders. The bath also has outdoor and indoor pools, saunas, and wellness treatments, making it a comprehensive spa destination.

In addition to these historic baths, Budapest is home to several other thermal spas, each with its unique charm and offerings. The Rác Bath, dating back to the 16th century, has recently been restored and reopened, blending historical elements with modern amenities. The Dandár Bath, a smaller and more intimate facility, offers a quiet retreat with thermal pools and wellness services. The Palatinus Bath, located on Margaret Island, is a favorite summer destination, featuring a large outdoor pool complex with wave pools, slides, and sunbathing areas.

The thermal bath culture in Budapest is not just about relaxation and health; it is deeply intertwined with the city's social fabric. Bathing in these historic spas is a communal activity where people of all ages come together to unwind, socialize, and enjoy the therapeutic benefits of the thermal waters. The baths often host cultural events, such as concerts, film screenings, and night parties, adding a modern twist to the traditional spa experience. These events attract both locals and tourists, creating a vibrant atmosphere that celebrates the city's rich heritage and contemporary culture.

Budapest's thermal baths also play a significant role in the city's tourism industry, drawing visitors from around the world who seek the unique experience of bathing in historic settings. The baths are an integral part of Budapest's identity, contributing to its charm and appeal as a travel destination. Whether it's soaking in the grandeur of the Széchenyi Bath, marveling at the Ottoman architecture of the Rudas Bath, or enjoying the elegance of the Gellért Bath, the thermal baths of Budapest offer a timeless and rejuvenating experience that reflects the city's storied past and dynamic present.

In recent years, there has been a growing interest in wellness tourism, and Budapest's thermal baths have adapted to meet this demand. Many of the baths now offer a range of wellness services, including massages, physiotherapy, mud treatments, and beauty therapies. These services are designed to complement the therapeutic effects of the thermal waters, providing a holistic approach to health and well-being. The integration of modern wellness practices with traditional thermal bathing has enhanced the appeal of Budapest's baths, attracting a diverse clientele seeking both relaxation and health benefits.

Moreover, the city has invested in the preservation and modernization of its thermal bath facilities to ensure they remain accessible and appealing to future generations. Efforts have been made to maintain the historical integrity of these sites while incorporating contemporary amenities and technologies. This balance of preservation and innovation has allowed Budapest to retain its status as a premier spa destination, where visitors can enjoy a blend of history, culture, and wellness.

Chapter 41: Damascus: Ancient Whisperings

Damascus, often considered one of the oldest continuously inhabited cities in the world, holds a wealth of history and cultural significance that spans millennia. Its strategic location at the crossroads of the Middle East made it a pivotal center for trade, culture, and politics throughout various eras. The ancient whisperings of Damascus are found in its streets, structures, and traditions, each narrating tales of civilizations that have left their mark on this timeless city.

The origins of Damascus can be traced back to prehistoric times, with archaeological evidence suggesting human habitation as early as 8,000 to 10,000 years ago. The city's prime location near the Barada River and the fertile Ghouta oasis made it an ideal settlement for early agricultural communities. These early inhabitants laid the foundation for what would become a thriving urban center, attracting settlers from diverse backgrounds.

By the time of the second millennium BCE, Damascus had already established itself as a significant city-state. It was mentioned in ancient Egyptian texts, including the Amarna letters, where it was referred to as "Dimašqa." During this period, Damascus was part of the Amorite kingdom and later came under the control of various empires, including the Egyptians and the Hittites. The city's strategic importance grew as it became a focal point in the trade networks connecting Mesopotamia, Egypt, and the Mediterranean.

The Assyrian Empire brought Damascus under its rule in the 8th century BCE, marking the beginning of a series of conquests that would shape the city's history. Following the Assyrians, the city fell to the Neo-Babylonian Empire and then to the Achaemenid Persians. Each of these empires left their imprint on Damascus, contributing to its cultural and architectural development. The influence of the Achaemenids, for example, is evident in the city's administrative structures and urban planning.

The arrival of Alexander the Great in 333 BCE heralded a new era for Damascus, as it became part of the Hellenistic world. Under the Seleucid Empire, the city was renamed "Demetrias" and experienced significant Hellenization. Greek culture, language, and architectural styles were introduced, blending with the existing Semitic traditions. The city's layout was transformed, with the construction of colonnaded streets, theaters, and temples. This fusion of cultures created a unique urban landscape that reflected the diverse heritage of Damascus.

Roman rule, beginning in 64 BCE, further enhanced the city's prominence. Damascus was integrated into the Roman Empire as part of the province of Syria. The Romans undertook extensive building projects, including the construction of the famous Straight Street (Via Recta) and the Temple of Jupiter. The city's prosperity continued to grow, becoming a key center for commerce, administration, and culture. The architectural legacy of the Romans is still visible today, with remnants of their grand structures scattered throughout the city.

The transition from Roman to Byzantine rule in the 4th century CE marked another chapter in Damascus's history. The city became an important center for early Christianity, with numerous churches and monasteries established. The influence of Christianity is evident in the architectural and artistic remnants from this period, including mosaics and religious structures. However, it was the arrival of Islam in the 7th century that would profoundly reshape Damascus.

In 635 CE, Damascus was conquered by the Rashidun Caliphate, marking the beginning of Islamic rule. The city quickly rose to prominence as the capital of the Umayyad Caliphate under Caliph Muawiya I. This period was a golden age for Damascus, as it became the political, economic, and cultural heart of the Islamic world. The Umayyad Caliphs invested heavily in the city's infrastructure, commissioning the construction of the Great Mosque of Damascus, also known as the Umayyad Mosque. This magnificent structure, built on the site of a Christian Basilica dedicated to John the Baptist, is an architectural marvel that exemplifies the synthesis of Byzantine and Islamic design elements.

The Umayyad Mosque remains one of the most significant religious sites in Islam, attracting pilgrims and visitors from around the world. Its grandeur, with its vast prayer hall, intricate mosaics, and towering minaret, reflects the zenith of Umayyad architectural and artistic achievement. The mosque also holds the shrine of John the Baptist, revered by both Christians and Muslims, symbolizing the city's long-standing tradition of religious coexistence.

Following the fall of the Umayyad Caliphate, Damascus continued to thrive under the Abbasid Caliphate, although the capital was moved to Baghdad. Despite this, the city remained a crucial center for trade, education, and culture. The Abbasids expanded and enhanced the city's infrastructure, building schools, libraries, and hospitals. Damascus became a hub of intellectual activity, attracting scholars, poets, and scientists who contributed to the flourishing of Islamic civilization.

The city's strategic importance made it a target for various conquerors over the centuries. In 1099, during the First Crusade, Damascus successfully repelled Crusader forces, maintaining its status as a Muslim stronghold. However, it was during the reign of the Ayyubid dynasty, established by Saladin in the 12th century, that Damascus once again rose to prominence. Saladin made Damascus his capital and fortified the city, building the Citadel of Damascus as a defensive stronghold. The Ayyubid period saw the construction of numerous madrasas (Islamic schools), mosques, and public buildings, further cementing the city's status as a center of learning and piety.

The Mamluks, who took control of Damascus in the 13th century, continued to invest in the city's development. They built new markets, khans (caravanserais), and public baths, enhancing the city's commercial and social infrastructure. The Mamluk era is notable for its contributions to the architectural heritage of Damascus, with structures characterized by elaborate stonework and intricate geometric designs.

The Ottoman Empire's conquest of Damascus in 1516 marked the beginning of a new phase in the city's history. Under Ottoman rule, Damascus retained its status as an important provincial capital. The Ottomans implemented administrative reforms, expanded the city's infrastructure, and fostered economic growth. They also preserved and restored many of the city's historical monuments, ensuring the continuity of its rich architectural heritage. The period of Ottoman rule lasted until the early 20th century, during which Damascus experienced relative stability and prosperity.

The modern history of Damascus is intertwined with the broader narrative of Syrian nationalism and independence. Following the collapse of the Ottoman Empire after World War I, Damascus became a focal point for the Arab nationalist movement. The city witnessed significant political upheaval, including the establishment of the short-lived Arab Kingdom of Syria in 1920. The French Mandate period that followed saw further political struggles and the eventual emergence of Syria as an independent nation in 1946.

Throughout its long and tumultuous history, Damascus has remained a beacon of cultural and intellectual life. The city's ancient souks (markets), such as the Souk al-Hamidiyah, continue to bustle with activity, offering a glimpse into the vibrant commercial traditions that have persisted for centuries. The narrow, winding streets of the Old City, with their historic homes, courtyards, and hidden gardens, preserve the charm and character of Damascus's past.

Damascus is also renowned for its contributions to the arts and literature. The city has produced countless poets, writers, and artists who have enriched the cultural tapestry of the Arab world. Traditional crafts, such as Damascene metalwork, wood inlay, and textile weaving, thrive in the city's artisan workshops, reflecting a deep respect for craftsmanship and heritage.

The rich culinary traditions of Damascus are another testament to its diverse cultural influences. The city's cuisine, characterized by dishes such as kibbeh, hummus, and baklava, combines flavors and techniques from various civilizations that have shaped its history. The bustling cafes and restaurants of Damascus offer a sensory experience that captures the essence of the city's culinary heritage.

Chapter 42: Warsaw: Phoenix Rising

Warsaw, the capital of Poland, embodies the spirit of resilience and rebirth, much like the mythological phoenix rising from its ashes. The city's history is marked by periods of prosperity, destruction, and remarkable recovery. From its origins as a modest settlement to its rise as a major European capital, Warsaw's journey is a testament to the enduring strength and determination of its people.

The early history of Warsaw dates back to the 9th and 10th centuries, when it began as a small fishing village on the banks of the Vistula River. The strategic location of the settlement on a major trade route facilitated its growth and development. By the 14th century, Warsaw had gained enough prominence to become a significant town, attracting merchants, craftsmen, and settlers. The construction of the Warsaw Castle in the early 14th century by the Dukes of Mazovia marked a turning point in the city's history. The castle became the seat of the Mazovian dukes, solidifying Warsaw's political and administrative importance.

In 1596, King Sigismund III Vasa moved the capital of Poland from Kraków to Warsaw, recognizing its central location and strategic advantages. This decision ushered in a golden age for Warsaw, as it became the political, cultural, and economic heart of the Polish-Lithuanian Commonwealth. The city flourished during this period, with the construction of grand palaces, churches, and public buildings. The Royal Castle, which served as the king's residence and the seat of government, was expanded and adorned with magnificent works of art and architecture.

The 17th century brought both challenges and growth to Warsaw. The city faced invasions and occupations, including the devastating Swedish Deluge in the mid-1600s, which caused significant destruction. Despite these hardships, Warsaw's resilient spirit prevailed, and the city embarked on a period of reconstruction and revitalization. The late 17th and 18th centuries saw the rise of the Baroque style in architecture, with the construction of beautiful structures like Wilanów Palace and St. John's Cathedral.

The partitions of Poland in the late 18th century by the neighboring powers of Russia, Prussia, and Austria marked a dark chapter in Warsaw's history. The city came under Prussian control and later Russian rule, experiencing political repression and cultural suppression. Despite these adversities, Warsaw remained a center of Polish nationalism and resistance. The city's intellectual and artistic communities played a crucial role in preserving Polish identity and fostering the spirit of independence.

The 19th century was a period of significant transformation for Warsaw. The city underwent industrialization, with the development of factories, railways, and modern infrastructure. This industrial boom attracted a diverse population, contributing to Warsaw's growth and cosmopolitan character. However, the city's aspirations for freedom and self-determination were met with harsh repression by the Russian authorities. The November Uprising of 1830-1831 and the January Uprising of 1863-1864 were pivotal moments in Warsaw's struggle for independence, although both uprisings were ultimately crushed.

World War I and the subsequent re-establishment of Poland as an independent nation in 1918 marked a new beginning for Warsaw. The city was once again the capital of a sovereign Poland, and it experienced a period of rapid growth and modernization during the interwar years. Warsaw became a vibrant cultural and intellectual hub, attracting artists, writers, and scientists. The city's architecture reflected a blend of historic styles and modernist influences, with new buildings and infrastructure projects transforming the urban landscape.

The outbreak of World War II in 1939 brought unprecedented devastation to Warsaw. The city was subjected to brutal occupation by Nazi Germany, which sought to annihilate the Polish population and culture. The Warsaw Ghetto, established by the Nazis in 1940, became a symbol of immense suffering and resistance. The ghetto, which confined hundreds of thousands of Jews, witnessed the heroic Warsaw Ghetto Uprising in 1943, a valiant but ultimately tragic revolt against the oppressive regime.

The Warsaw Uprising of 1944 was another defining moment in the city's history. Led by the Polish resistance Home Army, the uprising aimed to liberate Warsaw from German occupation. The 63-day struggle saw fierce urban warfare, with the city's inhabitants demonstrating extraordinary courage and resilience. However, the uprising was brutally suppressed, resulting in massive casualties and widespread destruction. In retaliation, the Nazis systematically razed much of Warsaw, leaving the city in ruins.

The end of World War II marked the beginning of Warsaw's most remarkable transformation. The city, reduced to rubble, faced the daunting task of rebuilding from scratch. The spirit of the phoenix rising from the ashes aptly describes Warsaw's post-war recovery. The Polish people, driven by a deep sense of patriotism and determination, undertook an ambitious reconstruction effort. Guided by historical photographs, paintings, and architectural plans, they meticulously restored the Old Town, faithfully recreating its pre-war appearance. This remarkable achievement earned the Old Town a place on the UNESCO World Heritage list as a symbol of human resilience and cultural preservation.

The post-war period also saw the construction of new residential districts, industrial areas, and public buildings. The Palace of Culture and Science, a towering skyscraper gifted by the Soviet Union, became a prominent landmark on the city's skyline. Despite its controversial origins, the building remains a symbol of Warsaw's resilience and adaptability. The city's infrastructure was modernized, and efforts were made to preserve and restore other historic sites, such as the Royal Castle and Wilanów Palace.

The Cold War era brought its own set of challenges and transformations to Warsaw. As the capital of a communist state, the city experienced political repression, economic difficulties, and social unrest. The workers' protests in 1956, 1970, and 1980, including the rise of the Solidarity movement, highlighted the growing discontent with the regime. Warsaw became a focal point for political activism and resistance, culminating in the eventual collapse of communism in Poland in 1989.

The transition to democracy and a market economy in the 1990s marked another period of profound change for Warsaw. The city embraced modernization and globalization, attracting foreign investment and fostering economic growth. Skyscrapers, shopping centers, and modern office buildings transformed the skyline, while new cultural institutions, such as the Warsaw Uprising Museum and the POLIN Museum of the History of Polish Jews, enriched the city's cultural landscape. The development of new residential areas, green spaces, and transportation infrastructure improved the quality of life for Warsaw's inhabitants.

Today, Warsaw stands as a dynamic and thriving European capital, embodying the resilience and determination of its people. The city's rich cultural heritage is celebrated through numerous festivals, museums, and artistic events. Warsaw's music scene, from classical concerts at the National Philharmonic to vibrant jazz and contemporary performances, reflects its diverse cultural influences. The city's culinary landscape, with its mix of traditional Polish cuisine and international flavors, offers a gastronomic journey that delights residents and visitors alike.

Warsaw's parks and green spaces, such as Łazienki Park and the Vistula River boulevards, provide tranquil retreats in the midst of urban life. The city's academic institutions, including the University of Warsaw and Warsaw University of Technology, contribute to its reputation as a center of education and innovation. The thriving business sector, with a growing number of startups and multinational corporations, underscores Warsaw's role as an economic powerhouse in the region.

Chapter 43: Baghdad: Stories of Mesopotamia

Baghdad, the capital of Iraq, is a city steeped in the rich and diverse history of Mesopotamia, often referred to as the "Cradle of Civilization." The region, nestled between the Tigris and Euphrates rivers, has been a fertile ground for human development for millennia, giving rise to some of the earliest and most influential cultures in human history. The story of Baghdad itself is deeply intertwined with the broader narratives of Mesopotamia, spanning from ancient times to the present day.

The region of Mesopotamia is renowned for its role in the dawn of civilization. Around 3500 BCE, the Sumerians established some of the world's first cities, such as Uruk, Ur, and Eridu, in the southern part of Mesopotamia. These early city-states developed complex societies characterized by innovations in writing, architecture, law, and governance. The invention of cuneiform writing by the Sumerians marked a significant milestone in human history, allowing for the recording of transactions, laws, and literature. The Epic of Gilgamesh, one of the earliest known literary works, emerged from this period, reflecting the profound cultural and intellectual achievements of the Sumerians.

Following the Sumerians, the Akkadian Empire rose to prominence under the leadership of Sargon of Akkad around 2334 BCE. This empire is often considered the world's first multi-national empire, uniting various city-states and regions under a centralized administration. The Akkadians further advanced the art of writing, governance, and warfare, leaving a lasting legacy in the annals of Mesopotamian history. The subsequent periods saw the rise and fall of several other influential civilizations, including the Babylonians and Assyrians.

The city of Babylon, situated near modern-day Baghdad, became a major cultural and political center during the reign of King Hammurabi in the 18th century BCE. Hammurabi is best known for his code of laws, one of the earliest and most comprehensive legal codes in history. The famous Ishtar Gate, a grand entrance to the city adorned with glazed bricks depicting dragons and bulls, exemplifies the architectural and artistic achievements of Babylon. The Hanging Gardens of Babylon, one of the Seven Wonders of the Ancient World, are also believed to have been located in this region, though their exact existence and location remain a subject of historical debate.

The Neo-Assyrian Empire, which emerged in the 10th century BCE, was another dominant force in Mesopotamia. The Assyrians are renowned for their military prowess, administrative efficiency, and monumental architecture. The city of Nineveh, the capital of the Assyrian Empire, featured impressive palaces, temples, and the extensive Library of Ashurbanipal, which housed thousands of cuneiform tablets and played a crucial role in preserving Mesopotamian literature and knowledge.

The fall of the Neo-Assyrian Empire in the 7th century BCE paved the way for the rise of the Neo-Babylonian Empire under Nebuchadnezzar II. This period is marked by a cultural and architectural renaissance, with the reconstruction of Babylon and the construction of iconic structures such as the Etemenanki ziggurat and the Processional Way. Nebuchadnezzar's reign also saw the flourishing of science, literature, and the arts, solidifying Babylon's status as a center of learning and culture.

The conquests of Alexander the Great in the 4th century BCE brought Mesopotamia under Hellenistic influence, integrating Greek culture with the rich heritage of the region. Following Alexander's death, the Seleucid Empire ruled over Mesopotamia, fostering a fusion of Greek and local traditions. The establishment of new cities, such as Seleucia on the Tigris, facilitated the spread of Hellenistic culture and commerce throughout the region.

The subsequent Parthian and Sassanian Empires, which controlled Mesopotamia from the 3rd century BCE to the 7th century CE, continued to shape the cultural and political landscape of the region. The Sassanians, in particular, left a significant legacy with their advancements in art, architecture, and administration. The capital city of Ctesiphon, near modern Baghdad, became a major center of power and culture during the Sassanian period, boasting grand palaces, temples, and the iconic Taq Kasra arch, one of the largest single-span brick arches in the world.

The advent of Islam in the 7th century CE marked a transformative era for Mesopotamia. The region rapidly embraced the new religion and became a crucial part of the expanding Islamic Caliphate. In 762 CE, the Abbasid Caliphate, under Caliph Al-Mansur, founded the city of Baghdad on the western bank of the Tigris River. Baghdad was meticulously planned and constructed to serve as the new capital of the Islamic world, reflecting the Abbasids' ambition to create a city that embodied their political, cultural, and intellectual aspirations.

Baghdad quickly grew into one of the most important cities in the world, earning the epithet "City of Peace" (Madinat al-Salam). The city's circular design, centered around the caliphal palace and the grand mosque, symbolized the unity and centrality of the Abbasid rule. Baghdad became a melting pot of cultures, attracting scholars, scientists, poets, and artists from across the Islamic world and beyond. The Bayt al-Hikma, or House of Wisdom, established in the 9th century, became a renowned center for learning and scholarship, where Greek, Persian, Indian, and other texts were translated into Arabic, fostering a golden age of intellectual and scientific achievements.

The period of the Abbasid Caliphate is often regarded as a golden age of Islamic civilization, with Baghdad at its heart. The city thrived as a hub of commerce, culture, and knowledge. Advances in various fields such as astronomy, mathematics, medicine, and philosophy were made, with prominent scholars like Al-Khwarizmi, Al-Razi, and Al-Farabi contributing to the rich intellectual heritage of Baghdad. The city also became famous for its literature, with the compilation of "One Thousand and One Nights" (Arabian Nights) capturing the imagination of audiences for centuries.

Despite its prosperity, Baghdad faced significant challenges over the centuries. The Mongol invasion in 1258, led by Hulagu Khan, resulted in the sacking of the city and the massacre of its inhabitants. This devastating event marked the end of the Abbasid Caliphate and a period of decline for Baghdad. The city's libraries, including the House of Wisdom, were destroyed, leading to an immense loss of knowledge and cultural heritage. The Mongol conquest was a turning point in the history of Baghdad, as the city struggled to recover from the destruction and chaos.

In the following centuries, Baghdad came under the control of various regional powers, including the Ilkhanate, the Timurids, and the Safavids. Each of these dynasties left their mark on the city, contributing to its architectural and cultural evolution. The Ottoman Empire, which gained control of Baghdad in the 16th century, brought a period of relative stability and economic revival. Under Ottoman rule, the city saw the restoration of key infrastructure, the construction of new mosques, and the revitalization of trade routes.

The 20th century brought further transformations and challenges to Baghdad. The city played a central role in the modern history of Iraq, from the establishment of the Kingdom of Iraq in 1921 to the subsequent periods of political upheaval and regime changes. The discovery of vast oil reserves in Iraq in the early 20th century brought newfound wealth and modernization to Baghdad, transforming it into a bustling metropolis with modern amenities and infrastructure.

However, the latter half of the 20th century and the early 21st century were marked by significant turmoil and conflict. The Iran-Iraq War in the 1980s, the Gulf War in 1991, and the Iraq War in 2003 brought immense suffering and destruction to Baghdad. The city witnessed widespread violence, political instability, and social upheaval, which took a heavy toll on its population and infrastructure.

Despite these challenges, Baghdad's resilient spirit continues to shine. The city's rich cultural heritage, embodied in its historic sites, museums, and monuments, serves as a testament to its enduring legacy. The Iraqi Museum in Baghdad houses an extensive collection of artifacts that chronicle the history of Mesopotamia, from ancient Sumerian tablets to Assyrian reliefs and Babylonian artifacts. The preservation and restoration of historic sites, such as the Abbasid Palace and the Al-Mustansiriya School, reflect ongoing efforts to safeguard Baghdad's cultural heritage.

Baghdad's contemporary cultural scene is vibrant and diverse, with a thriving arts community, bustling markets, and lively cafes. The city's literary tradition continues to flourish, with poets, writers, and intellectuals contributing to Iraq's rich cultural tapestry. Baghdad's culinary heritage, featuring dishes such as kebabs, dolma, and masgouf, reflects the diverse influences that have shaped the city's cuisine over millennia.

The future of Baghdad holds promise and potential, as the city seeks to rebuild and revitalize in the face of ongoing challenges. Efforts to restore infrastructure, improve public services, and promote economic development are crucial for the city's recovery and growth. The resilience and determination of Baghdad's inhabitants, who have endured and overcome countless adversities, remain a source of inspiration and hope.

Chapter 44: Manila: The Pearl of the Orient

Manila, the capital city of the Philippines, is often referred to as the "Pearl of the Orient," a testament to its historical significance, cultural richness, and enduring beauty. Situated on the eastern shores of Manila Bay and adjacent to the Pasig River, Manila has long been a center of commerce, culture, and political power in the archipelago. Its history is a captivating tale of indigenous heritage, colonial encounters, and a journey toward modernity, punctuated by periods of prosperity and adversity.

Long before the arrival of European colonizers, Manila was already a thriving settlement and a significant center of trade and culture. The earliest evidence of human habitation in the Manila area dates back thousands of years, with archaeological findings indicating the presence of ancient communities that engaged in fishing, farming, and trading. The region's strategic location along the trade routes of Southeast Asia made it an ideal meeting point for merchants from China, India, and the Malay Archipelago. The indigenous Tagalog people, who inhabited the area, had developed a sophisticated society with intricate systems of governance, commerce, and culture.

The arrival of the Spaniards in the 16th century marked a pivotal moment in Manila's history. In 1571, Spanish conquistador Miguel López de Legazpi claimed the settlement of Manila for the Spanish Crown, effectively establishing it as the capital of the newly formed Spanish East Indies. This event marked the beginning of over three centuries of Spanish colonial rule, which would profoundly shape the cultural, social, and architectural landscape of Manila. The Spanish colonizers introduced Christianity, and Manila became a crucial hub for the spread of Catholicism throughout the

Philippines. The construction of grand churches, convents, and schools underscored the city's role as a religious center.

Intramuros, the "Walled City," stands as a testament to Manila's colonial past. Constructed by the Spaniards in the late 16th century, Intramuros served as the political, military, and religious center of Spanish Manila. Enclosed by massive stone walls, the city within a city housed the colonial administration, military garrisons, churches, convents, and residences. The San Agustin Church, a UNESCO World Heritage Site, is one of the oldest stone churches in the Philippines and a magnificent example of Baroque architecture. Intramuros also featured plazas, cobblestone streets, and an intricate system of fortifications, including Fort Santiago, which played a critical role in the city's defense against foreign invasions and local uprisings.

During the Spanish colonial period, Manila became a bustling port city and a vital link in the global trade network. The Manila Galleon Trade, which operated between Manila and Acapulco, Mexico, from 1565 to 1815, facilitated the exchange of goods, ideas, and cultures between the East and the West. The galleons carried precious commodities such as spices, silk, porcelain, and silver, making Manila a cosmopolitan melting pot where Asian, European, and American influences converged. This period of economic prosperity also led to the growth of a diverse and multicultural population, with communities of Chinese, Japanese, Indian, and Spanish settlers contributing to the city's vibrant social fabric.

The 19th century brought significant changes to Manila and the Philippines. The decline of the Spanish Empire and the increasing influence of European Enlightenment ideas fueled a growing sense of nationalism and desire for independence among Filipinos. The opening of the Suez Canal in 1869 further integrated the Philippines into global trade networks and exposed Filipinos to new ideas and technologies. The rise of the Filipino middle class, composed of educated and wealthy individuals known as the ilustrados, played a crucial role in the intellectual and political awakening of the nation. Prominent figures such as José Rizal, whose writings and activism inspired the Filipino nationalist movement, emerged during this period.

The culmination of these growing nationalist sentiments was the Philippine Revolution against Spanish rule, which began in 1896. The revolution was a complex and multifaceted struggle, characterized by a series of armed uprisings, political maneuverings, and the formation of revolutionary organizations such as the Katipunan. The execution of José Rizal in 1896 further galvanized the revolutionaries, leading to intensified efforts to achieve independence. The revolution ultimately led to the proclamation of Philippine independence on June 12, 1898, although the subsequent Treaty of Paris ceded the Philippines to the United States, marking the beginning of a new era of colonial rule.

The American period in Manila's history brought about significant transformations in the city's urban landscape, governance, and society. The Americans introduced modern infrastructure, public education, and democratic institutions, which had a lasting impact on Manila and the Philippines as a whole. The construction of wide boulevards, parks, and government buildings, following the City Beautiful movement, aimed to create a modern and orderly urban environment. Iconic landmarks such as the Manila Hotel, the University of the Philippines, and the Philippine General Hospital were established during this period, contributing to the city's development as a center of education, health, and hospitality.

World War II was a dark chapter in Manila's history, as the city became a battleground during the Japanese occupation and the subsequent liberation by Allied forces. The Battle of Manila in 1945 resulted in widespread destruction and significant loss of life, as intense urban warfare ravaged the city. Historical landmarks, cultural treasures, and much of the city's infrastructure were destroyed, leaving a lasting scar on Manila's physical and cultural landscape. Despite the devastation, the resilient spirit of the people of Manila endured, and efforts to rebuild and restore the city began in the post-war years.

The post-war period saw Manila's transformation into a bustling metropolis, grappling with the challenges of rapid urbanization, population growth, and political change. The declaration of Manila as an open city during the Japanese invasion had resulted in an influx of migrants seeking refuge and opportunities, contributing to the city's population boom. The rebuilding efforts focused on reconstructing essential infrastructure, revitalizing the economy, and addressing the social needs of a growing population. The establishment of new residential districts, commercial centers, and industrial zones reflected Manila's evolution into a modern and dynamic capital.

The 20th and early 21st centuries in Manila were marked by periods of political upheaval, social change, and economic development. The declaration of martial law by President Ferdinand Marcos in 1972 brought about a period of authoritarian rule, which significantly impacted the city's political and social landscape. The People Power Revolution of 1986, a peaceful uprising that led to the ousting of Marcos, underscored the resilience and collective will of the Filipino people to restore democracy and uphold human rights. Manila played a central role in these historic events, with key sites such as EDSA and Rizal Park becoming symbols of the struggle for freedom and justice.

In the contemporary era, Manila continues to evolve as a dynamic and vibrant city, balancing its rich historical heritage with the demands of modernization and globalization. The city's cultural scene is a testament to its diversity and creativity, with a thriving arts community, numerous festivals, and a burgeoning culinary landscape. Manila's museums, such as the National Museum of the Philippines and the Ayala Museum, preserve and showcase the nation's artistic and historical treasures, offering insights into the Philippines' rich cultural heritage. The city's performing arts venues, including the Cultural Center of the Philippines, host a wide array of performances, from traditional Filipino dances to contemporary theater and music.

Manila's culinary heritage is a reflection of its multicultural history, with a rich tapestry of flavors and influences from various cultures. Filipino cuisine, characterized by dishes such as adobo, sinigang, and lechon, is a delicious fusion of indigenous, Spanish, Chinese, and American culinary traditions. The city's vibrant street food scene, with popular treats like balut, taho, and halo-halo, offers a unique and authentic taste of Manila's diverse culinary landscape. The proliferation of food markets, trendy restaurants, and fusion cuisine establishments highlights Manila's evolving gastronomic scene and its role as a culinary destination.

The city's bustling markets and shopping districts, such as Divisoria, Quiapo, and Greenhills, offer a vibrant and dynamic shopping experience, reflecting Manila's role as a commercial hub. These markets are not only centers of commerce but also cultural microcosms where people from all walks of life converge, trade, and interact. The Mall of Asia, one of the largest shopping malls in the world, exemplifies Manila's embrace of modern retail culture and its appeal to both locals and tourists.

Manila's educational institutions, including the University of Santo Tomas, Ateneo de Manila University, and De La Salle University, continue to play a crucial role in shaping the intellectual and cultural landscape of the city. These institutions, with their long histories and traditions of academic excellence, contribute to the development of a well-educated and socially conscious populace. The city's commitment to education and innovation is evident in its growing tech and startup ecosystem, which fosters entrepreneurship and creativity.

Despite the challenges of urbanization, Manila's green spaces and parks, such as Rizal Park, Arroceros Forest Park, and the Manila Zoo, provide much-needed oases of tranquility and recreation. These green spaces serve as important cultural and historical landmarks, offering residents and visitors a place to relax, reflect, and connect with nature. The Pasig River, once heavily polluted, has been the focus of rehabilitation efforts aimed at restoring its ecological health and enhancing its role as a vital urban waterway.

The future of Manila holds promise and potential as the city continues to navigate the complexities of modernization, economic development, and cultural preservation. Efforts to address urban challenges, such as traffic congestion, pollution, and housing shortages, are crucial for ensuring the city's sustainable growth and enhancing the quality of life for its residents. The development of infrastructure projects, such as new transportation networks and green initiatives, reflects Manila's commitment to building a resilient and livable city for future generations.

Chapter 45: Stockholm: Archipelago Ancestry

Stockholm, the capital of Sweden, is a city renowned for its stunning archipelago, rich history, and cultural vibrancy. Often referred to as the "Venice of the North," Stockholm is spread across 14 islands where Lake Mälaren meets the Baltic Sea, and it is connected by 57 bridges. This unique geographical setting has profoundly influenced the city's development, culture, and identity. The history of Stockholm and its archipelago ancestry is a captivating tale that spans millennia, from its early settlement and Viking heritage to its rise as a major European capital and a hub of innovation and design.

The origins of Stockholm can be traced back to the Viking Age, around the 8th to 11th centuries, when the region was inhabited by seafaring Norsemen. These Vikings were not only fierce warriors but also skilled traders and explorers who established extensive trade networks across Europe, Asia, and beyond. The strategic location of the Stockholm archipelago made it an ideal base for Viking activities, facilitating trade, exploration, and conquest. Archaeological findings, such as burial mounds, rune stones, and ancient artifacts, provide evidence of the Vikings' presence and their influence on the region's early development.

The name "Stockholm" is believed to derive from the Old Norse words "stock" (log) and "holm" (islet), reflecting the city's origins as a fortified settlement on a small island. The earliest recorded mention of Stockholm dates back to the mid-13th century, when it was established as a trading post by Birger Jarl, a powerful Swedish statesman and founder of the city. Birger Jarl's establishment of Stockholm was aimed at protecting Sweden from foreign invasions and promoting trade with other Baltic Sea regions. The city's strategic location at the juncture of important trade routes contributed to its rapid growth and economic prosperity.

During the medieval period, Stockholm flourished as a center of commerce and trade. The city's membership in the Hanseatic League, a powerful confederation of merchant guilds and market towns in Northern Europe, further boosted its economic significance. The Hanseatic League facilitated the exchange of goods, ideas, and cultures, bringing wealth and influence to Stockholm. The city's medieval architecture, characterized by narrow cobblestone streets, Gothic churches, and historic buildings, reflects this period of prosperity and cultural exchange. Notable landmarks from this era include Storkyrkan (the Great Church), Riddarholmen Church, and the Royal Palace.

The 16th and 17th centuries marked a period of significant political and cultural transformation for Stockholm and Sweden as a whole. The reign of Gustav Vasa, who became King of Sweden in 1523, ushered in a new era of centralization and modernization. Gustav Vasa's efforts to strengthen the monarchy, reform the church, and promote economic development laid the foundations for Sweden's emergence as a major European power. Stockholm, as the capital, became the focal point of these reforms and played a crucial role in the nation's political and cultural life.

The 17th century, known as the Swedish Empire period, was a time of expansion and conquest for Sweden. Under the rule of King Gustavus Adolphus and his successors, Sweden extended its territories through military campaigns and strategic alliances. Stockholm benefited from this era of imperial expansion, becoming a vibrant and cosmopolitan city. The construction of grand palaces, government buildings, and cultural institutions reflected the city's growing importance and ambition. The founding of the University of Stockholm and the establishment of various academies and societies fostered intellectual and artistic pursuits, contributing to the city's cultural renaissance.

The 18th century brought both challenges and opportunities for Stockholm. The Great Northern War (1700-1721), which pitted Sweden against a coalition of European powers, resulted in territorial losses and economic hardship. However, the post-war period saw efforts to rebuild and modernize the city. The Age of Liberty (1718-1772), characterized by parliamentary rule and increased political freedoms, encouraged economic growth and cultural development. Stockholm's role as a center of trade, industry, and culture continued to expand, with innovations in science, literature, and the arts flourishing.

The 19th century was a transformative period for Stockholm, marked by industrialization, urbanization, and social change. The Industrial Revolution brought significant technological advancements and economic growth to the city. The construction of factories, railways, and infrastructure projects spurred urban development and increased population density. The expansion of the city's boundaries and the establishment of new residential and industrial districts reflected the changing dynamics of urban life. Social reforms, including improvements in public health, education, and labor rights, addressed the challenges posed by rapid industrialization and urbanization.

The 20th century was a period of remarkable progress and innovation for Stockholm. The city's commitment to modernization, social welfare, and environmental sustainability set it apart as a model of urban development. Stockholm's progressive policies in areas such as housing, transportation, and public services earned it a reputation as one of the world's most livable cities. The development of extensive public transportation networks, including the iconic Stockholm Metro with its art-adorned stations, enhanced the city's connectivity and accessibility. The creation of green spaces, parks, and waterfront promenades reflected Stockholm's dedication to preserving its natural beauty and promoting a high quality of life.

Stockholm's cultural scene in the 20th and 21st centuries has been characterized by creativity, diversity, and innovation. The city's rich artistic heritage is evident in its numerous museums, galleries, theaters, and cultural institutions. The Nobel Prize, established by Swedish inventor Alfred Nobel, is awarded annually in Stockholm, highlighting the city's global significance in science, literature, and peace. Stockholm's vibrant music scene, which gave rise to internationally acclaimed artists and bands such as ABBA, Roxette, and Avicii, underscores the city's influence in popular culture. The Stockholm International Film Festival, the Stockholm Design Week, and other cultural events attract visitors from around the world, showcasing the city's dynamic and cosmopolitan spirit.

The Stockholm archipelago, with its thousands of islands and islets, remains a defining feature of the city's identity and heritage. The archipelago's natural beauty, with its rugged coastlines, lush forests, and pristine waters, offers a serene escape from urban life and a connection to Sweden's maritime traditions. The islands of the archipelago are home to charming villages, historic landmarks, and recreational opportunities that attract both locals and tourists. Activities such as boating, fishing, hiking, and island-hopping provide a unique way to explore and experience the archipelago's diverse landscapes and cultures.

Stockholm's commitment to sustainability and environmental stewardship is reflected in its innovative urban planning and green initiatives. The city's efforts to promote renewable energy, reduce carbon emissions, and enhance public transportation have earned it recognition as one of the world's most sustainable cities. The development of eco-friendly neighborhoods, such as Hammarby Sjöstad and Norra Djurgårdsstaden, showcases Stockholm's dedication to creating livable, resilient, and environmentally conscious communities. The city's green spaces, such as Djurgården, Hagaparken, and Tantolunden, offer residents and visitors a harmonious blend of nature and urban life.

The people of Stockholm, known for their openness, creativity, and forward-thinking mindset, play a crucial role in shaping the city's vibrant and inclusive culture. The city's diverse population, with a mix of Swedes and immigrants from around the world, contributes to its rich cultural tapestry. Stockholm's reputation as a hub of innovation and design is reflected in its thriving tech and startup ecosystem, which fosters entrepreneurship and creativity. The city's universities, research institutions, and cultural organizations continue to drive advancements in science, technology, the arts, and humanities.

Chapter 46: Algiers: Mediterranean Mosaic

Algiers, the capital city of Algeria, is often referred to as the "Mediterranean Mosaic" due to its rich tapestry of history, culture, and architecture that spans millennia. Situated on the western shore of the Mediterranean Sea, Algiers has been a crucial crossroads for various civilizations, including Phoenicians, Romans, Byzantines, Arabs, Ottomans, and French. This diverse heritage has shaped Algiers into a city of contrasts, where ancient ruins coexist with modern structures, and traditional customs blend seamlessly with contemporary lifestyles. The story of Algiers is a fascinating narrative of resilience, transformation, and cultural fusion, reflecting the broader history of Algeria itself.

The history of Algiers dates back to antiquity, with the earliest known inhabitants being the Berber tribes. The region's strategic location along the Mediterranean made it an attractive destination for early settlers and traders. The Phoenicians, renowned maritime traders from the eastern Mediterranean, established trading posts along the coast of North Africa, including in the area that would become Algiers. These early settlements laid the foundation for the city's development as a vital hub of commerce and cultural exchange.

During the Roman period, Algiers, known as Icosium, became an important part of the Roman Empire. The Romans established a colony in the area, integrating it into their vast network of trade and communication. The remnants of Roman architecture, such as roads, aqueducts, and ruins of buildings, bear witness to the city's significance during this era. Roman rule brought about significant economic and cultural development, with the introduction of Roman law, language, and infrastructure. The legacy of this period is still evident in the archaeological sites and artifacts scattered throughout the region.

The fall of the Western Roman Empire in the 5th century AD led to a period of instability and transformation in North Africa. The region saw the arrival of the Vandals, a Germanic tribe, who established a kingdom in the area. However, their rule was relatively short-lived, as the Byzantine Empire, under Emperor Justinian I, reconquered North Africa in the 6th century. Byzantine rule restored some stability and brought about a revival of Roman culture and administration. The influence of Byzantine architecture and art can still be seen in the remnants of churches and mosaics from this period.

The arrival of Islam in the 7th century marked a significant turning point in the history of Algiers and North Africa. The Arab conquests led to the spread of Islam and the establishment of new political and social structures. Algiers became part of the Islamic Caliphate, and the city began to flourish as a center of learning, trade, and culture. The construction of mosques, madrasas (Islamic schools), and other religious institutions underscored the city's new Islamic identity. The Great Mosque of Algiers, built in the 11th century, is one of the oldest and most significant examples of Islamic architecture in the city.

The medieval period in Algiers was characterized by a series of dynastic changes and external influences. The city came under the control of various Berber dynasties, including the Almoravids and the Almohads, who ruled vast territories in North Africa and Spain. These dynasties contributed to the cultural and architectural development of Algiers, blending Berber, Arab, and Andalusian influences. The city's strategic location made it a target for foreign powers, including the Spanish and Portuguese, who sought to control the lucrative trade routes and resources of the region.

The 16th century witnessed a dramatic transformation in the history of Algiers with the arrival of the Ottoman Empire. In 1516, the legendary pirate brothers, Aruj and Hayreddin Barbarossa, seized control of Algiers and pledged allegiance to the Ottoman Sultan. This marked the beginning of Algiers' role as a prominent center of Ottoman power in North Africa. The city became a base for the infamous Barbary pirates, who conducted raids and engaged in maritime warfare against European powers. The Ottoman period brought about significant urban development, with the construction of fortifications, palaces, and public buildings. The Kasbah of Algiers, a UNESCO World Heritage Site, is a remarkable example of Ottoman-era architecture and urban planning, with its maze-like streets, historic buildings, and stunning views of the Mediterranean.

The influence of the Ottoman Empire on Algiers extended beyond architecture and urban development. The city became a melting pot of cultures, attracting traders, scholars, and artisans from across the Mediterranean and the Islamic world. This cultural fusion is evident in the art, cuisine, and traditions of Algiers, which reflect a unique blend of Arab, Berber, Turkish, and Mediterranean influences. The city's vibrant markets, known as souks, buzzed with activity as merchants traded goods such as spices, textiles, ceramics, and jewelry. The rich cultural heritage of this period is preserved in the traditional crafts and artisanal products that continue to be made in Algiers today.

The 19th century marked another significant chapter in the history of Algiers with the arrival of French colonial rule. In 1830, French forces invaded and occupied Algiers, initiating a period of colonization that would last for over 130 years. The French occupation brought about profound changes to the city's landscape, society, and economy. Algiers was transformed into a modern colonial capital, with the construction of wide boulevards, European-style buildings, and infrastructure projects. The French sought to impose their culture and institutions on the local population, leading to a complex and often contentious relationship between the colonizers and the indigenous people.

The colonial period in Algiers was marked by significant economic development, driven by investments in agriculture, industry, and trade. The city became a major center for the export of goods such as wine, olive oil, and citrus fruits, which were cultivated on large colonial estates. The construction of ports, railways, and roads facilitated the movement of goods and people, further integrating Algiers into the global economy. However, the benefits of this economic growth were unevenly distributed, with the indigenous population often facing exploitation, discrimination, and marginalization. The colonial era also witnessed the emergence of a vibrant cultural scene in Algiers, with the establishment of theaters, cafes, and literary salons. French intellectuals, artists, and writers were drawn to the city, contributing to its reputation as a center of creativity and intellectual exchange. This period saw the rise of prominent figures such as Albert Camus, who was born in Algeria and drew inspiration from its landscapes and people in his literary works.

The struggle for independence from French colonial rule was a defining moment in the history of Algiers. The Algerian War of Independence (1954-1962) was a brutal and protracted conflict that saw widespread violence, repression, and resistance. Algiers became a focal point of the liberation movement, with nationalist leaders, freedom fighters, and intellectuals playing key roles in the struggle. The Casbah of Algiers, with its labyrinthine streets and historic buildings, served as a stronghold for the resistance, symbolizing the resilience and determination of the Algerian people. The war culminated in the signing of the Evian Accords in 1962, leading to Algeria's independence and the end of French colonial rule.

The post-independence period in Algiers was characterized by efforts to rebuild and modernize the city while preserving its rich cultural heritage. The Algerian government implemented policies aimed at promoting economic development, social justice, and national unity. Algiers underwent significant urban expansion, with the construction of new housing, infrastructure, and public facilities to accommodate the growing population. The city's educational institutions, including universities and research centers, played a crucial role in fostering intellectual and scientific advancements.

In the contemporary era, Algiers continues to be a vibrant and dynamic city, reflecting the diversity and resilience of its people. The city's cultural scene is a testament to its rich heritage and creativity, with a thriving arts community, numerous festivals, and a burgeoning music and film industry. Traditional Algerian music genres, such as raï and chaabi, blend with contemporary influences to create a unique and dynamic sound. Algiers' theaters, galleries, and cultural centers host a wide array of performances, exhibitions, and events, showcasing the talents of local and international artists.

Algiers' culinary heritage is a reflection of its multicultural history, with a rich tapestry of flavors and influences from Berber, Arab, Turkish, and French cuisines. Traditional dishes such as couscous, tagine, and mechoui are celebrated for their complexity and depth of flavor, often accompanied by fresh vegetables, herbs, and spices. The city's bustling markets and street food vendors offer a taste of Algiers' diverse culinary landscape, with an array of savory pastries, grilled meats, and aromatic stews. The Mediterranean diet, characterized by its emphasis on fresh ingredients, olive oil, and seafood, is an integral part of the culinary traditions of Algiers.

The architecture of Algiers is a visual testament to its historical and cultural mosaic. The city's skyline is dotted with a mix of Ottoman-era palaces, French colonial buildings, and modern high-rises. The iconic Martyrs' Memorial, a towering monument commemorating the sacrifices of the Algerian people during the War of Independence, stands as a symbol of national pride and resilience. The preservation and restoration of historic sites, such as the Casbah and the Ketchaoua Mosque, underscore the city's commitment to honoring its past while embracing the future.

Algiers' role as a political and economic center continues to shape its development and influence in the region. The city is home to the Algerian government, foreign embassies, and numerous international organizations, making it a hub of diplomatic and political activity. Algiers' strategic location along the Mediterranean Sea positions it as a key player in regional trade and economic partnerships. The city's ports, airports, and transportation networks facilitate the movement of goods and people, enhancing its connectivity and global reach.

In recent years, Algiers has faced challenges and opportunities as it navigates the complexities of modernization and globalization. Issues such as urbanization, economic diversification, and environmental sustainability are at the forefront of the city's agenda. Efforts to promote renewable energy, reduce pollution, and enhance public transportation reflect Algiers' commitment to sustainable development. The city's dynamic youth population, with its entrepreneurial spirit and innovative mindset, is driving new initiatives in technology, culture, and social change.

Chapter 47: Prague: The City of a Hundred Spires

Prague, often called "The City of a Hundred Spires," is the capital of the Czech Republic and one of the most enchanting cities in Europe. This moniker, although poetically imprecise as Prague actually boasts over five hundred spires, reflects the city's skyline dominated by Gothic and Baroque architecture. Prague's history spans over a millennium, during which it has been the seat of Bohemian kings, a significant cultural hub in the Holy Roman Empire, and a center of arts, science, and politics in modern Europe. Its enchanting blend of historical and architectural heritage, along with its vibrant cultural scene, makes Prague a living museum and a beacon of European culture.

The origins of Prague date back to the Paleolithic Age, but it was during the late 9th century that the area began to take shape as a settlement with the establishment of Prague Castle by Prince Bořivoj of the Přemyslid dynasty. This castle, strategically situated on a hill overlooking the Vltava River, became the center of power and has remained the political and cultural heart of Prague to this day. The Castle complex, which has been expanded and modified over the centuries, includes palaces, churches, and gardens, making it the largest ancient castle in the world and a symbol of Czech heritage.

The development of Prague accelerated during the 10th and 11th centuries, with the establishment of Vyšehrad Castle, another significant fortification on the opposite bank of the Vltava River. By the 12th century, Prague had grown into a significant economic and cultural center, benefiting from its position on important trade routes. The city's prosperity was further enhanced by the reign of Charles IV, Holy Roman Emperor and King of Bohemia, in the 14th century. Charles IV envisioned Prague as a grand imperial city, and his ambitious architectural and urban planning projects transformed it into one of the most magnificent cities in Europe.

One of Charles IV's most notable contributions was the founding of Charles University in 1348, making it the first university in Central Europe. This institution became a center of learning and intellectual activity, attracting scholars from across the continent and laying the groundwork for Prague's long-standing tradition of academic excellence. Charles IV also initiated the construction of the iconic Charles Bridge, connecting the Old Town with the Lesser Town (Malá Strana) and facilitating the city's expansion. The bridge, adorned with statues of saints and lined with Gothic towers, remains one of Prague's most recognizable landmarks.

Under Charles IV's patronage, Prague's architectural landscape flourished with the construction of numerous churches, monasteries, and public buildings. The St. Vitus Cathedral, a masterpiece of Gothic architecture located within Prague Castle, began construction during his reign and became the spiritual and cultural heart of the city. The cathedral, with its soaring spires, intricate stained-glass windows, and elaborate sculptures, is a testament to the artistic and architectural achievements of medieval Prague.

The Hussite Wars of the early 15th century, sparked by religious and political conflicts, marked a turbulent period in Prague's history. The followers of Jan Hus, a reformist preacher who criticized the corruption of the Catholic Church, clashed with the ruling authorities, leading to widespread violence and upheaval. Despite the destruction and chaos, the Hussite movement had a lasting impact on Prague and the broader Czech lands, fostering a spirit of resistance and shaping the city's identity as a center of reformist thought.

The Renaissance period brought renewed prosperity and cultural flourishing to Prague. The Habsburgs, who gained control of the Bohemian crown in the early 16th century, were great patrons of the arts and sciences. Under Emperor Rudolf II, who made Prague his residence in the late 16th century, the city became a hub of artistic and scientific innovation. Rudolf II's court attracted renowned artists, alchemists, and scholars, including Johannes Kepler and Tycho Brahe, who made significant contributions to astronomy and other fields.

The architectural landscape of Prague was enriched during the Renaissance and Baroque periods with the construction of magnificent palaces, churches, and gardens. The Clementinum, a sprawling complex of historic buildings housing the National Library, is a prime example of Baroque architecture and intellectual heritage. The Church of St. Nicholas in the Lesser Town, with its grand dome and lavish interior, exemplifies the opulence and artistic mastery of Baroque Prague.

The Thirty Years' War (1618-1648), a devastating conflict that engulfed much of Europe, had a profound impact on Prague. The city suffered from battles, sieges, and occupations, leading to significant loss of life and damage to its infrastructure. Despite these hardships, Prague's resilient spirit prevailed, and the post-war period saw efforts to rebuild and revitalize the city. The Baroque era continued to shape Prague's architectural and cultural landscape, with the construction of numerous churches, palaces, and public buildings that added to its charm and grandeur.

The 18th and 19th centuries witnessed significant social, economic, and cultural changes in Prague. The city experienced industrialization and urban expansion, transforming it into a modern metropolis. The development of transportation networks, including the introduction of trams and railways, facilitated the movement of people and goods, enhancing Prague's connectivity and economic growth. The National Revival movement of the 19th century, aimed at promoting Czech language, culture, and national identity, had a profound impact on Prague. The construction of the

National Theatre, a symbol of Czech cultural resurgence, and the establishment of various cultural institutions underscored the city's role as a center of Czech nationalism and artistic expression.

The early 20th century brought both challenges and opportunities to Prague. The city became the capital of the newly established Czechoslovakia in 1918, following the collapse of the Austro-Hungarian Empire after World War I. This period of independence and democratic governance fostered economic growth, cultural development, and political stability. The interwar years saw the flourishing of modernist architecture and art, with notable contributions from Czech architects such as Josef Gočár and Adolf Loos. The vibrant cultural scene, characterized by avant-garde literature, theater, and visual arts, positioned Prague as a leading cultural hub in Europe.

The outbreak of World War II and the subsequent Nazi occupation brought immense suffering and hardship to Prague and its inhabitants. The city was subjected to brutal repression, and its Jewish community, one of the oldest in Europe, faced systematic persecution and annihilation. The Old Jewish Cemetery, the Jewish Quarter (Josefov), and the Old-New Synagogue stand as poignant reminders of this tragic period in Prague's history. Despite the horrors of the war, Prague's architectural heritage remained largely intact, preserving its historic buildings and cultural landmarks.

The post-war period saw the establishment of a communist regime in Czechoslovakia, which had a profound impact on Prague's political, social, and cultural life. The communist government implemented policies aimed at industrialization, collectivization, and centralization, leading to significant changes in the city's urban landscape and economic structure. The construction of large-scale housing projects, industrial facilities, and infrastructure projects reflected the regime's focus on modernization and socialist ideals. The suppression of political dissent, censorship, and state control over cultural institutions stifled artistic and intellectual freedom, but Prague's resilient spirit persisted.

The Prague Spring of 1968, a brief period of political liberalization and reform, was a moment of hope and aspiration for many Czechoslovakians. The movement, led by Alexander Dubček, aimed at creating "socialism with a human face" through political, economic, and cultural reforms. The Soviet-led invasion of Czechoslovakia in August 1968 abruptly ended the Prague Spring, leading to a period of repression and normalization. The legacy of the Prague Spring, however, continued to inspire resistance and dissent, contributing to the eventual downfall of the communist regime.

The Velvet Revolution of 1989 marked a peaceful and dramatic end to communist rule in Czechoslovakia. Mass protests, led by students, intellectuals, and dissidents, culminated in the resignation of the communist government and the establishment of a democratic republic. Václav Havel, a playwright and leading dissident, became the first president of the newly democratic Czechoslovakia. The subsequent peaceful dissolution of Czechoslovakia in 1993 resulted in the creation of two independent states, the Czech Republic and Slovakia, with Prague becoming the capital of the Czech Republic.

In the contemporary era, Prague has emerged as a vibrant and dynamic city, blending its rich historical heritage with modern innovation and development. The city's cultural scene is thriving, with numerous theaters, galleries, museums, and music venues showcasing a diverse array of artistic and cultural expressions. The Prague Spring International Music Festival, the Prague Quadrennial of Performance Design and Space, and the Karlovy Vary International Film Festival are just a few examples of the cultural events that attract artists, performers, and audiences from around the world.

Prague's culinary landscape reflects its diverse cultural influences and rich gastronomic traditions. Traditional Czech cuisine, characterized by hearty dishes such as roast pork with dumplings and sauerkraut, goulash, and svíčková (marinated beef with creamy vegetable sauce), is celebrated for its robust flavors and comforting appeal. The city's cafes, bistros, and fine dining establishments offer a wide range of culinary experiences, from traditional Czech fare to international cuisine. Prague's thriving craft beer scene, with its historic breweries and modern microbreweries, adds to the city's culinary allure.

The architectural beauty of Prague continues to captivate visitors and residents alike. The city's historic districts, including the Old Town (Staré Město), the Lesser Town (Malá Strana), and the New Town (Nové Město), are a testament to its architectural diversity and historical significance. The Old Town Square, with its Gothic Tyn Church, Baroque St. Nicholas Church, and the Astronomical Clock, is a focal point of Prague's historical and cultural heritage. The Charles Bridge, the Prague Castle complex, and the iconic spires of St. Vitus Cathedral are enduring symbols of Prague's architectural splendor.

Prague's urban development and infrastructure have evolved to meet the needs of a modern metropolis while preserving its historical charm. The city's public transportation system, including an extensive network of trams, buses, and the metro, facilitates efficient and convenient movement within the city. Efforts to promote sustainable urban development, green spaces, and environmental conservation reflect Prague's commitment to enhancing the quality of life for its residents and visitors.

Chapter 48: Antananarivo: Island of Intrigues

Antananarivo, the capital city of Madagascar, often called "Tana" by the locals, is a city steeped in history, mystery, and cultural richness, making it truly an "Island of Intrigues." This city, which dates back to the early 17th century, is not just the political and economic center of Madagascar but also a vibrant cultural hub that reflects the unique blend of African, Asian, and European influences that have shaped the island over centuries. The city's intriguing past and its evolution into a bustling modern metropolis offer a captivating narrative of resilience, adaptation, and cultural fusion.

The history of Antananarivo is deeply intertwined with the Merina Kingdom, one of the prominent kingdoms of Madagascar. The Merina people, originally from the central highlands, established Antananarivo as their capital in the early 17th century under the leadership of King Andrianjaka. According to legend, the city was named Antananarivo, meaning "City of the Thousand," after the thousand soldiers Andrianjaka stationed there to protect the hilltop capital. The strategic location of Antananarivo on a high ridge overlooking the surrounding plains provided both a natural defense and a vantage point for controlling the central highlands.

The Merina kings played a crucial role in unifying the various ethnic groups of Madagascar and expanding their territory through alliances and conquests. King Andrianampoinimerina, who reigned in the late 18th and early 19th centuries, was particularly instrumental in consolidating power and laying the foundations for a centralized kingdom. His vision of a united Madagascar under Merina rule set the stage for significant political and social transformations. The royal palace, known as the Rova, built on the highest hill in Antananarivo, became the symbol of Merina authority and the epicenter of political and cultural life.

Antananarivo's importance grew as it became the seat of power for successive Merina monarchs. Under the reign of King Radama I in the early 19th century, the kingdom experienced significant modernization and opening to foreign influences. Radama I established diplomatic relations with European powers, particularly the British, and embraced educational and military reforms. The introduction of the Latin alphabet and the establishment of schools marked a pivotal shift in the cultural and intellectual landscape of Antananarivo. The influence of European missionaries also led to the spread of Christianity, which began to take root alongside traditional beliefs.

The reign of Queen Ranavalona I in the mid-19th century was a period of intense intrigue and dramatic shifts in Antananarivo's history. Known for her fierce opposition to foreign influence and her efforts to preserve traditional Malagasy culture, Ranavalona I implemented policies that isolated Madagascar from European powers. Her reign was marked by a strong centralized authority, harsh laws, and efforts to maintain the sovereignty and cultural integrity of the kingdom. The queen's resistance to European colonial ambitions, coupled with her formidable and often controversial leadership, has made her a complex and intriguing figure in Madagascar's history.

The late 19th century brought significant changes to Antananarivo with the advent of French colonial rule. After a series of military campaigns, the French captured Antananarivo in 1895, marking the end of the Merina Kingdom and the beginning of Madagascar's colonization. The imposition of French administration brought about profound transformations in the city's political, economic, and social structures. The French colonial government undertook extensive infrastructure development, including the construction of roads, railways, and public buildings, which facilitated the integration of Madagascar into the global economy.

Antananarivo under French rule became a focal point of colonial administration, education, and commerce. The city's architecture began to reflect a blend of Malagasy and European styles, with colonial buildings, churches, and schools dotting the urban landscape. The establishment of institutions such as the University of Madagascar and the National Library underscored the city's growing role as an intellectual and cultural center. The French influence permeated various aspects of life in Antananarivo, from language and education to architecture and cuisine.

The struggle for independence from French colonial rule in the mid-20th century was a pivotal chapter in the history of Antananarivo and Madagascar. The nationalist movement, fueled by a desire for self-determination and the preservation of Malagasy identity, gained momentum in the years following World War II. The 1947 Malagasy Uprising, a major anti-colonial rebellion, highlighted the growing resistance against French rule and the demand for independence. Despite being suppressed by the colonial authorities, the uprising marked a significant step towards decolonization.

Madagascar gained its independence from France on June 26, 1960, and Antananarivo became the capital of the newly independent nation. The post-independence period was marked by efforts to build a cohesive national identity and address the challenges of economic development and social change. The city's role as the political and administrative center of Madagascar was reaffirmed, and it continued to be a hub of cultural and intellectual activity. The legacy of French colonialism, however, left lasting imprints on the city's infrastructure, institutions, and cultural landscape.

In the decades following independence, Antananarivo has experienced significant urban growth and transformation. The city's population has expanded rapidly, leading to the development of new residential areas, commercial districts, and public amenities. The challenges of urbanization, including housing, transportation, and infrastructure, have been central to the city's development agenda. Efforts to modernize the city's infrastructure while preserving its historical and cultural heritage have shaped the urban planning and development strategies of Antananarivo.

Antananarivo's cultural heritage is a rich tapestry of traditions, languages, and artistic expressions. The city's diverse population includes various ethnic groups, each contributing to the cultural mosaic of the capital. Traditional Malagasy music, dance, and crafts are celebrated in cultural festivals and events, reflecting the vibrancy and resilience of local traditions. The Hira Gasy, a traditional form of musical theater, is a unique cultural expression that combines music, dance, and storytelling, often performed in open-air settings. This art form, rooted in the highlands, continues to be a vital part of Antananarivo's cultural life.

The architectural heritage of Antananarivo is a testament to its historical evolution and cultural influences. The Rova of Antananarivo, the royal palace complex, remains a symbol of the Merina monarchy and a significant historical site. The palace, along with the Andafiavaratra Palace and other historic buildings, provides insights into the architectural styles and craftsmanship of different periods. The colonial-era buildings, with their distinctive European architectural elements, add to the city's historical charm and architectural diversity.

The natural environment of Antananarivo and its surroundings is characterized by the highland landscapes, with rolling hills, valleys, and rivers. The city's elevated position provides stunning panoramic views of the surrounding countryside. The Anosy Lake, located in the heart of the city, is a popular recreational area and a scenic spot for both locals and visitors. The parks and gardens of Antananarivo, such as the Tsimbazaza Zoo and Botanical Garden, offer green spaces for relaxation and exploration of Madagascar's unique flora and fauna.

The culinary traditions of Antananarivo are a reflection of Madagascar's diverse cultural influences. Malagasy cuisine is characterized by the use of rice as a staple, accompanied by a variety of dishes made from meat, fish, vegetables, and spices. Traditional dishes such as Romazava (a meat stew with greens), Ravimbomanga sy Henakisoa (sweet potato leaves with pork), and Koba (a sweet made from rice, peanuts, and banana) are celebrated for their unique flavors and culinary heritage. The city's markets and street food vendors offer a wide array of local delicacies, providing a taste of Antananarivo's vibrant food culture.

Antananarivo's contemporary art and cultural scene is dynamic and evolving, with a growing community of artists, musicians, and performers. The city's galleries, theaters, and cultural centers host a variety of events, exhibitions, and performances, showcasing both traditional and contemporary artistic expressions. The annual Madajazzcar festival, one of the largest jazz festivals in Africa, attracts international musicians and jazz enthusiasts to Antananarivo, highlighting the city's role as a cultural hub.

The social and economic development of Antananarivo faces both opportunities and challenges. The city's growing population and urban expansion require innovative solutions for housing, transportation, and public services. Efforts to improve education, healthcare, and employment opportunities are central to enhancing the quality of life for the residents of Antananarivo. The city's economic activities are diverse, ranging from traditional markets and crafts to modern industries and services. Antananarivo's strategic position as the economic center of Madagascar positions it as a key player in the nation's development and regional trade.

Antananarivo's political landscape has been shaped by the broader dynamics of Madagascar's political history. The city has been the focal point of political movements, protests, and changes in governance. The resilience of its people and the city's ability to adapt to political shifts underscore the dynamic nature of Antananarivo's political life. The democratic processes and political reforms of recent years reflect the aspirations of the Malagasy people for stability, transparency, and inclusive governance.

Chapter 49: San Juan: Fortress of the Caribbean

San Juan, the capital of Puerto Rico, stands as a historical and cultural gem in the Caribbean, embodying centuries of rich history, vibrant culture, and strategic significance. Known as the "Fortress of the Caribbean," San Juan's history is a captivating tale of exploration, colonization, military fortifications, and cultural fusion.

San Juan's origins date back to the early 16th century, shortly after Christopher Columbus's voyages opened the New World to European exploration. In 1508, the Spanish explorer Juan Ponce de León, who had accompanied Columbus on his second voyage, founded the original settlement of Caparra, located to the west of present-day San Juan. However, due to the unhealthiness of the site and its distance from the sea, the settlement was relocated in 1521 to a more suitable location on the islet of San Juan Bautista, which offered better defensive capabilities and access to the harbor. This new settlement was named Puerto Rico, meaning "Rich Port," in recognition of the natural harbor's importance.

The strategic location of San Juan quickly became evident to the Spanish Crown. Positioned at the northernmost point of the Caribbean, San Juan served as a key outpost for Spanish ships traveling between Europe and the Americas. The city's natural harbor provided a safe haven for the Spanish treasure fleets that transported gold, silver, and other valuable resources from the New World to the Old. Recognizing the importance of securing this vital port, the Spanish began constructing fortifications to protect San Juan from potential threats, including pirates and rival European powers.

The first major fortification in San Juan was La Fortaleza, built between 1533 and 1540. Originally intended as a defense against

Carib attacks, La Fortaleza also served as the governor's residence, a role it continues to fulfill today as the official residence of the Governor of Puerto Rico. As the oldest executive mansion in continuous use in the Americas, La Fortaleza is a symbol of San Juan's enduring political and historical significance.

The construction of additional fortifications followed, most notably Castillo San Felipe del Morro, commonly known as El Morro. Construction of El Morro began in 1539 and continued for more than 200 years, with various modifications and expansions made over the centuries. Perched on a promontory overlooking the entrance to San Juan Bay, El Morro was designed to protect the harbor from seaborne attacks. Its massive walls, towering bastions, and strategically placed cannons made it one of the most formidable fortresses in the Caribbean. El Morro's distinctive six-level design and triangular shape allowed for optimal defense against enemy ships, and its commanding position provided a panoramic view of the surrounding waters.

El Morro was not the only fortification in San Juan. In the 1630s, the Spanish began constructing Castillo San Cristóbal, a sprawling fortress complex located to the east of El Morro. San Cristóbal was designed to protect against land-based attacks, particularly from the east, where the city was most vulnerable. Covering 27 acres, San Cristóbal is the largest fortification built by the Spanish in the New World. Its intricate system of walls, tunnels, and dry moats, along with its multiple bastions and gun batteries, made it a critical component of San Juan's defensive network.

The fortifications of San Juan were tested numerous times throughout the city's history. One of the earliest and most significant tests came in 1595 when the English privateer Sir Francis Drake attempted to capture San Juan. Despite his formidable reputation and fleet, Drake's assault on El Morro was repelled by the fort's defenders, who inflicted heavy casualties on the attackers. Just two years later, in 1598, another English expedition led by George Clifford, the Earl of Cumberland, successfully breached San Juan's defenses and occupied the city for several months before being forced to withdraw due to disease and supply shortages.

In 1625, San Juan faced another major threat when a Dutch fleet under the command of Boudewijn Hendricksz attacked the city. The Dutch managed to breach San Juan's outer defenses and set fire to much of the city, but they were ultimately unable to capture El Morro and were forced to retreat. These repeated attacks underscored the strategic importance of San Juan and the need for robust fortifications to protect the city and its harbor.

Throughout the 17th and 18th centuries, San Juan continued to play a crucial role in Spain's colonial empire. The city's fortifications were continually upgraded and expanded to address evolving military threats and technological advancements. The construction of additional bastions, walls, and powder magazines strengthened San Juan's defenses, making it one of the most heavily fortified cities in the Caribbean.

San Juan's military significance was not limited to its fortifications. The city also served as a hub for Spanish naval operations in the region. The harbor of San Juan provided a safe anchorage for Spanish warships and supply vessels, and the city became a key staging point for expeditions and campaigns throughout the Caribbean and beyond. San Juan's shipyards and naval facilities supported the maintenance and repair of the Spanish fleet, further enhancing the city's strategic value.

The strategic importance of San Juan and its fortifications was highlighted once again during the Spanish-American War of 1898. As tensions between Spain and the United States escalated, San Juan became a focal point of military operations. On May 12, 1898, a U.S. naval squadron under the command of Rear Admiral William T. Sampson bombarded San Juan in an attempt to weaken Spanish defenses and gain control of the island. Despite the intensity of the bombardment, the fortifications of El Morro and San Cristóbal withstood the attack, and the Spanish defenders managed to inflict damage on the U.S. fleet.

The Spanish-American War ultimately resulted in Spain's defeat and the cession of Puerto Rico to the United States. Under American rule, San Juan underwent significant changes. The new administration introduced various infrastructure improvements, including modern roads, bridges, and public utilities. The U.S. military also made modifications to the city's fortifications, converting some areas into military bases and facilities.

Despite these changes, San Juan's historical and cultural heritage remained deeply ingrained in the city's identity. The fortifications of El Morro and San Cristóbal, recognized for their historical significance and architectural grandeur, were preserved and eventually designated as part of the San Juan National Historic Site. Today, these iconic landmarks stand as testament to San Juan's storied past and its role as a fortress of the Caribbean.

Beyond its military history, San Juan has evolved into a vibrant cultural and economic center. The city's colonial-era architecture, cobblestone streets, and colorful buildings in Old San Juan create a picturesque and historically rich environment that attracts visitors from around the world. The preservation of historic sites, including La Fortaleza, El Morro, and San Cristóbal, along with the restoration of historic buildings, has contributed to San Juan's status as a UNESCO World Heritage Site.

San Juan's cultural scene is a dynamic blend of Puerto Rican traditions and contemporary influences. The city is renowned for its music, dance, and art, which reflect the island's diverse heritage. Traditional Puerto Rican music, such as bomba and plena, can be heard alongside salsa, reggaeton, and other modern genres. The annual San Sebastián Street Festival, held in Old San Juan, is one of the island's most celebrated cultural events, featuring live music, parades, and vibrant street performances.

The city's culinary scene is equally diverse, offering a fusion of Spanish, African, Taíno, and international flavors. From traditional dishes like mofongo and lechón to innovative culinary creations, San Juan's restaurants and food markets showcase the island's rich gastronomic heritage. The city's nightlife, with its lively bars, clubs, and casinos, adds to the vibrant atmosphere, making San Juan a popular destination for both locals and tourists.

San Juan's economic importance extends beyond its cultural and historical attractions. As the capital of Puerto Rico, the city serves as the political and administrative center of the island. Government institutions, including the Capitol Building and various executive agencies, are located in San Juan, making it the hub of political activity. The city's economy is driven by a diverse range of industries, including finance, tourism, manufacturing, and services. The San Juan metropolitan area is a major economic engine for Puerto Rico, contributing significantly to the island's GDP and employment.

San Juan's port remains a critical asset, serving as one of the busiest in the Caribbean. The Port of San Juan handles a substantial volume of cargo, facilitating trade between Puerto Rico and the rest of the world. The port is also a major destination for cruise ships, welcoming millions of visitors each year. The tourism industry is a vital component of San Juan's economy, with the city's historic sites, beaches, and cultural attractions drawing tourists from around the globe.

In recent years, San Juan has faced challenges related to economic fluctuations, natural disasters, and infrastructure needs. The impact of Hurricane Maria in 2017 highlighted the vulnerabilities of the island's infrastructure and the need for resilient and sustainable development. Efforts to rebuild and modernize the city's infrastructure, enhance disaster preparedness, and promote economic diversification are ongoing. These initiatives aim to ensure San Juan's long-term viability and improve the quality of life for its residents.

San Juan's future is shaped by its ability to balance preservation with innovation. The city's rich historical and cultural heritage provides a strong foundation for sustainable tourism and cultural exchange. Investments in education, technology, and infrastructure are essential to fostering economic growth and resilience. Community engagement and collaboration between public and private sectors are crucial to addressing the city's challenges and leveraging its opportunities.

Chapter 50: Addis Ababa: The Heart of Africa

Addis Ababa, the capital of Ethiopia, stands as a vibrant and dynamic city at the heart of Africa. Its name, which means "New Flower" in Amharic, reflects its growth and development from a modest settlement into a bustling metropolis that plays a crucial role in the political, economic, and cultural life of both Ethiopia and the African continent. The story of Addis Ababa is a fascinating tapestry woven from threads of history, tradition, modernization, and international significance.

The origins of Addis Ababa can be traced back to the late 19th century when Emperor Menelik II, one of Ethiopia's most renowned rulers, sought to establish a new capital. Prior to this, the Ethiopian Empire's capital was a mobile one, with the imperial court moving from place to place. Menelik II and his wife, Empress Taytu Betul, decided to settle in a location that offered both strategic and environmental advantages. The site they chose was the Entoto Hills, which provided a vantage point overlooking the surrounding plains and access to vital water sources. The initial settlement, established in 1886, was known as Finfinne, but Empress Taytu named it Addis Ababa, a name that resonated with the vision of a flourishing new capital.

The establishment of Addis Ababa marked a significant shift in the history of Ethiopia. Under Menelik II's leadership, the city began to grow rapidly. The emperor initiated the construction of key infrastructure, including roads, bridges, and buildings, which laid the foundation for the city's development. One of the earliest significant structures was the Menelik Palace, which served as the imperial residence and a symbol of the new capital's importance. The city's growth was also supported by the construction of the Addis

Ababa-Djibouti Railway, completed in 1917, which connected the landlocked country to the Red Sea and facilitated trade and communication with the outside world.

Addis Ababa's development was further accelerated by its role as a center of political power and administration. As the seat of the Ethiopian government, the city attracted a diverse population, including nobles, government officials, merchants, and artisans. The establishment of various government institutions and ministries in Addis Ababa solidified its status as the heart of the Ethiopian state. The city's administrative and political significance was underscored by the construction of the Jubilee Palace in the 1950s, which became the official residence of Emperor Haile Selassie I.

The early 20th century was a period of modernization and expansion for Addis Ababa. Emperor Haile Selassie I, who ascended to the throne in 1930, embarked on a series of ambitious reforms aimed at modernizing Ethiopia and its capital. Under his reign, Addis Ababa witnessed the construction of new roads, schools, hospitals, and public buildings. The establishment of Addis Ababa University, originally known as the University College of Addis Ababa, in 1950, marked a significant milestone in the city's educational development. The university became a center of higher learning and intellectual activity, contributing to the growth of a skilled and educated workforce.

Addis Ababa's status as the political and diplomatic heart of Africa was further cemented in 1963 with the founding of the Organization of African Unity (OAU), now known as the African Union (AU). The OAU's headquarters were established in Addis Ababa, symbolizing the city's importance as a hub for African unity and cooperation. The decision to locate the OAU in Addis Ababa was influenced by Ethiopia's historical role as a symbol of African independence and resistance to colonialism. Ethiopia, under the leadership of Emperor Haile Selassie, was one of the few African countries that successfully resisted European colonization, and it played a pivotal role in supporting the decolonization movements across the continent.

The presence of the OAU, and later the AU, in Addis Ababa transformed the city into a focal point for African diplomacy and international relations. The AU headquarters, located in the Addis Ababa Conference Center, became a venue for important meetings, summits, and negotiations involving African leaders and representatives from around the world. The city's diplomatic significance was further enhanced by the establishment of numerous embassies, consulates, and international organizations in Addis Ababa, making it one of the most important diplomatic centers in Africa.

The cultural richness of Addis Ababa is another defining feature of the city. As a melting pot of various ethnic groups and cultures, Addis Ababa offers a vibrant and diverse cultural scene. The city is home to numerous cultural institutions, including museums, theaters, and art galleries. The National Museum of Ethiopia, located in Addis Ababa, houses a vast collection of artifacts that showcase the country's rich history and cultural heritage. Among its most famous exhibits is the skeletal remains of "Lucy," a hominid that lived over three million years ago and is considered one of the earliest known ancestors of modern humans.

Addis Ababa is also a center for traditional Ethiopian music and dance. The city hosts a variety of cultural events and festivals that celebrate Ethiopia's diverse traditions and artistic expressions. The Ethiopian National Theatre, established in 1955, is a prominent venue for performances of traditional and contemporary music, dance, and theater. The city's vibrant nightlife, with its numerous clubs and entertainment venues, reflects the dynamic and youthful energy of Addis Ababa's population.

The culinary scene in Addis Ababa is a reflection of the city's cultural diversity. Ethiopian cuisine, known for its rich flavors and unique ingredients, is a highlight of the city's food culture. Traditional dishes such as injera (a sourdough flatbread), doro wat (spicy chicken stew), and kitfo (minced raw meat) are widely enjoyed by locals and visitors alike. The city's numerous restaurants and cafes offer a range of dining experiences, from traditional Ethiopian meals to international cuisine. Coffee, an integral part of Ethiopian culture, is celebrated in Addis Ababa through the traditional coffee ceremony, which is a social and cultural ritual that brings people together to enjoy freshly brewed coffee.

Addis Ababa's economy has evolved significantly over the years, transitioning from a primarily agrarian economy to a more diversified and modern one. The city's economic growth has been driven by various sectors, including manufacturing, services, construction, and trade. The establishment of industrial zones and business parks has attracted domestic and international investors, contributing to the city's economic development. Addis Ababa's role as a commercial and financial center is supported by its modern infrastructure, including a network of roads, highways, and public transportation systems.

The city's Bole International Airport, one of the busiest airports in Africa, serves as a major gateway for international travel and trade. The airport's expansion and modernization have enhanced its capacity to handle a growing number of passengers and cargo, further boosting Addis Ababa's connectivity with the rest of the world. The presence of Ethiopian Airlines, the national carrier, has also played a significant role in establishing Addis Ababa as a key aviation hub in Africa.

In recent years, Addis Ababa has undergone significant urban development and modernization. The city's skyline has been transformed by the construction of high-rise buildings, modern office complexes, and luxury hotels. The development of new residential areas, commercial centers, and public spaces has improved the quality of life for the city's residents. The Addis Ababa Light Rail, inaugurated in 2015, is the first light rail system in sub-Saharan Africa and has greatly enhanced public transportation within the city.

Despite its rapid growth and modernization, Addis Ababa faces various challenges, including urbanization, population growth, and infrastructure demands. The city's population has increased significantly over the years, leading to pressures on housing, public services, and transportation. Efforts to address these challenges include urban planning initiatives, investment in infrastructure, and sustainable development projects. The city's leadership is focused on creating a resilient and livable urban environment that balances growth with environmental sustainability.

Addis Ababa's future is shaped by its vision for sustainable development and innovation. The city's leadership is committed to creating a smart and inclusive city that leverages technology and innovation to address urban challenges and improve the quality of life for its residents. Investments in renewable energy, waste management, and green spaces are integral to Addis Ababa's vision for a sustainable and resilient city. Community engagement and collaboration between government, private sector, and civil society are crucial to achieving this vision.

Epilogue

As our journey through the hidden histories of major cities draws to a close, we find ourselves enriched by the profound tapestry of human experience that these urban landscapes have revealed. Each city we have explored is more than just a collection of buildings, streets, and landmarks; it is a living chronicle, a testament to the resilience, creativity, and enduring spirit of humanity.

Throughout our travels, we have uncovered the forgotten tales and unsung heroes that have shaped the destinies of these cities. We have walked through the ancient ruins of Rome, where the echoes of a mighty empire still resonate, and marveled at the grandeur of Cairo's pyramids, standing as timeless sentinels of a civilization that once flourished along the banks of the Nile.

In Athens, we traced the roots of democracy and philosophy, immersing ourselves in the intellectual currents that have flowed through the ages. Jerusalem offered us a mosaic of faiths and cultures, each layer of its history adding depth to its spiritual and historical significance. From the bustling streets of Beijing to the vibrant heart of Mexico City, we witnessed the dynamic interplay of tradition and modernity, each city a testament to the enduring power of cultural heritage.

As we journeyed through Istanbul, Paris, and Kyoto, we encountered a rich diversity of cultures and histories, each city offering its unique perspective on the human experience. In the shadows of Moscow's Kremlin and Delhi's Mughal monuments, we saw the complexities of power and the intricate dance of history that has shaped these iconic cities.

London, with its echoes of empire, and Buenos Aires, with its passionate rhythms, revealed the vibrant, evolving narratives that define them. The colonial echoes of Lagos and the maritime tales of Sydney's harbor offered us insights into the global forces that have shaped these cities. Each chapter of this book has illuminated a different aspect of the human journey, a different facet of the rich mosaic that is our shared history.

In exploring these hidden histories, we have also discovered a common thread that binds these cities together—a shared legacy of human endeavor, innovation, and resilience. Despite the diverse cultural, political, and historical contexts of each city, we see a reflection of our own humanity in their stories. The triumphs and tragedies, the moments of greatness and the struggles for survival, remind us of the enduring spirit that has driven us forward through the ages.

As we reflect on the tales we have uncovered, we are reminded that history is not just a collection of dates and events, but a living narrative that continues to shape our present and future. The stories of these cities are not confined to the past; they are woven into the very fabric of our daily lives, influencing our identities, our communities, and our world.

In the hidden histories of these cities, we find lessons that resonate deeply with our contemporary experience. The challenges of governance, the quest for justice, the struggles for freedom and equality, and the pursuit of innovation and progress—all are themes that echo across the centuries and continue to shape our world today.

As we close the final chapter of this book, we are left with a profound appreciation for the richness and complexity of our shared history. We are reminded that each city, no matter how modern or cosmopolitan, carries within it the echoes of its past, a legacy that continues to influence its future. These cities are not just places on a map; they are vibrant, dynamic entities, each with its own unique story to tell.

In the end, "Hidden Histories of Major Cities" is more than just a collection of stories; it is a celebration of the human spirit, a tribute to the resilience and creativity that have shaped our world. It is an invitation to look beyond the surface, to explore the layers of history that lie hidden beneath the streets we walk every day, and to discover the rich and diverse heritage that connects us all.

As we move forward, let us carry with us the lessons and inspirations we have gained from this journey. Let us continue to explore, to question, and to uncover the hidden histories that shape our world. And in doing so, let us celebrate the rich tapestry of human experience that makes each city, and each of us, a unique and vital part of the ongoing story of our shared humanity.

The End.